HISTORIC COURTHOUSES
of the State of New York

BY
JULIA C. ROSENBLATT
AND
ALBERT M. ROSENBLATT

TURNER
PUBLISHING COMPANY

Dedication

To the Historical Society of the Courts of the State of New York,
which chronicles the history of the New York Courts and the
dedicated people who serve in them.

Turner Publishing Company

424 Church Street, Suite 2240
Nashville, TN 37219

445 Park Avenue, 9th Floor
New York, NY 10022

www.turnerpublishing.com

Library of Congress Control Number: 2006932081

ISBN-10: 1-59652-200-3
ISBN-13: 978-1-59652-200-8

Printed in the United States of America.

0 9 8 7 6 5 4 3 2

Contents

Acknowledgements

We never could have written this book without the assistance of numerous local historians, judges, and others, who supplied us with information about their counties and pointed us toward relevant material. We have recognized them on their respective county pages and thank them heartily.

Our thanks to Frances Murray, the librarian of the New York Court of Appeals, for her acquisitional talents. Nothing seems beyond her reach. The Dutchess County Historical Society has been a great resource. Our thanks goes to Eileen Hayden, Joyce Ghee, and Stephanie Mauri, along with Dutchess County Historian Stanley Mersand, not only for their help with Dutchess County historical materials, but for their generous efforts in all spheres.

We thank the Trustees of the Historical Society of the Courts of the State of New York, who encouraged this project, particularly Sue Nadel, our past Executive Director, Marilyn Marcus, the present director, also to Judicial Institute Dean Robert Keating and Assistant Joy Beane. Our Historical Society interns were of great assistance at both the beginning and end of the project. Jennifer Sculco helped locate material and contact information. Indira Satarkulova organized the bibliography. We took inspiration from Whitney North Seymour and Catryna Seymour who have made a splendid hobby of painting and photographing courthouses.

We are grateful as well to Rosemary "Snookie" Fitzgerald and Gail Fillion for various and sundry administrative tasks, to Pat Ryan for her creative artistry in the Court Historical Society's Calendars that we drew upon. Thanks also goes to Scott Baright and to Thomas X. Casey for their expertise in postcards. After we selected the images for this book, Dean DiMarzo did excellent work scanning them for publication.

The local history section of the State Library proved a particularly valuable resource. We thank Nancy Horan, for helping us find a wealth of information.

It was a pleasure to work with Marsha Newsom and Randy Baumgardner of Turner Publishing Company. We thank them for their expertise and cooperative spirit.

Our utmost gratitude goes to New York's Chief Judge Judith S. Kaye, a boundless source of support and inspiration, to our daughter, Betsy Rosenblatt, for her keen editorial comments, and our enormous thanks to Inez Tierney, who has helped in countless ways.

– Julia and Albert Rosenblatt
Pleasant Valley, New York, December 2006

Because the authors have written this book pro bono, the proceeds of this book will go to the Historical Society of the Courts of the State of New York, a non-profit entity created to preserve the legal history of New York. The Society, based in White Plains, New York, conducts programs, generates exhibits, and preserves materials relevant to the history of New York State Courts. This book was issued under the auspices of the Society, which thanks Thompson West for helping toward its publication.

Preface

Surely there is no other book like this one–a history of New York State told through picture postcards of the courthouses of its 62 highly diverse counties. What's more, it's a history delightfully recounted by Julie and Al Rosenblatt, both ardent historians, courthouse devotees, and magnificent writers. All in all, it's a winning combination.

I have a few special perspectives on this book.

First, as Chief Judge of the State of New York, with oversight of most of the facilities pictured here–some have been razed, some transmogrified, one never actually constructed–I have a new appreciation of what these formidable structures have been through, physically and operationally. It's amazing, but shouldn't be, that so much of New York's history took place in and around our courthouses.

Second, that all this can be told through picture postcards is itself wondrous. For me, picture postcards mean pleasure travel to far-off places. A picture postcard conveys to friends and family a taste of the beauty of exotic stops more than words can say. I hardly think I would select a picture of a courthouse (well, I might, but I can't recall ever having been presented with the choice at newsstands). Hard to imagine that someone would have selected a <u>courthouse</u> photograph to write a friend, "Hoping to see you on Thursday evening." Or, "Wish you were here." That choice in itself says so much about the popular regard for courthouses a century or so ago–or alternative sites in the area.

Finally, just a word or two about the authors. Plainly, for the Rosenblatts this has been a labor of love. I can only imagine the hours and hours of pleasure they had collecting all of these postcards. Surely they have dozens of stories about chancing on these treasures in musty backrooms piled high with "antiques." But I do know something of the pleasure they have had collecting the courthouse histories. Often in Albany, as the Judges of the Court of Appeals would gather for dinner after afternoon arguments at Court of Appeals Hall, we would stop to "collect" Julie, who had spent her afternoon at the State Library researching county history. Then, at dinner, they both would regale us with stories of facades and foibles now so masterfully gathered in this volume.

Yes indeed, a winning combination. A truly unique, and pleasurable, opportunity to learn something new.

– Judith S. Kaye
New York City

Introduction

istoric courthouses evoke a sort of nostalgia. Without quite being able to put a finger on it, we somehow sense that the courthouse has a different place in our society than it did even a few decades ago. In this book, we trace the story of courthouses in New York, county by county. Things, we conclude, have changed.

Courthouses are still in use, today more than ever, for everyday court-related business. But they are no longer celebrated for their individuality and service as community centers. In some instances, court matters take place in buildings called by other names: "Court Facility" or "Hall of Justice," as part of a larger "Government Center." An older building may retain the title "Courthouse," while

This image of the Dutchess County Courthouse is printed on leather. On the reverse side, it has a space for the address, and a box indicating where the stamp should go, but it has never been mailed.

accommodating something other than the courts; say, a museum or other county offices. The transition has been a natural consequence of the ever-growing need for space and modernization.

In the first half of the 20th Century, courthouses and postcards each had a sort of heyday. Both survive, to be sure, but their uses have evolved. Each in its own way reflects the shift to a more rapid pace of life in the last half of the 20th and the beginning of the 21st. Century.

We still use and appreciate post cards. Then, as now, tourists send postcards to greet the folks back home and show landmarks from their travels. In this day of telephone, e-mail, and text messaging, we seldom use a postcard to say, for example, "I hope to see you on Thursday," or "I've finished the project. Expect the manuscript soon."

Look through the rotating postcard racks anywhere, and you will encounter few courthouses. Usually there are none. This contrasts with the early 20th Century, in which most of the depictions in this volume were produced. Then almost every county had its courthouse photographed from different angles and vantage points.

It is hard to imagine that something as simple as a postcard is a relatively recent invention. Take a card, add a picture perhaps, write a message, address it, and affix a stamp. Simple. Yet credit for inventing the postcard goes to Dr. Emmanuel Hermann of the Vienna Military Academy, who wrote a letter to a Vienna newspaper suggesting such a thing. Dr. Hermann may not have been the first to have the idea, but he was the

This postcard of the Onondaga County Courthouse in Syracuse is printed on a thin sheet of metal. Although it has space for a stamp and address, it also bears the notation, "This card must be sent under cover only." The sender has addressed the card, but it is not stamped.

first to make it happen. The Austrian government issued the first "Korrespondenz Karten" in 1869. Great Britain, under Prime Minister William Gladstone, followed suit a year later. The public caught on quickly. During the first three months, the Austro-Hungarian Empire sold 2,926,102 of the buff-colored cards. Great Britain sold 575,000 cards on the first day alone.

The United States was relatively slow in adopting the postal card. Although the government considered the idea in 1870, the Post Office did not issue any until May 1873. More than 60 million sold within the first six months.

Picture postcards were the logical next step. The German postal service authorized them in 1872. American greeting card companies took to printing greetings on government issued cards shortly after they were introduced. Again, the United States government was slow in warming to the idea. Although privately printed picture post cards were sold at the World Colombian Exhibition of 1893, it took another five years, until May 19, 1898, before the government authorized their use.

Postcard collecting soon followed. It has been said that even Queen Victoria fell into line with this hobby. Although the types of messages on postcards may have shrunk over the decades, people still send them, and collectors abound.

Anything that goes through the mails has to conform to postal service regulations. At first, only the address could appear on the side that bears the stamp. Any message had to share space with the picture on the other side. The U.S. Post Office changed this in 1907, making it easy to distinguish a pre-1907 from post-1907 card. Occasionally a postcard of some unusual material turns up from that era: metal or leather, for example.

As the United States lagged behind Europe in adopting the post card, it also lagged in production. Many American publishers had their wares printed in Germany. This changed, of course, with World War I.

Post cards appeared in color long before color photography. The publisher began with a black and white image and had it hand colored. Starting from the same photo, different colorists could work in their individual styles. Two postcards of the Wayne County Courthouse in Lyons, for example, obviously based on the same photograph, give two entirely different effects. Sometimes the colorist took artistic license by painting a building in a different hue. Although the Ontario County Courthouse in Canandaigua never was red, a widely distributed postcard of the building depicted it in that color anyway.

The history of county courthouses in New York State is two centuries longer than that of postcards. It follows the settlement and growth of New York State from colonial times and the formation of 62 counties from the original ten. The story behind each of these counties has certain common elements. First, people living far from the county seat would clamor for a closer one, citing time and expense of travel. The State Legislature made the final decision on drawing county lines, locating the county seat, and authorizing a courthouse.

At the formation of each county, communities would vie for the honor of being the shire town, or county seat. Rival communities cited their virtues of central location, ease of transportation, and sufficient development to support the influx of visitors on court days. Politics also played a role. At times, the decision hinged on the influence of an important individual or on the effectiveness of a well-organized lobby. Often the Legislature declined to create a new county, but divided it into half-shires, each with its own county seat. Steuben County had the unique arrangement of three county seats.

Designation as county seat brought more than honor. It stimulated commerce. Court was not then, as it is now, an everyday affair. In the early days, people traveled long distances to register deeds or serve as jurors. Being the county seat generated, not only court-related business, law offices, and the like, but hotels and restaurants did a booming business when court was in session. Sometimes the influx of visitors made court sessions times of great festivity, producing an almost carnival atmosphere about town.

Before the building of a courthouse, court had to meet somewhere. In the late 18th Century, a tavern often served the purpose. Even when the record said "at the house of," it was frequently a home with a tavern attached. In the 19th Century, more likely a school, or even a church, served as temporary quarters. This change in usual venue was probably a matter of choosing the biggest meeting place, not a change in sensibilities about the morality of taverns.

It was not uncommon for congregations of various religious denominations to meet in courthouses until they were able to build their own buildings.

Notions of the First Amendment or what constituted "establishment' were different then. And in no instance was the courthouse reserved for the exclusive use of any denomination.

The jail was also an integral part of early courthouse plans, and usually shared the building. The settlers wanted to be sure the bad guys were locked up. Not just bad guys; this was the era of debtors' prisons. Because debtors weren't necessarily dangerous characters, and if they were locked up had no way of settling their debts, officials sometimes set out boundaries, called jail limits, within which debtors could roam. Sometimes this comprised the business district or the whole town. In the early days, defining jail limits was often the first order of business, even before a jail was built.

The early courthouses were usually two story buildings placing the jail and residence for jailer or sheriff in the basement or on the first floor. County offices also often occupied the first floor. The courtroom usually occupied the second. Sometimes it had a separate, outdoor entrance and staircase. Only recently, with the passage of the Americans with Disabilities Act of 1990, did handicapped accessibility become an essential consideration.

Many a courthouse succumbed to fire. The inclusion of a jail complicated matters. Some courthouses burned through care-

Court House and Indian Treaty Rock, Canandaigua, N. Y.

This postcard shows a bright red Ontario County Courthouse, but the courthouse never was red.

lessness or when a prisoner set a fire in order to escape. At times, a prisoner would fall victim to a courthouse fire, unable to get out.

The vulnerability of county clerk's records often prompted a county to build a separate fireproof clerk's office. Sometimes this spared the records in a courthouse fire. But on Staten Island, the supposedly fireproof clerk's office, built in 1827, burned shortly thereafter.

Like all buildings, courthouses require constant maintenance, repair, and modernization. As a county grows, its government expands along with it. No matter how commodious a courthouse may have been at the outset, it always becomes cramped or outmoded within a few decades. Sooner or later, the building's fate hangs in the balance as officials decide whether or not it merits saving. Sometimes the courthouse wins, and the county embarks on a major renovation and expansion. Other times it loses and is razed.

The courthouse and postcard heyday may be over, but both remain relevant to our time. Seeing the architecture through postcard images illuminates the role of the courthouse in making New York State what it is today.

Right: For this view of the Ontario County Courthouse, the colorist has given the scene the appearance of sunrise or sunset.

Below: The colorist of this postcard of the Wayne County Courthouse has given the scene a delicate watercolor appearance.

CANANDAIGUA, N.Y.

COURT HOUSE

a beautiful spot

COURT HOUSE, LYONS, N.Y.

CITY HALL,
ALBANY, N. Y.

The courts shared space with city
government in this City Hall from
1883 to 1916. The building was designed by noted architect Henry
Hobson Richardson, after whom the
style "Richardson Romanesque" was
named.

Albany County

Third Judicial District

In his introduction to the *Temple of Justice, a Celebration of the 75th Anniversary of the Albany Court House*, Joseph C. Williams noted, "What the temple is to the religious life of a people, the court is to its civil life." The life of Albany courthouses is about as long as any in the United States. The earliest one, which served for some 70 years, was built around 1634 near where Madison Avenue meets Broadway. Next came the 1670 Stadt Huys, which in 1740 was replaced by City Hall, a brick, three-story building on the northeast corner of Broadway and Hudson Avenue. The First Congress of the Colonies, presided over by Benjamin Franklin, was held there in 1754. At this site, the Declaration of Independence was read to the Continental troops on July 19, 1776. The building was destroyed by fire in 1836.

Facing Eagle Street, the Old Capitol (1808-1883) designed by Phillip Hooker, served as a courthouse and for other governmental functions. In 1883, it was removed to create a park in front of the present State Capitol. One of America's greatest architects, Henry Hobson Richardson (1838-1886) of Brookline, MA, designed the present City Hall, for which the cornerstone was laid in 1881. This was the last stopover for the courts until they had their own independent quarters.

In 1912, the Albany County Board of Supervisors acted on the public sentiment that the county courts should be separated from city matters and chose architects Hoppin and Koen of New York City to design a "Temple of Justice." The Classic Revival structure of Indiana limestone with granite steps sits on one of the highest points in the city. The foundation, using three million bricks, was built to hold 34,000 tons.

A maze-like geometric pattern, called a "meander," ties together the decorative components of the inside and outside. The pattern appears in the hallways, railings, and on the front of the elevators. A spacious concourse in the center of the building provides a dramatic setting for swearing in newly-elected officials. Tall columns of Belgian marble with Roman-type bases and capitals of

Hoppin and Koen of New York City designed Albany's "Temple of Justice." It has remained much the same as when dedicated in 1916 except for modernization of heating and electrical wiring. The building underwent renovation and expansion in 2006.

NEW COUNTY COURT HOUSE, ALBANY, N. Y.

a variant on the Ionic style dominate the interior. The building has remained essentially the same as when dedicated in 1916, except for changes in electrical and heating components. For many years, the courthouse was also the home of the Supreme Court, Appellate Division, Third Department. The Court of Appeals sat there as well during its 1958-1959 renovation.

One of Albany County's most publicized trials involved the kidnapping of John J. O'Connell, Jr., nephew of the then-Democratic leader Daniel P. O'Connell. On July 7, 1933, John J. ("Butch") O'Connell, Jr., a 24-year-old National Guard Lieutenant and nephew of Albany political bosses Edward J. and Daniel P. O'Connell was abducted. The captors sought $250,000 ransom, and the entire Albany police force was directed to undertake the search.

Governor Herbert Lehman offered a reward and invoked the state's energies. After almost a month in captivity, young O'Connell was released when the O'Connells gave $42,000 in cash to Manning Strewl, an intermediary. Strewl was charged with kidnapping in a trial that drew national attention.

Strewl was found guilty, and Judge Earl H. Gallup sentenced him to a 50-year term. He was carted off to Dannemora in an armored patrol wagon surrounded by police with machine guns. The aftermath of Strewl and the actual kidnappers is a fascinating story that took a number of twists and turns. The kidnapping is recounted in *People v. Strewl*, 240 App. Div. 400 (3rd Dept 1936).

New York's highest court, the Court of Appeals, was created by the Constitution of 1846, and began holding its sessions in the old Capitol building. When the new Capitol went up in the mid-1800's, Henry Hobson Richardson designed a magnificent courtroom on the second floor. On January 14, 1884, the court held its first session there. The Richardson Courtroom is an architectural masterpiece, combining beauty and tranquility. The hand-carved oak paneled walls, bench, and intricately crafted furniture create a setting not of opulence, but of grace that is impervious to time.

By the early 1900's, the Capitol, which had been damaged by fire in 1911, needed more room. Officials began to contemplate moving the Court of Appeals from the Capitol to the State House on Eagle Street. The Legislature took steps to alter the State House, an 1842 building, to accommodate the Court. The building is Greek-Revival-Ionic on the outside. Its exterior front capitals and bases were copied from those of the Temple of Nike Apteros on the Acropolis.

By 1917, the Court moved in, Richardson Courtroom and all. The courtroom was moved, piece by piece, with its oak walls and its huge fireplace of marble, onyx, and bronze. Louis F. Pilcher, the State Architect, designed a rear addition to the State House so that it could accommodate the courtroom.

By the 1940's, Court of Appeals Hall had seriously deteriorated. The wiring and heating systems had suffered a century of wear and tear. Governor Averill Harriman authorized a renovation plan that began in 1957 and was continued by Governor Nelson Rockefeller in 1959.

The program was under the direction of State Architect Carl Larson, with interiors by designer H. Clifford Burroughes. There were setbacks. Soon after construction began, a fire broke out in October 1958. The fire destroyed the roof and dome, but miraculously spared the Richardson Courtroom.

Construction continued, and the much of the exterior was replaced with Vermont marble, up to a foot in thickness. The original marble had been quarried at the State Prison at Mount Pleasant, now known as Sing Sing. The building's footings were replaced

COURT OF APPEALS, ALBANY, N. Y. 2

Court of Appeals Hall, where New York State's highest court sits, was originally constructed in 1842 as a State Office Building and converted in 1916 to its present use. In 1959 and in 2003 it underwent renovations, but from this angle, it looks much the same today.

with concrete and a new dome erected. The dome's interior was painted on slices of canvas that artist Eugene Savage fitted together. The mural, "The Romance of the Skies," depicted celestial bodies.

By the end of the 20th Century, Court of Appeals Hall was again in need of major repair. The building's electrical, plumbing, ventilation, and telecommunications systems had to be replaced, with an eye toward preserving the 1959 furnishings. Under the architectural aegis of the De Wolff Partnership of Rochester, with the State Dormitory Authority as project manager, the building took on two new additions. Marble for the addition was quarried from the same Danby, Vermont quarry as in the 1958-1959 project.

During the renovation, court operations moved to a building on Washington Avenue Extension. However, the judges continued to hear arguments in the Richardson courtroom, making their way through construction materials and debris to get to court. In all, 60,000 feet of existing space were refurbished and 33,000 square feet of spaced added. As a result of the additions, what once were exterior walls now serve as interior walls in offices throughout the building.

The architects and contractors created the final product, but the inspiration and touch flowed from Chief Judge Judith S. Kaye, who oversaw every detail, and assured a blend of elegance, preservation, and utility. Judge Richard C. Wesley served ably as liaison. The Richardson courtroom is not only intact, but also has been refurbished with new carpeting and chandeliers similar in design to the 1884 originals.

The Judges of the Court of Appeals have come from all over the state, but those who hailed from Albany County include Rufus W. Peckham, Sr. (1809-1893), Rufus W. Peckham, Jr. (1838-1901), Francis Bergan (1902-1998), Joseph W. Bellacosa (1937-), and Victoria A. Graffeo (1952-). J. Newton Fiero (1847-1931) was State Reporter of 63 volumes of New York Reports and Dean of Albany Law School.

The courtroom of the New York Court of Appeals, designed by H. H. Richardson, opened in 1884 on the second floor of the State Capitol.

When the New York Court of Appeals moved out of the Capitol to 20 Eagle Street, the Richardson courtroom was moved there piece by piece. After the 2002-2004 renovation, the courtroom looks much the same as it did in 1884.

Allegany County Court House, Belmont, N. Y.

The Allegany County Courthouse, circa 1909.

Allegany County

Eighth Judicial District

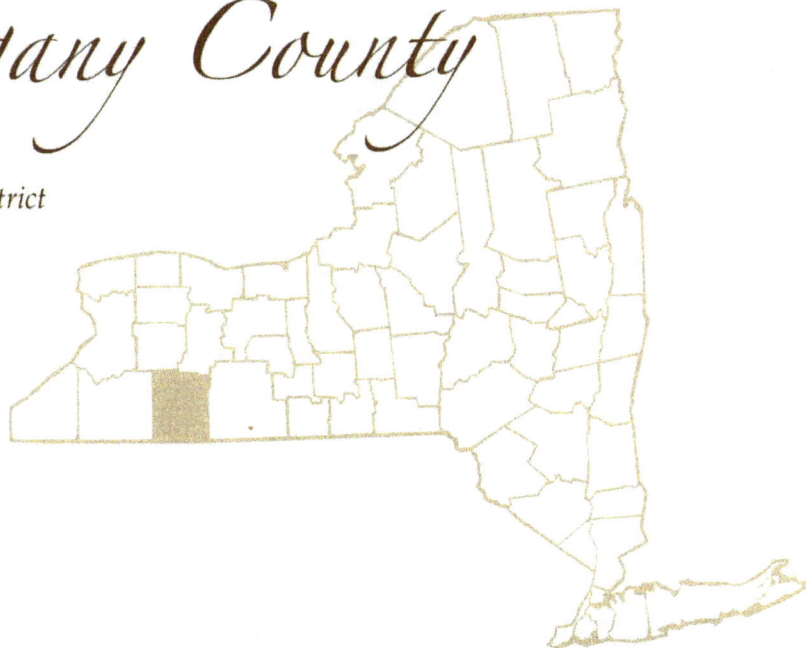

In 1804, Philip Church, Alexander Hamilton's nephew, took possession of a large tract of land owned by his father and moved there. At that time it was wilderness. He founded a town and named it Angelica in honor of his mother, Angelica Schuyler Church. When the 1000 square miles of Allegany County was formed from part of Genesee County two years later, this town became the county seat. Church became Judge of the Allegany County Court of Common Pleas and served for 14 years.

In 1808, the county built a County Clerk's office and jail, but there was not enough money for a courthouse. Court was held in various places, including the home of Revolutionary War hero Moses Van Campen, until 1823 when the County's first courthouse was finished. In 1849, a grand jury decreed the jail unfit, and the county built a new one.

In 1851, the Erie Railroad came through Allegany County, but not to Angelica. By 1857, there was some sentiment in favor of moving the county seat to a town located on the Erie line, either Belvidere or Philipsville, named for Philip Church. Philipsville, later renamed Belmont, built a courthouse in 1859 and won the contest.

Losing the county seat greatly displeased the residents of Angelica. They protested vigorously enough that, in 1860, the Legislature enacted a compromise. The Angelica courthouse would be repaired and court would be held alternately in the two towns. This practice lasted until 1892 when Belmont became the sole county seat. At that time a new jail was built in Belmont. The jail was enlarged in 1910 and a Surrogates office was built to the east of the courthouse.

By 1937, the county government was squeezed into 12,000 square feet and spread out over five buildings, not counting the jail. The time had come for a new courthouse, and the old courthouse was demolished. The Board of Supervisors solicited proposals from several architects and chose one by Carl Ade of Rochester. The county financed the $217,000 project with bonds at 2.4% interest. The final payment was made March 28, 1952.

Underneath the coats of paint, the courtroom walls are of matched cherry paneling. The white plaster ceiling is said to be of a secret Italian formula. The marble came from a Carolina quarry, especially opened for the purpose. Most of the built-in furnishings were custom made in Jamestown. The new courthouse provided 28,000 square feet of space. To accommodate the ever-expanding needs of government, the county built a county office building adjacent to the courthouse in 1976.

Martin Grover (1811-1875) was one of Allegany County's most eminent jurists. Born October 11, 1811, in Otsego County, he began is law practice in Angelica, Allegany County. As a country lawyer, Grover was more powerful than polished but stunningly successful with juries. He goes down in history as having an irrepressible sense of humor, which he made no effort to contain.

An able debater and adroit politician, he was elected in 1844 to the House of Representatives as a Democrat, serving from March 4, 1845 to March 3, 1847. At the 1853 political convention, he took part in the slavery debates, opposing the extension of slavery into Free Territory.

Grover was designated to serve ex officio on the Court of Appeals in 1859. He was elected to the Court in 1867 for an eight-year term, and after the 1870 Constitution, was elected to a 14-year term. In 1875, Grover died at his home in Angelica and is buried in Angelica Cemetery in Angelica, New York.

Thanks to Judge James Euken and Allegany County Historian Craig Braack.

COURT HOUSE AND JAIL, BELMONT, N. Y.

Allegany County's 1859 courthouse was demolished to make way for its present courthouse.

Allegany County's present courthouse, built in 1938, was designed by Carl Ade of Rochester.

The present Bronx County Courthouse was completed in 1934 at the cost of $7,000,000. Courtesy of the Thomas X. Casey Collection.

Bronx County

Twelfth Judicial District

The Bronx is the home of the New York Yankees (the Bronx bombers), the Bronx Zoo, and, of course, the Bronx cheer. The Bronx has its own distinctive character. It is New York State's newest county, the only one created in the 20th Century, and the only one of New York City's five boroughs not one of the original ten counties of 1683.

The Bronx is unique in its affinity for the definite article. When referring to counties, one does not speak of "The Erie," or "The Albany," or "The Ulster." The Bronx acquired its name from Jonas Bronck, a Scandinavian immigrant who in 1639, through an arrangement with the Dutch West India Company, took title to about 500 acres just north of the Harlem River. Even after Bronck disposed of the land, it was known by his name, which eventually morphed into "The Bronx."

The unofficial usage of the definite article has even had its day in court. An enterprising defendant in a criminal case challenged his indictment, which alleged that he committed the crime in the "County of The Bronx." The Court agreed that the "County of The Bronx" was not the correct designation, but that the borough was called "The Bronx," and the technical defect in the indictment did not warrant its dismissal. The Court (Hon. Dominic R. Massaro) wrote a lengthy and entertaining decision on the history of Bronx County, or if you like, The Bronx. [*People v. Riedd*, 160 Misc. 2nd 733 (1993)].

The early history of the Bronx is tied to Westchester County, of which the Bronx was a part. The Bronx, separated from Manhattan by the Harlem River and divided by the Bronx River, is the only borough of New York City on the mainland of the United States. Mid-19th-Century settlement in the Bronx included a region known as Morrisania, said to be the first commuter village of lower Westchester County. The name of this part of the Bronx owes its origin to the family of Gouverneur Morris (1752-1816), a member of the Constitutional Convention of 1787 and American Minister to France. The Morris family had vast holdings in part of what is now the Bronx.

NEW COURT HOUSE, 3RD AVENUE, BRONX, NEW YORK CITY.

The first Bronx County Courthouse was completed in 1914 at a cost of $2,000,000. Note the curving elevated railroad tracks at the far right. The frequent trains made it impossible for the grand jurors to hear testimony. Courtesy of the Thomas X. Casey Collection.

Westchester County lost the Bronx in 1874. New York City annexed the land, apparently believing it was in a better position than Westchester to provide the infrastructure to support the growing population. The City delegated this task to the Parks Department, and improvements proceeded at a snail's pace. New York annexed more of Westchester in 1895. The Bronx became a borough in 1898, but it remained a part of New York County.

By 1911, there was a considerable movement within the Bronx to become its own county. In a December 1911 meeting of the Taxpayers' Alliance of the Bronx, real estate broker Julius Haas declared, "The Bronx is a clean, decent place, a home of law-abiding and peace-loving citizens…We have no Tenderloins here, no criminal element, then why should we pay for prosecutions in which we have no concern?"

Bronx Senator Stephen J. Stillwell, who introduced the bill of separation in the legislature, expressed concern that New York County had proposed spending $25 million on a new courthouse. "We can build our own courthouse, and still have $2,000,000 left on the deal to invest in some other way," he said.

Whether the Bronx would actually save money with independence was open to question. In a November 5, 1912 editorial, urging voters to decide against secession, the *New York Times* estimated that just filling the 54 county offices, District Attorney, Sheriff, County Clerk, and the like, for a new county would cost the taxpayers $193,000 a year. In addition, the construction of new county building, and the support staff to fill the offices would run up still more costs. The *Times* further advocated the abolition of all counties within New York City. "They are not real counties, they are vermiform appendixes. In them politicians grow and fester…. The voters in the Bronx who want the luxury of a new county would find it costly."

The bill creating Bronx County passed the legislature April 19, 1912. It was then left to the voters in the Borough of Bronx to decide. The following November they voted 38,872 to 28,274 to become a separate county. In November 1913, the county officers were elected. The Bronx took its place officially as New York's 62nd county on January 1, 1914.

Lewis D. Gibbs was elected County Judge and Francis Martin, District Attorney. Martin later had a distinguished career on the bench, eventually becoming Presiding Justice of the Appellate Division, First Department, serving until his death on June 1, 1947. His daughter Edith married Adrian P. Burke who later served on the New York Court of Appeals.

A criminal defendant figured in the jurisdiction of the newly formed Bronx. Joseph P. McKenna challenged his conviction in New York County, claiming that the court had no jurisdiction because Bronx County – the location of the crime – had already been created by virtue of 1912 N.Y Laws 548. The New York Court of Appeals, however, upheld the conviction. It also upheld the constitutionality of the law creating Bronx County [People ex. rel. Unger v. Kennedy 207 NY 533 (1913)] over the objection of some residents of Manhattan who asserted that voters in all of New York County should have had a say in the creation of the Bronx.

Even before the Bronx became a county, its citizens felt the need for a courthouse of their own. Municipal Court sessions were held in a commercial building on the corner of Third Avenue and 158th St. The basement below the courtroom served as a sort of jail, with generally acknowledged crowded and unsanitary conditions. Those advocating a new courthouse chose a site at Third Ave. and East 161st Street. They believed they were well on their way to achieving it in 1902. The City bought the land and, in 1904, appropriated $800,000 to build the structure. Two years later, with the entire appropriation spent, only the beginnings of the foundation showed. Delay upon delay ensued.

Countyhood brought the completion of the project after the expenditure of some two million dollars. The Bronx celebrated its new status and new courthouse January 1, 1914. By the following June, the building had already achieved disrepute. The elegantly appointed Grand Jury room lay on the same level as the Third Avenue elevated railroad, almost adjacent to it. Here the tracks curve, and the cars make the turn with a loud screeching noise. When the trains passed every few minutes, the grand jurors could not hear the witnesses. In those pre-air-conditioning days, they had to choose between hearing the proceedings or closing the windows and enduring stifling heat. This historic structure, nicknamed the "Gray Lady" has stood empty since sometime in the 1970's, at about the same time the elevated railroad tracks were taken down. After 91 years, the building is slated for new life as a charter school. As reported in a 2006 New York Times article, the old hall of justice was yielding to halls full of children.

In June 1930, the county began constructing the present 10-story courthouse. The $7,000,000 building was dedicated in a three-day ceremony in June 1934. It stands at the corner of 161st Street and the Grand Concourse, occupying the entire city block. It features Art Deco styling, balustrade terraces, entry porticos supported by columns, and vertically ribboned windows. Two massive blocks of Georgia marble flank the steps leading to each of the four entrances. In 1934, these blocks were valued at $5,000 apiece. The granite and limestone façade is ornamented with marble statuary and friezes, symbolizing law and justice.

Inside, the grandeur is carried forth in arched marble entrances, vaulted lobbies, and bronze ornamental door. The Supreme, Surrogate's, and City Civil court rooms are wood paneled and embellished with classical themes.

The Concourse Plaza Hotel, across from the courthouse, was a home away from home for the New York Yankees. When the Yankees were in town, the two buildings could wink at each other – court proceedings in one building, the New York Yankees overnighting in the other.

Thanks to Judge Dominic R. Massaro, Thomas X. Casey, Dr. Gary Hermalyn, and the Bronx County Historical Society.

Court House, Binghamton, N. Y.

The Broome County Courthouse is shown here in a postcard mailed in 1919. The building was designed by Isaac G. Perry and built in 1898.

Broome County

Sixth Judicial District

Broome County was named after John Broome (1738-1810) who was Lt. Governor when Broome County was established in 1806 from a portion of Tioga County. At that time, Binghamton, or Chenango Point, as it was then known, had already been a half-shire town of Tioga. A small courthouse, built in 1802, had a two-celled log jail attached to it. The jailer lived on the first floor. The courtroom was on the second. Before that, court proceedings took place in the home of Josiah Whitney, who managed the immense acreage owned by William Bingham of Philadelphia. Bingham had promised the county land for a courthouse. After his death in 1804, his executors arranged for the county to take possession of it, and the courthouse was placed there. It was crude and unpretentious, but it sufficed for 25 years.

In 1829, Broome built a plain two-brick courthouse with cupola and a clock. The courtroom and jury room occupied the second floor. The jailer lived on the first floor, and the jail was in the basement.

It served for about 30 years, when the demand for a larger building arose along with the notion of separating the jail from the court facilities. John Stuart Wells of Broome County built the new courthouse in 1857 at a cost of $32,000. It was a brick, two-story structure with a dome and cupola surmounted by a statue of justice, reaching a height of 120 feet.

By 1890, the population had doubled, and the supervisors chose Alexander B. Carman to build an addition on each end. The additions cost $19,000. On December 28, 1896, the courthouse burned, causing the destruction of many records and damaging the extensive law library.

Broome County immediately started work on the new courthouse, choosing Isaac Perry as architect and Miles Leonard as contractor. It was built in the Classic Revival similar to its predecessor, but grander with a wider portico. The dome was of copper and featured a large clock. When it was completed in 1898, the citizens marveled at its grandeur. It was built of Ohio sandstone with bluestone trimmings and a copper dome. Combination gas-electric chandeliers illuminated the Supreme Courtroom. Gold leaf ornamented the capitals of the interior columns.

Even the grandest of courthouses will suffer from deterioration over time. Renovations will introduce elements far removed from the architect's original vision. Lucky is the courthouse whose citizens appreciate it. What began as a relatively modest asbestos abatement project in 2001, led to an extensive restoration project. The removal of a 1950's drop ceiling revealed the beauty of the original, but heavily damaged, tin ceiling.

The few surviving light fixtures were repaired and made consistent with modern lighting requirements. Further fixtures resembling the originals were purchased. An expert in Rhode Island examined paint samples taken from every one of the 12 to 15 layers on walls, pilasters, capitols, beams, and ceiling and matched them to currently available paint colors.

A 1911 photograph shows a Seth Thomas clock hanging on the wall behind the juror's box. If only it could be found. When the county purchased it, the timepiece cost only $15, but now its collectors' value is in the thousands of dollars. A newspaper article about the clock brought a response from Simon O'Neil, a retired attorney and clock collector. He had acquired the clock and offered to donate it back.

Before accepting the gift, the County wanted to make sure it was the same clock and not one that merely looked like it. Those who repaint walls will usually paint around an object like a clock rather than to remove it and paint underneath it. The object will then show small bits of paint from each re-painting. An examination of the edges of the clock revealed traces of paint that matched the courthouse paint samples precisely. The clock now has resumed its place in the courtroom.

Celora E. Martin (1834-1909), born in Newport, NY, served as a Judge of the New York Court of Appeals from 1895 to 1904. Ransom Balcom (1818-1879), born in Oxford, NY, served ex officio on the Court in 1863. The Judge Ransom Balcome House, built in 1836, is still featured in a walking tour of Oxford.

Thanks to Judge Robert S. Rose and Attorney William E. Night.

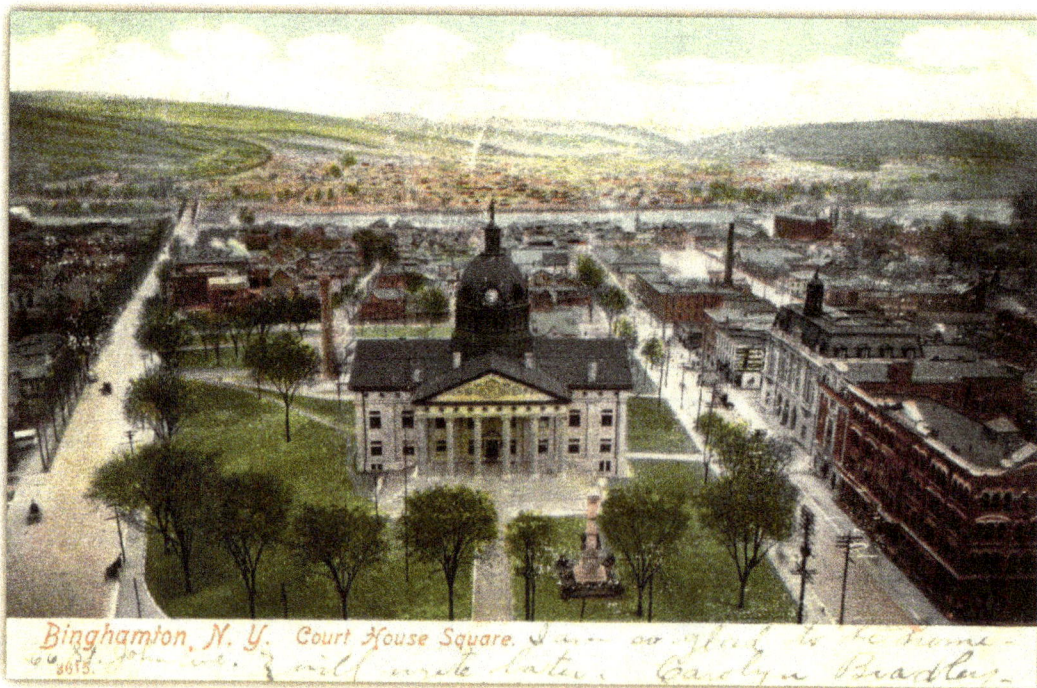

A broader view of the Broome County Courthouse, as shown around 1907.

Broome County Court House and Office Building, Binghamton, N. Y.

Right: The Broome County Courthouse as it looked in the 1940's.

Below: On this pre-1907 card, the Broome County Courthouse looks festive decked out in bunting.

The Cattaraugus County Courthouse was built in 1868 after the county seat was moved to Little Valley to be near the Erie Railroad line.

Cattaraugus County

Eighth Judicial District

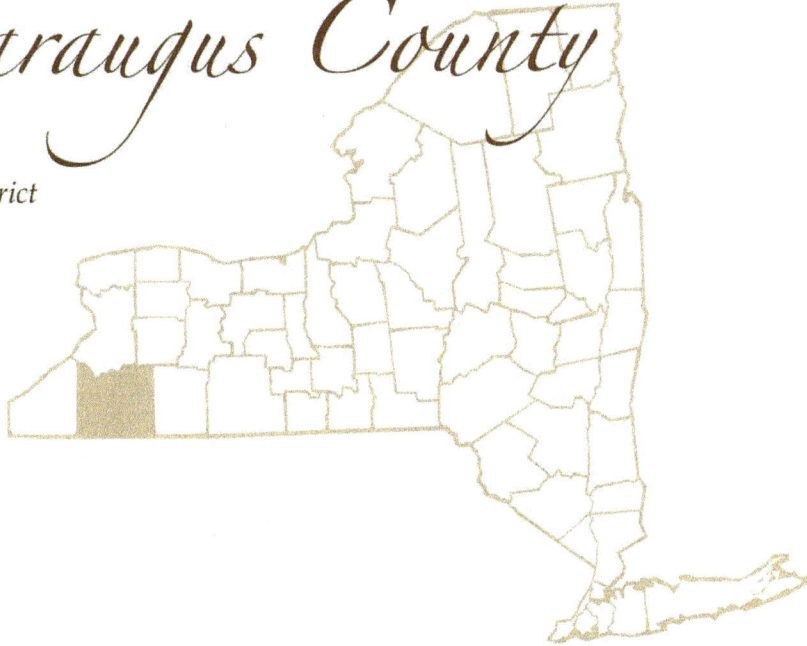

Cattaraugus County lies at the eastern border of the large tract that the Holland Land Company, a group of Dutch investors, had purchased to sell to settlers. The entire county, except for three Indian reservations, was part of this purchase.

Cattaraugus was made a provisional county in 1808, to become official as soon as it had the requisite number of citizens. Ellicottville, named for Joseph Ellicott, the resident land agent for the Holland Land Company, was named county seat at that time. The company laid out the streets and left a public square in the center, anticipating a courthouse.

Cattaraugus fulfilled the population quota in 1817. The first session of court was held in Olean, but in 1818, the Legislature decreed that court be held in Ellicottville. The residents of Olean were not happy about this. Those from Olean who came to the first session of court in Ellicottville brought tents and their own provisions with them so that the Village of Ellicottville should not receive any economic benefit from hosting court. Eventually, they cooled down

and stayed at the hotels in Ellicottville. Court took place at the house of Baker Leonard during the building of the courthouse.

The Holland Land Company conveyed the land, and the building was put up in 1820. It was typical for its time, with the jail on the first floor and the courthouse on the second. A fire took the building in the winter of 1829. Fearing the new courthouse might be built somewhere else, Ellicottville residents were relieved to learn in April 1829 that the Legislature had authorized the rebuilding in Ellicottville. This prompted great celebration.

The new courthouse was a brick structure. The building was ready for use in January 1830, although evidently not complete because the legislature authorized an additional $1200 to complete the courthouse and jail. It had a belfry, and sometime after 1862, a bell.

In 1845, disaffected purchasers of land from the Holland Land Company started a disturbance called the Dutch Hill War in the Town of Ischua. The sheriff, alarmed that the rioters would come to

Ellicottville and destroy the land offices and county buildings, as a mob had nine years earlier in Chautauqua County, called out two companies of militia on Sunday, Jan. 26, 1845 to guard the courthouse.

In 1865, the Legislature voted to move the county seat to Little Valley because it was located on the Erie Railroad line. The move was completed in 1868. The Town of Ellicottville bought the old county buildings for $1000 for eventual use as a Town Hall.

The Little Valley courthouse, designed by Horatio Nelson White of Syracuse, was 82 by 52 feet, built of brick with a stone foundation and a slate roof. The first story, which housed among other offices, a fireproof room for the county clerk, was 13 feet tall. The second story contained the courtroom, judge's chambers, grand jury, jury, and janitor's rooms.

A fire, starting in the belfry in April 7, 1946, destroyed the upper part of the courthouse. The bell plummeted to the first floor, narrowly missing several firemen. When the courthouse was repaired, the bell was moved to the courthouse lawn. The courthouse continued to deteriorate. In the quest for space, some county offices were dispersed to other parts of the county. During the 1960's the historic courthouse was demolished and replaced by a new courthouse, county office building, and jail.

Although the old courthouse building in Ellicottville burned in 1969, it survives. The fire started downstairs, but it destroyed mainly the attic, roof, and tower. The brick walls remained intact. After the building lay empty and unprotected for a couple of years, the town was able to raise the funds to repair and restore the building. In June 2004, Governor George Pataki announced an additional $192,500 grant to restore the brick masonry on the exterior walls of the Ellicottville Town Hall. The Old Cattaraugus County Courthouse will remain with us.

Among the county's legal figures, Albert Haight (1842-1926) was born in Ellicottville and went on to serve on the Court of Appeals from 1889 to 1892 and 1895 to 1912.

Thanks to Cattaraugus County Historian Carol A. Ruth.

CATTARAUGUS COUNTY, LITTLE VALLEY, N.Y.

Above: The courthouse, shown among other county buildings.

Left: After the belfry burned in 1946, the bell and the eagle from the top were moved to the front lawn of the courthouse.

Copyright 1905 by the Rotograph Co.

G 4285 Court House, Auburn, N. Y.

This 1905 postcard shows Cayuga County's Greek Revival courthouse, designed by John I. Hagaman in 1835.

Cayuga County

Seventh Judicial District

A large bronze plaque in honor of Harriet Tubman (c. 1821-1913) adorns the entrance of the Cayuga County Courthouse. The tablet was erected by the citizens of Auburn and describes Tubman as the "Moses" of her people. "With rare courage," the plaque reads, "she led over three hundred Negroes up from slavery to freedom…" in her brave actions in support of the Underground Railroad. The plaque was erected in 1914 in the courthouse that has endured since1835 and serves today.

Cayuga was originally part of Onondaga County, from which it was separated in 1799 and eventually was made smaller by the removal of Seneca County and a part of Tompkins County. Before 1804, court usually took place in the village of Cayuga. A log jail was built at Cayuga, by the lake, underneath the tollhouse at the East End of the Cayuga bridge. Prisoners entered the jail by descending ladders through a trap door in the tollhouse.

When Seneca County was carved out of Cayuga County on March 27, 1804, the village at Cayuga was no longer a central location for the remainder of the county. The jail was transferred to Aurora. In the law creating Seneca County, the legislature inserted a provision to the effect that the courthouse for Cayuga County be located at Sherwood Corners in the town of Scipio. The Cayuga residents, irked by what they viewed as a sneaky act, voiced their objection with such vigor that this portion of the law was repealed and the question of county seat reopened. Aurora, Sherwood, Cayuga, and Levanna all campaigned for it, but Auburn won. William Bostwick owned the land at Hardenburg Corners in Auburn on which the courthouse was to be built. The condition of the county seat's location was that the land be donated. A citizens group raised $200 to compensate Bostwick, and Cayuga County's buildings have been there ever since.

The first Auburn courthouse was a log building, completed in 1809 at a cost of $10,000. It had a jail in the first story, the courtroom on the second. While the courthouse was being built, County Clerk Peter Hughes kept the records in his house. He kept them there until 1814 when the county built a separate county clerk's office.

This building sufficed until 1835 when the county expended $30,000 to build its present courthouse. The county began building its courthouse during a period of economic boom, when it seemed reasonable to build a grand Greek Revival building with a large dome supporting a Statue of Justice, and a Statue of Liberty and Temperance adorning the portico. Then the Panic of 1837 hit. The plans for the statuary had to be abandoned. The remaining plans went forward, however. In the beginning, the acoustics were poor, but subsequent renovations lessened that problem.

In 1922, the courthouse was seriously damaged by fire. The dome collapsed into the building, but the structure survived. Architect Samuel Hillger designed its restoration and added a third floor. In 1979, the building underwent a major renovation which, among other things, provided handicapped accessibility. The site now functions as both a County and a Federal courthouse. It has been on the National Register of Historic Places since 1991 and has become a source of pride for the county.

Several miles south of Auburn is Locke, N.Y., which marks the southern border of Cayuga County. President Millard Fillmore was born in there in 1800. Another prominent figure from Cayuga County was Charles C. Dwight (1830-1902), who served ex officio on the New York Court of Appeals in 1868.

Seward House and Museum sits not far from the courthouse. William H. Seward (1801-1872) was one of Cayuga's most prominent attorneys. He was a New York Governor, United States Senator, and as Secretary of State for President Abraham Lincoln, was active in the purchase of Alaska. In 1846, at the Cayuga County courthouse, Seward represented William Freeman in a landmark case [*Freeman v. People* 4 Denio 9 (1847)] that pioneered the insanity defense in New York and represented a call for fairness across racial lines.

In 1851, early proceedings in the "Jerry Rescue" indictments were held at the courthouse. "Jerry" was a freed slave who was arrested in Syracuse. After the rescuers were taken to the Auburn courthouse for arraignment, Seward bailed them out. Of the 20 rescuers indicted for violating the Fugitive Slave Law, only one was convicted. The rescuers had been arrested elsewhere. Because of the strong public sentiment against slavery in Cayuga County, no one was ever charged locally for violating the Fugitive Slave Law. In 1998, the United States Congress established the National Underground Railroad Network to Freedom Act, which includes the Cayuga County Courthouse among its program members and sites.

Thanks to Sheila Tucker, County Historian and to County Judge Peter Corning.

COURT HOUSE, AUBURN, N. Y.

The large dome of the Cayuga County Courthouse collapsed in a 1922 fire. Samuel Hillger designed this restoration, adding a third floor.

GENESEE STREET LOOKING EAST SHOWING POST OFFICE AND CAYUGA COUNTY COURT HOUSE, AUBURN, N. Y.

E-8064

A later photo shows the vine-covered Cayuga County Courthouse with other buildings on Genesee Street.

Old Court House, Mayville, N. Y. *At last I found one of three cards in Sugargrove. D.M.S.*

PS will send a picture of the new court house if you if I haven't one. Be careful failure.

When this Chautauqua County Courthouse was built in 1834, some residents thought it was too expensive. It served for 70 years before it was demolished to make way for a larger building.

Chautauqua County

Eighth Judicial District

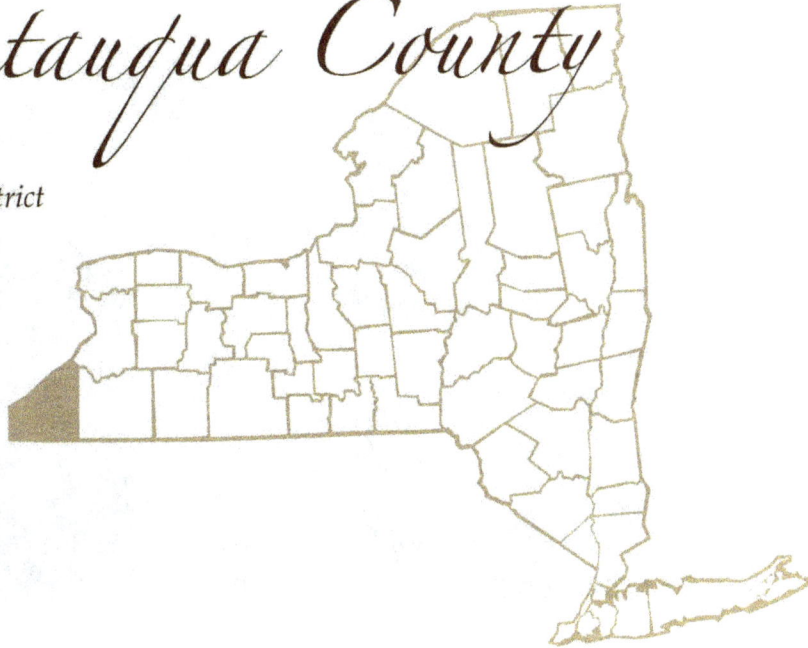

After it was created in 1808, Chautauqua County took three years to complete its governmental organization. In order for the county to gain full status, it needed 500 taxable inhabitants, and it took until 1810 before the assessment rolls revealed that many people. When the three commissioners appointed to select the county seat in 1808 decided on Mayville, they put up a large hemlock post to mark the courthouse site so that there should be no question about the location when the time came. The county began to build a courthouse in 1811, but the War of 1812 delayed the completion until 1815. The two-story structure, costing $1500, was the first frame building in the county. The first floor housed the jailer and his family and provided three jail cells, two for miscreants and one for debtors. The second floor was for court, jury, and other public meetings.

Even in 1811, $1500 did not buy much. Cheap construction soon deteriorates. In 1831, a grand jury declared the jail dilapidated and unsafe, but the supervisors failed to act. The next year, the State Legislature ordered a new jail to be built, and the county borrowed the money.

By 1834, the courthouse had obviously become inadequate for the county's needs. The county was still paying off the loan for the jail. Nevertheless, the Board of Supervisors had the county borrow $5000 for a new courthouse. The commissioners chose Benjamin Rathbun of Buffalo to erect the exterior of the two-story brick building. After he completed that, the entire $5000 was gone. The county had to raise an additional $4000 to furnish and decorate it. Some citizens grumbled that the county was spending too much to make the building larger and grander than necessary, thereby improving Mayville at the expense of the rest of the county. The sum proved to be a good investment, however. This courthouse served the county for almost 70 years.

Chautauqua County was within the large acreage purchased by Dutch investors known as the Holland Land Company. Many of the settlers who had bought land from the company were poor and

Mayville, N.Y., Old Holland Land Co. Vault, Built about 1802.

Before Chautauqua became a county, the Holland Land Company came to Mayville, opened a land office and sold land to settlers. In 1836, disgruntled purchasers stormed the land office and destroyed it, leaving only the vault.

had purchased their land on generous credit terms. Whether from neglect or inability, many owed much of the principal and interest on these contracts. For years, the Holland Land Company had dealt leniently with them, but eventually new management took sterner measures to secure payment.

On Feb. 7, 1836, a mob destroyed the land office at Mayville, leaving only the vault intact. The rioters, and those who supported them, rejoiced that the records of indebtedness were destroyed. Most of the records were recovered and sent elsewhere for safe-keeping.

One of the last trials held in the original courthouse, before its demolition, was that of Joseph Damon for killing his wife. [*People v. Damon*, 13 Wend. 351 (1835)] He was convicted and hanged. A crowd numbering in the thousands attended the hanging. It was the last public execution in the state.

By 1906, the county needed more space and the following year razed the 1834 courthouse. The county clerk and treasurer had already moved their offices across the street. The Board of Supervisors allocated $135,000 for a new courthouse. Construction began in 1908 with the firm of Shellberg, Lindquist, and Bailey of Jamestown, NY

as contractors. The 90 by 140 square foot building, of Ohio sandstone with a tile and copper roof, consists of two stories, each 18 feet high. Marble and quartered oak finish the interior.

Most of the American courthouses depicted on the millions of post cards sent are of an early vintage, when the penny post card was a handy way to deliver a greeting. For a variety of reasons, courthouse postcards are now far less popular than they once were. A modern-looking courthouse seldom appears on a post card. One from Chautauqua depicts the 1969 addition to the courthouse, named for Supreme Court Judge Joseph Gerace, Chautauqua's first County Executive. The trees in the postcard are no longer standing, having been removed during the summer of 2005 to widen the street.

United States Supreme Court Justice Robert H. Jackson (1892-1954) is the most renowned jurist to hail from Chautauqua County. Justice Jackson was educated in Frewsburg, Chautauqua County. He was a Justice of the United States Supreme Court (1941-1954) after having spent a substantial part of his legal career as a country lawyer in Jamestown. He had a considerable influence on national and world affairs, serving as United States Attorney General

(1940-1941), and Chief Prosecuting Attorney at the Nuremberg War Trials. He died on October 9, 1954 at the age of 62 and is buried at the Maple Grove Cemetery in Frewsburg. The Robert H. Jackson Center is located on East Fourth Street in Jamestown.

Other notable Chautauqua legal figures include Marvin R. Dye (1895-1997), who served on the Court of Appeals from 1944 to 1965; Charles E. Goodell (1926-1987), a United States Senator from 1968 to 1971; and Bainbridge Colby (1869-1950), a founder of the Bull Moose Party in 1912 and law partner of Woodrow Wilson from 1921 to 1923.

Richard P. Marvin (1803-1892) was a Member of Congress from 1837 to 1841 and served ex officio on the New York Court of Appeals in 1855 and 1863. James Mullett (1784-1851) served ex officio on the Court in 1851. Reuben E. Fenton (1819-1885) was Governor of New York from 1865 to 1869 and is buried in Jamestown, as is Gilbert Dean (1819-1870) who served ex officio on the Court of Appeals in 1855.

Thanks to Michelle Henry, Chautauqua County Historian and County Judge John T. Ward.

Chautauqua County Court House, Mayville, N. Y.

Above: In 1908, Chautauqua County began construction of its present courthouse..

Right: To meet the need for more space, Chautauqua County built a modern addition to its courthouse in 1969.

Court House and Soldiers Monument, Elmira, N. Y.

This Horatio Nelson White masterpiece, with necessary upkeep, modernization, and expansions, has served Chemung County well since 1861.

Chemung County

Sixth Judicial District

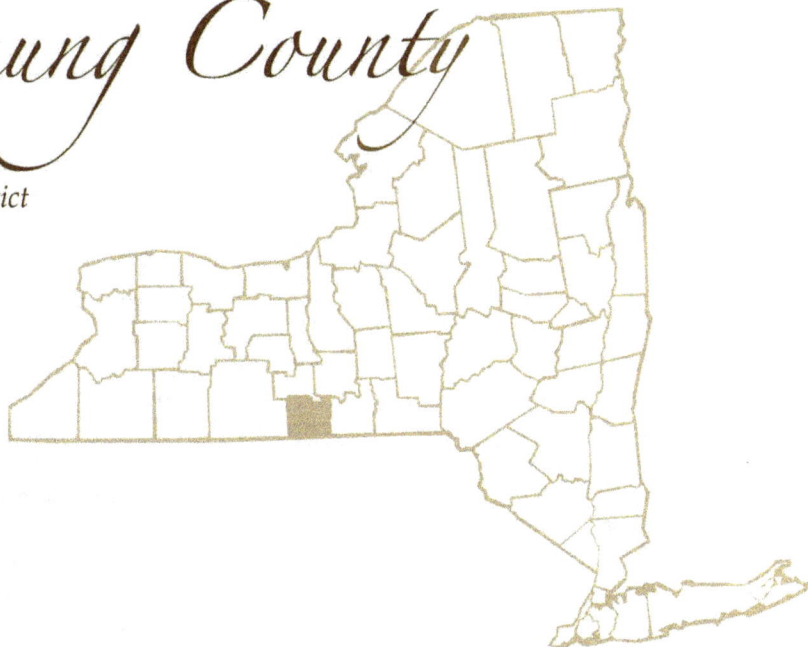

The Chemung County Courthouse on Lake Street in Elmira is a splendid example of the work of noted Syracuse architect Horatio Nelson White and of the Anglo-Norman style of architecture. It was built in 1861 of red brick with lime putty mortar and finished with hand-tooled limestone. It has had five additions in its lifetime, each of a slightly different shade of brick. A painted exterior masks the differences in color. The building is 84 feet high with a 15-foot tower extending above the roof. The façade on Lake Street features massive stone pillars and heavy brick arches, giving an appearance of solidity and durability. The foundation, of native stone faced with limestone, includes some of the foundation of the previous courthouse, which had been moved to make way for the new one.

The building cost $21,205, all financed by bonds, which were paid by 1884. The total cost, including interest, amounted to $25,000. David Wilcox of Syracuse, NY served as contractor: Thomas Gerrity of Elmira was subcontractor for the masonry. All the workmen lived in Chemung County.

This courthouse came about largely through the efforts of Col. Samuel Gilbert Hathaway, Jr., who toward the end of an illustrious legal career sought election to the Board of Supervisors solely to see to it that a new courthouse would be built. A graduate of Union College, he was admitted to the practice of law in 1836. He was elected to the State Assembly in 1841, and ran unsuccessfully for Congress in 1856 and 1862.

Hathaway joined the military in 1862 and saw action in the Civil War. He had to leave his command and return to Elmira, owing to a heart condition. He never regained his health and died in 1864. A niche in the courtroom holds a white marble bust of Col. Hathaway.

The first courthouse in Elmira was built in 1792, when Chemung was part of Tioga County and Elmira was known as Newtown, on land provided by Col. Brinton Paine. A simple building with no steeple, bell, nor porches, it served nonetheless as a hub of village activity.

In 1822, the county seat was moved to Spencer, but the 1792 courthouse was still used for civic functions, church services, and a jail. When the Spencer Courthouse burned in 1822, the Tioga County Board of Supervisors divided the county into two shires, with county seats at both Owego and Newtown.

The county did not move into the old courthouse, which had been allowed to deteriorate. County officials obtained land on Lake Street for a new building. The former site and courthouse reverted to Col. Paine, and in 1823 he moved his family into the building.

The 1824 courthouse was a two story Greek Revival style building framed with hand-hewn logs and covered with painted siding. The courtroom was on the second floor. The first floor provided Judges' chambers, an office for the District Attorney, a jury room, and the jail. It had a full basement, which housed the under sheriff and his family. The plaster walls were whitewashed. The building had no plumbing and was heated only by open fireplaces on each side of the courtroom. It was illuminated by candlelight.

Like the 1792 building, this courthouse served as a multi-purpose civic center. Various groups met there. The Methodists held services; political parties held conventions; and all special meetings took place there. This was the courthouse when Chemung County was created in 1836.

In 1860, the Village of Elmira bought the building to use as a Village Hall and moved it to another location. It served all municipal needs until 1896 when Elmira built its present City Hall. It later passed into private hands.

Elmira's present courthouse has been continually upgraded. In its history can be seen the history of technology itself. Like the 1824 courthouse, it was first heated only by fireplaces. It was illuminated by gaslight in 1901, and electric lights were installed as soon as they were available. Toilets were installed in 1911. Ventilation was accomplished by opening the windows until air conditioning was added in 1975. It was placed on the National Register of Historic Places in 1970.

Several jurists of note hail from Chemung County. Frederick Collin (1850-1939) was born in Elmira and served as its Mayor from 1894 to 1898. He was a Judge of the New York Court of Appeals from 1910 to 1920. Hiram Gray (1801-1890) served ex officio on the Court of Appeals in 1851. Walter B. Reynolds (1901-1991) served on the Appellate Division, Third Department, from 1985 to 1976. He was President of the New York State District Attorney's Association in 1943, as was his law clerk, Judge John O'Mara in 1972 to 1973, and his nephew, Appellate Division Justice D. Bruce Crew III in 1976 to 1977.

Thanks to J. Arthur Kieffer, Chemung County Historian.

Court House, West Lake Street,
ELMIRA, N. Y.

This view shows a quiet Lake Street at the front of the courthouse in 1908.

COURT HOUSE, NORWICH, N. Y. IN ICE STORM FEB. 16TH. 1909.

An ice storm damaged a tree in front of the Chenango County Courthouse in 1909. The 1837 building is among the oldest courthouses in New York still in use today.

Chenango County

Sixth Judicial District

The citizens of Chenango are rightfully proud of their 1837 Greek Revival courthouse. It is one of the oldest courthouses in New York still functioning for its original purpose. The building owes its longevity, in part, to the community's appreciation of its beauty and historical significance.

The genealogy of Chenango County begins with Albany County and continues through Tioga County and Herkimer County. It became a county of its own in 1798, with courts alternating between two county seats, Hamilton and Oxford. In 1806, when Madison County was created from part of Chenango, Hamilton went with it. The State Legislature, bypassing Oxford, appointed Norwich as Chenango's county seat.

Peter and Polly Garnsey donated about an acre and a half in Norwich village for the courthouse and jail. The first court held in Norwich was the Court of Common Pleas in 1809. The first Circuit Court was held in the courthouse in 1810, presided over by Smith Thompson who 13 years later would become a United States Supreme Court Justice.

The county quickly outgrew its first courthouse. The $6500 two-story frame building soon became cramped, and the jail proved a problem when prisoners escaped easily. In 1830, the county alleviated the pressure by building a separate jail with a fenced-in yard to the north of the courthouse.

Oxford had not given up its hope to regain its position as county seat. As the need for a new courthouse became increasingly evident, Oxford petitioned the State Legislature to become the county seat. The ensuing three months of intense debate ended March 24, 1837 when the Legislature directed the new courthouse to be built at Norwich. Both towns had sent delegations to lobby for the county seat. The returning Norwich delegation received a hero's welcome.

The county budgeted $7,000 for the building. The old courthouse was sold at auction for $5.22, with the stipulation that it by removed from the site but that the stone be reserved.

Even as the cost of the structure was mounting, there remained substantial public sentiment for a building worthy of the growing and promising county. By the time it was finished, the cost was some $9,000 over budget. The result was an elegant Greek-Revival style building of which the citizens were proud. It was built of stone quarried near Oxford. Four massive Corinthian columns graced the front. A seven-foot statue of Lady Justice stood upon its dome.

The building went through a series of repairs and alterations during the ensuing century. In 1946, the building's future became threatened when the Board of Supervisors proposed construction of a new courthouse and office building at the site of the old one. This prompted an unexpected outcry, first from preservationists and later from the general public.

Oxford, still not having given up its dream of recapturing the county seat, sensed an opening. The town invited members of the Board of Supervisors to visit proposed sites there. Despite this lobbying, the Supervisors eventually responded to the groundswell of pressure from the public and in June 1947 voted to keep and repair the century-old building.

In December 1977, the county embarked on an extensive three-year restoration of the courthouse to bring back its historic character and to bring it up to modern building and safety codes. The most outstanding conservation feat was the preservation of the seven-foot statue of Lady Justice. The white-pine sculpture had suffered much damage throughout the years, and the Herculean job was undertaken by Faye Wrubel, a student in the Cooperstown Graduate Program in Conservation of Historic and Artistic Works. The statue now resides inside the courthouse, encased in glass, while a replica graces the dome.

The Chenango County Courthouse is the 14th oldest courthouse in New York and is listed on the National Register of Historic Places.

Irving M. Ives (1896-1962) was born and resided in Chenango County. He served as State Assembly Speaker (1936), United States Senator (1947-1959), and was candidate for Governor in 1954. He is interred in Greenlawn Cemetery, Bainbridge, Chenango County.

Thanks to Dale C. Storm, Chenango County Historian; to Hon. W. Howard Sullivan, County Court Judge; to Thomas Kelly, Esq.; and to Patricia Scott, City of Norwich Historian.

This view shows the courthouse with other county buildings, including a jail completed in 1903.

COURT HOUSE AND COUNTY BUILDINGS, NORWICH, N. Y.

Above: This view from a hilltop shows the Chenango County Courthouse and nearby county buildings.

Left: In 1996, the Chenango County Courthouse still shines following its 1977-1980 renovation. Note the new statue of Lady Justice on the golden dome and the modern county buildings in the background.

COURT HOUSE, PLATTSBURG, N. Y.

107836

The 1889 courthouse in Plattsburgh was designed by Marcus F. Cummings of Troy.

Clinton County

Fourth Judicial District

There are strong links between Clinton County and our nation's beginnings, developed by people who played roles in both. In 1788, Judge Zephaniah Platt (1735-1807) of Poughkeepsie was a member of the convention that ratified the United States Constitution. He was one of the founders of Plattsburgh, along with his brother, Nathaniel Platt (1741-1816), a captain in the French and Indian War of 1760. Judge Zephaniah Platt's son Jonas Platt (1769-1834) was a member of the (old) State Supreme Court from 1814 to 1821 and a delegate to the State's Constitutional Convention in 1821.

Another Plattsburgh pioneer, Melancton Smith (1744-1798) of Dutchess County, was a pivotal figure at the Convention to Ratify the United States Constitution in 1788. The convention was chaired by George Clinton (1739-1812) after whom Clinton County was named. Clinton was also New York State's first Governor and served as Vice President under Thomas Jefferson and James Madison.

In 1788, the very year New York ratified the Constitution, Clinton County was created, taken from Washington County. The next year, the county built a log blockhouse adjacent to the shore of Lake Champlain. It was built as a jail, but officials voted 40 dollars to expand it for use as a courthouse, which was completed in 1796. In 1803, the county oversaw the construction of a new $2,751 courthouse. That building lasted until 1814 when, during the siege of Plattsburgh, it was burned by order of American General Alexander Macomb.

Rebuilt in 1815-1816, it was again destroyed by fire in 1836 and rebuilt again. In the meantime, Essex County and Franklin County were carved from Clinton County in 1799 and 1808 respectively. At a December 5, 1888 meeting, the Clinton County Board of Supervisors authorized a $40,000 bond issue to finance a new courthouse and jail. The Supervisors ordered the construction with care that "so much of the material of the old courthouse as can be used with profit, be used in the new buildings." The Supervisors made this resolution at the Surrogate's building, which went up in 1884 and is now the county's oldest building.

The 1889 county courthouse is a magnificent Romanesque Italianate structure, designed by Marcus F. Cummings of Troy. It was built of locally quarried stone and cast iron lintels made from melted-down Civil War cannons. After Plattsburgh became a city in 1902, City Court shared the county courthouse from 1906 to 1919.

The first trial in the 1889 courthouse was a murder prosecution against Joseph Chapleau. His conviction was affirmed by the Court of Appeals [*People v. Chapleau*, 121 NY 266 (1890], after which Governor David B. Hill commuted the death sentence to life imprisonment.

The 1889 courthouse has been on the National Register of Historic Places since 1982. Today it houses the County Health Department and the Stop DWI Program. The current courthouse is in the Clinton County Government Center, built in the 1970's.

Zephaniah Platt and Jonas Platt are buried at Riverside Cemetery in Plattsburgh, as is Henry T. Kellogg (1869-1942), who served on the New York Court of Appeals from 1927 to 1934. Clinton County can also boast Reuben H. Walworth (1788-1867), who practiced law there and was New York's Chancellor from 1828 to 1848. Charles Mason (1810-1879) was born in Plattsburgh and served on the New York Court of Appeals from 1868 to 1869.

Thanks to Clinton County Historian Addie Shields and Judge Penelope Clute.

This 1915 view of Trinity Park shows the Clinton County Courthouse in the background.

ark and Court Hous
ttsburgh, N. Y.

219537

Court House, Hudson, N.Y.

This building burned down last sunday. How is Lena I have not heard from you in months Feb 4th 07. Catharine Miller

This courthouse, the pride of Columbia County for almost six years, burned in 1907 as the writer of this postcard noted.

Columbia County

Third Judicial District

Columbia County is an "O.K." county, considering that the expression "O.K." was popularized in 1840 when Martin Van Buren, known as Old Kinderhook" or "O.K." was up for re-election. The presidential campaign took place 44 years after the county was created, and 235 years after Henry Hudson stopped there and recorded in his journal that he found "very loving people" and "caught great stores of very good [or at least O.K.] fish."

When the 415,000 acres of Columbia County were carved out of Albany County in 1796, Claverack became the county seat. The county expended $9,000 to build a courthouse. It was ready in 1788, in time to convict three men for stealing horses. They were hanged on May 30.

At about the same time, freedom of the press became an issue. Harry Croswell, editor of a local newspaper, was convicted of libel for criticizing President Thomas Jefferson. Alexander Hamilton defended him successfully on appeal in a decision written by James Kent. [*People v. Croswell*, 3 Johns. Cas. 337 (N.Y.Sup. Ct. 1804)]

By 1801, the Claverack courthouse needed repairs. The City of Hudson had begun to build a city hall in 1786, a plain square brick building. Hudson agreed to share this building with the county. Over the strong opposition of Claverack, the county seat was moved to Hudson in 1805, and the city hall was repaired and finished for the purpose. The cost for these renovations and to build a jail amounted to $7,000. The courthouse served as a gathering place for most public purposes and as a place of worship for several denominations. When, by 1835, the county had outgrown the structure, the Presbyterian society bought it.

Columbia County's third courthouse, completed in 1835 at a cost of $35,000, was built on a four-acre park donated by the City of Hudson. The city and the county shared this building, as they had its predecessor. It was built of Stockbridge marble and Blue Mountain limestone. The east wing comprised the jail, and the west wing housed the county clerk and the Hudson Common Council Chambers. A large dome topped the two-story center of the building.

By the end of the 19th Century, the county had outgrown its third courthouse. The State had condemned the jail, and the county sent its prisoners to Albany temporarily. In 1900, the Board of Supervisors voted to raze the courthouse, construct a new one in its place, and build a sheriff's residence to the southeast of the building.

The new courthouse opened May 13, 1901. For the first time in the county's history, all the departments, courts, and the jail were housed in the same building. The two-story building was of Stockbridge marble and featured a portico and pediment supported by eight Corinthian columns. It was crowned by a grand dome made of glass and metal with a statue of Justice on top. On the landing of the central staircase, a stained glass window depicted the county seal. The building cost $60,000, and was the pride of Columbia County.

On January 27, 1907, fire swept through the building. Within two hours all that remained were the outside walls and the jail at the rear of the building. The county commissioned the firm of Warren and Wetman of New York City, who later designed Grand Central Station, to design the county's fifth and present courthouse. The cornerstone laying took place September 14, 1907, and the $100,000 structure was ready for occupancy on December 8, 1908. In the near future Columbia County will enlarge this building and renovate it to provide full handicapped access and to meet the needs of the 21st Century.

For a rural county of small population, Columbia County has produced an impressive number of eminent legal figures. Martin Van Buren (1782-1862), the eighth President of the United States, was born in Kinderhook. Ambrose Spencer (1765-1848), who practiced law in Hudson, was New York State Attorney General from 1802 to 1804 and Chief Justice of the (old) Supreme Court from 1819-1823.

Theodore Miller (1816-1895), who was born in Hudson and served on the New York Court of Appeals from 1874 to 1886, is also remembered for preserving peace in Columbia County when the anti-rent disputes broke out there in the 1840's.

John Worth Edmonds (1799-1874), a famed prison reformer, was born in Hudson and served on the Court of Appeals in 1852. Daniel Cady (1773-1859) was born in Canaan. He was the father of Elizabeth Cady Stanton and served on the Court of Appeals in 1849.

Born in Columbia County in 1808, Judge Henry Hogeboom died in Hudson in 1872, after having served on the Court of Appeals in 1864. In a September 13, 1872. *New York Times* obituary, he was said to have been the most eminent jurist on New York's trial bench.

Thanks to Mary Howell, Columbia County Historian and Hon. Paul Czajka.

Court House, Hudson, N.Y.

This is almost done.

Warren and Wetman of New York City, who later designed Grand Central Station, designed Columbia County's fifth and present courthouse. The writer of this postcard, in 1908, observed that it was nearing completion.

Court House, Cortland, N. Y.

214947

Cortland County's second official courthouse was built in the 1830's. The jail was in the basement. By 1924, the county had outgrown both the courthouse and the jail and built new ones. The Cortland Free Library stands near this site today.

Cortland County

Sixth Judicial District

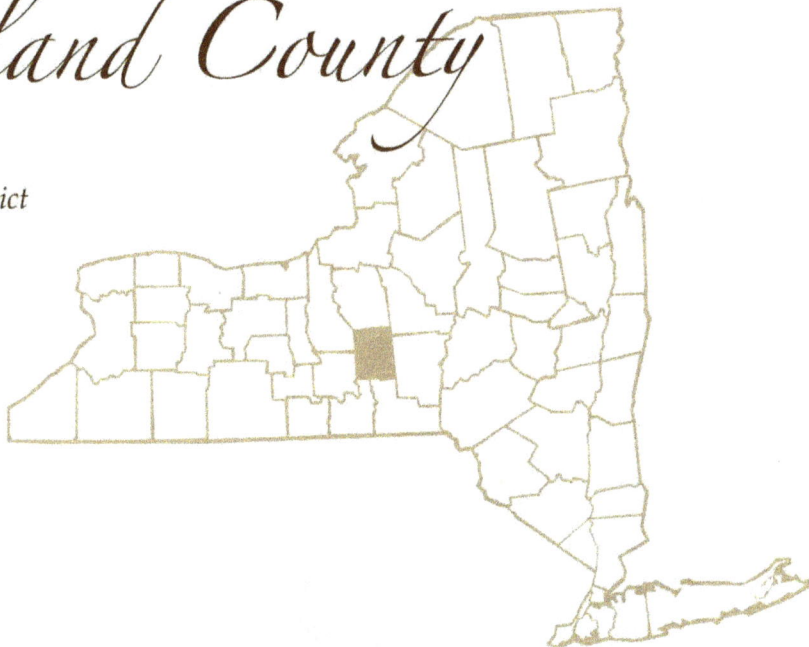

A statue of Themis, Goddess of Law and Justice, stands on top of the Cortland County Courthouse. In one hand, she holds a set of scales; in the other, a twelve-foot sword, pointing north toward Onondaga County, as if to recognize Cortland County's parentage. The county was founded in 1808 from land taken from Onondaga.

Court was first held in a school in Homer Village on Lot 45 until about 1813 when an official courthouse was built. Meanwhile, intense competition arose over which village should become the county seat. Port Watson was a thriving commercial village. Homer was the first village to be settled and the first to have a newspaper. It seemed to have an advantage. Cortland, on the other hand, had Jonathan Hubbard who lobbied intensely and put up $1000 of his own money for the purpose. Cortland prevailed.

The county built its first courthouse between 1812 and 1813 on a hill near where Cortland College is today. Built of wide pine clapboards, it had a circular roof covered with tin and topped with an iron spire. It was a majestic location, visually impressive, but it was a strenuous hike for judges, lawyers, and litigants to ascend the hill to get to court.

In the mid-1830's, the Board of Supervisors decided to place a courthouse in a more convenient location. The old structure was abandoned, and a new red brick building with white trim was constructed at a cost of about $7,000. The Cortland Free Library is located near that site today.

The courthouse had a jail in the basement, but it was small, dank, and often overcrowded. The state ordered the county to build a new jail. At that time the Supervisors recognized that the courthouse had become inadequate and decided to replace it as well.

In 1924, the Supervisors decided on a location in central Cortland on Greenbush Street, on a site of the former Normal School, which had burned in 1919. They chose James Reilly Gordon as architect, who designed the courthouse to resemble the U.S. Capitol. It is built of Indiana limestone, granite, marble, oak, and mahogany. Stained glass on the interior of the dome features a county seal, designed by Gordon, which depicts the union of agriculture and industry. The building cost $800,000, a hefty sum for the time. The courthouse, still in use, was placed on the National Register of Historic Places in 1974.

Among Cortland County's legal figures, several stand out. Born in Cortland, Alton B. Parker (1852-1926) was elected Chief Judge of New York's highest court in November 1897 and served in that capacity until he resigned on August 5, 1904 to run as the Democratic nominee for President of the United States. Theodore Roosevelt defeated him. Today the Alton B. Parker Elementary School is located at 89 Madison Street in Cortland.

Nathan L. Miller was born in Solon, Cortland County in 1868. Miller was State Comptroller (1901-1903) and then, at age 36,

Justice of the Supreme Court Appellate Division from 1905-1913. He was named to the Court of Appeals in 1913, serving until 1915. From 1921-1923, Miller served as New York's Governor, defeating Democrat Alfred E. Smith in the 1920 election. In the 1922 election, Smith turned the tables, defeating Miller. In 1953, Miller died and is buried in the Cortland County Rural Cemetery.

William H. Shankland (1804-1883) served on the New York Court of Appeals in 1849 and 1857. Samuel Nelson (1792-1873) was a Justice of the United States Supreme Court (1845-1872) after having been Chief Justice of the (old) New York Supreme Court (1827-1845).

Thanks to Cathy A. Barber, Cortland County Historian.

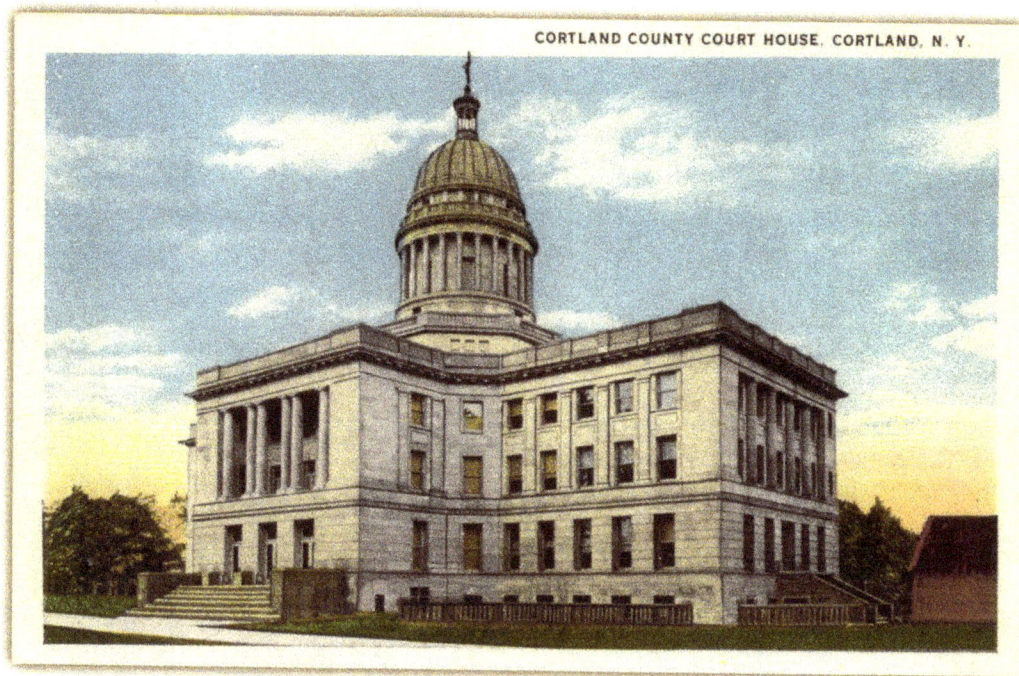

CORTLAND COUNTY COURT HOUSE, CORTLAND, N. Y.

James Reilly Gordon designed the Cortland County Courthouse to resemble the United States Capitol. A statue of Themis, Goddess of Law and Justice, stands on top of the dome, her sword pointing northward toward Onondaga County, from which Cortland County was formed.

VIEW OF COURT HOUSE AND PARK, SHOWING FIRST METHODIST CHURCH, CORTLAND, N. Y.

E-8933

A side view of the 1924 courthouse, still in use today, peeking out from behind the trees and a row of 1940's automobiles.

SOLDIERS MONUMENT AND COUNTY BUILDINGS, DELHI, N. Y.

The Delaware County Courthouse, dedicated in 1871, was designed by Isaac G. Perry. The *Saturday Evening Post* considered the Courthouse Square to be so typically American that the magazine featured it on the cover of its July 7, 1951 issue.

Delaware County

Sixth Judicial District

When in 1951 the *Saturday Evening Post* wanted a cover for a typical July 4th celebration, the editors depicted a brass band in a gazebo in front of the Delaware County Courthouse. It was a slice of Americana.

The history of Delaware County goes back to the 18th Century. The county was named after Lord Thomas West Delaware (De La Warr) (1577-1618), in recognition of his early service to the Colonies. Settled before the Revolution, Delaware became a county in 1797, with Delhi as its county seat. The first session of the Court of Common Pleas took place that year at Gideon Frisbee's home and tavern at the junction of Elk Creek and the West Branch of the Delaware River. Juries deliberated under a large butternut tree on the property. The tree survived until the latter part of the 19th Century. The county began construction of its first courthouse and jail in 1798, on land taken from Levi Baxter and George Fisher on the "Main Road" to Catskill. Pending its completion, court continued to meet at Frisbee's tavern. The courthouse, completed in 1799, cost $2000.

There was not much business for the courts in those days and, it would seem, even less crime. The jail was said to have remained unused for 14 years. The courthouse saw so little use that, in 1812, the legislature authorized its use as a tavern. This building burned in 1820, destroying most of the county records in the process.

The county received an $8000 loan to build a new courthouse, jail, and county clerk's office. Until the buildings were finished, prisoners were held in the Greene County jail, and court sessions held in the house of Jesse C. Gilbert.

This courthouse was the scene of a significant event in the "Anti-Rent Wars," the controversy surrounding the last vestiges of feudalism in New York. Descendants of gentlemen who had received land grants from King George III leased parcels of land to farmers under terms that proved onerous. The settlers who had first tenanted the land were the ones who turned it from wilderness into productive farms. Typically the rents would have covered the full purchase price of the land each 15 years, had the land been for sale, but the tenants could never purchase the land. Should the farmer default any portion of the rent, the landlord could repossess the land and sell the farmer's livestock without any compensation for the improvements to the land.

On the one side, the prominent landowning families – Livingstons, Montgomerys, Verplancks – had contracts and centuries of feudalism. On the other side, the farmers had something no less powerful, the American ideals of fair play, notions of public policy, and the principle that people should be allowed to reap the fruits of their labors.

The issue came to a head in Delaware County in 1845, when a group of protestors dressed as Indians protested the sale of a farmer's stock in Andes. Someone shot and killed the unpopular Under-Sheriff Osman Steel, and rioting ensued. The Governor sent a battalion of 300 men, half of them mounted, to quell the uprising.

Because no one could identify the shooter, 94 men were indicted for murder and 148 for lesser crimes. Two men were sentenced to be hanged, and four sentenced to life imprisonment. Shortly thereafter, Governor Silas Wright commuted the death sentences to life imprisonment. In 1846, John Young, running on an Anti-Rent platform, defeated Wright and in 1847, pardoned all the Anti-Rent convicts.

When in 1866, the county proposed building a new courthouse, the Town of Walton bid for becoming the county seat, offering to build the new courthouse should it be located there. Delhi held on by putting up $10,000 toward the new building, which eventually cost $20,000. The Village of Delhi bought the old frame courthouse, moved it further back on the lot, and used it as a village hall until the late1980's.

Isaac G. Perry designed the courthouse, dedicated in 1871. As state architect, Perry supervised the completion of the New York State Capitol and the construction of a host of armories.

This courthouse remains in use, having received regular repairs, improvements, and modifications over the years. In 1966, the area between the courthouse and county clerks office was enclosed, providing a common entrance and handicapped access for both buildings. The entire Courthouse Square is on the National Register of Historic Places, including the present courthouse, county clerk's office, jail, and the 1820 courthouse.

Delaware County has had its share of judges who served on the State's highest court, including Amasa J. Parker (1807-1890) and William Murray (1820-1887), both ex-officio, and Isaac H. Maynard (1838-1896)

Charles Evans Hughes (1862-1948), who taught school in Delhi, later became Governor of New York (1907-1910) and Chief Justice of the United States Supreme Court (1930-1941).

Thanks to Judge Carl F. Becker and to Shirley Houck, Delaware County Records Clerk.

Delaware County's Courthouse Square as seen in winter.

COURT HOUSE, POUGHKEEPSIE, N. Y.

The Dutchess County Courthouse was designed by William J. Beardsley of Poughkeepsie and was ready for occupancy December 1903. On this site in 1788, New York State ratified the United States Constitution, thus joining the Union.

Dutchess County

Ninth Judicial District

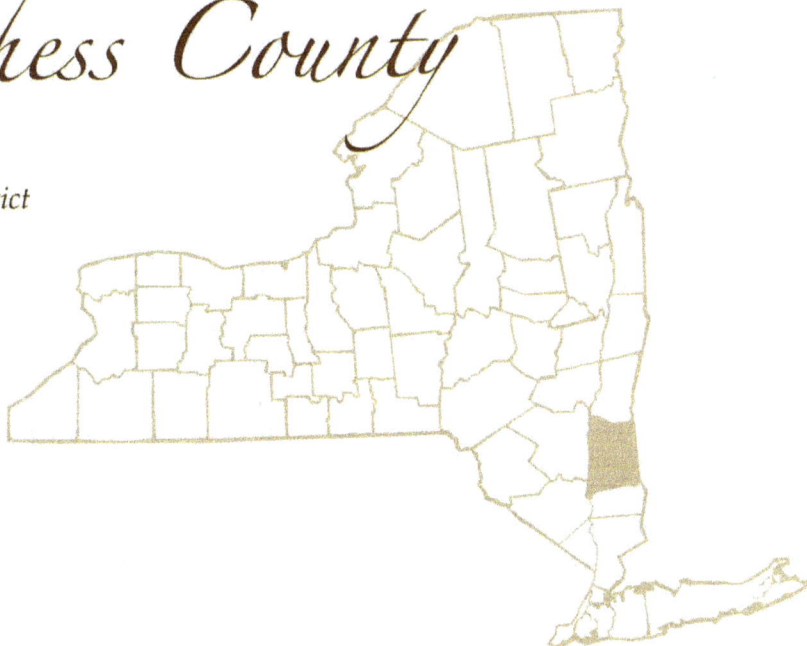

In her *History of New York*, Martha J. Lamb stated that the ratification of the Constitution at the Poughkeepsie courthouse in 1788 "turned the pivot in the history of the English-speaking race." A sweeping claim, but not extravagant. She makes the case that, when New York joined the Union, it formed the United States and cemented a political compact unique in the world's history. What began with Magna Carta in 1215 culminated in the creation of a democracy based on freedom, political balance, and a framework for the rule of law.

The setting was the summer of 1788, on Market Street in Poughkeepsie, two courthouses ago. Poughkeepsie was then the capital of the eleven-year-old State of New York. Dutchess County's third courthouse was newly built – only three days old – when on June 3, 1788, Stephen Hendricksen paid for the steps that led to the building's front door.

Delegates from all over what was then New York State entered and debated whether New York should adopt the Constitution drafted in Philadelphia the previous summer. As Federalists, Alexander Hamilton and John Jay were the principal proponents of the Constitution. They were opposed and initially outnumbered by Anti-federalists, led by Governor George Clinton and Melancton Smith, who resisted the idea of a Constitution that made no provision for a Bill of Rights, but took local and regional power from the states with questionable controls on a central federal government. Eventually New York ratified, a Bill of Rights was enacted by Congress in 1791, and our country set out on an unprecedented political journey – carried on to this day – balancing individual, local, and national interests.

Dutchess was among the original counties established in 1683 by the Duke of York, later to become King James II. It is generally believed that the county's name honored Elizabeth, Duchess of York, just as Kings County recognized Charles II and Queens was named for his wife, Catherine of Braganza. The unique spelling of the county, with the "t" in Dutchess, may be taken to commemorate the Dutch origins of New York, but no one knows for sure.

In its earliest days, Dutchess County was too sparsely populated to have its own government and shared its administration with Ulster County at Kingston. In 1715, the Colonial Assembly authorized the construction of a courthouse in Poughkeepsie. Officials chose a site on the corner of "The Kings Road," now Main and Market Streets. At a cost of 250 pounds, they built a simple stone structure from 1717 to 1720 on land granted by Jacobus Van den Bogart, who along with Barent Van Kleeck, was in charge of the construction. The land grant carried an ironclad provision that the parcel be used for a courthouse and jail or reverts to Van den Bogart or his heirs.

As the county grew, it needed a more elaborate courthouse. In 1745, the county completed its second courthouse and jail, containing offices for the county supervisors, sheriff, and rooms for the clerk, and treasurer. This building existed during the Revolution while Kingston was the state's capital. After the British burned the Kingston courthouse, the State Legislature began to meet at Poughkeepsie. This courthouse might well have served during the 1788 ratification debates had it not been destroyed by fire in 1785.

In 1806, the Ratification Courthouse, like its predecessor, succumbed to fire. Nothing remained but stone walls, the dungeon, and the salvaged county clerk's records. During the next five years, court proceedings took place at the Dutch Reformed Church across the street.

Dutchess County's fourth courthouse, completed in 1811, was a two-story $25,000 building with an attic and basement. Large enough to house the courts, all county offices, and the jail, it still had room for a few businesses. Among these was Matthew Vassar's Oyster and Ale Bar. Vassar became a highly successful brewer who went on to found Vassar College in 1860.

The 1811 courthouse may have been spacious when built, but by the 1860's, it was bursting at the seams. The county put up a small one-story brick building for the Surrogate in 1847. The dungeon in the courthouse basement was condemned in 1856, prompting the county to provide jail space upstairs and build an annex for the jail in 1861. For almost forty years, the county improvised adaptations to the cramped quarters, with offices doing double duty as courtrooms or jury rooms.

In 1901, the Board of Supervisors resolved to raze the court-

house and build a new one – the fifth – in its place. The Board commissioned a young Poughkeepsie architect, William J. Beardsley, to design it. Beardsley went on to become prominent in his field with ten courthouses to his credit as well as Attica Prison, in addition to numerous other buildings, including the 1923 renovation of the Bardavon 1869 Opera House on Poughkeepsie's Market Street.

The county's fifth and present courthouse cost $268,000 and was ready December 1903. Beardsley took care to design it to be fireproof so that it would not meet the fate of Dutchess's second and third courthouses. The effectiveness of the fireproofing was proven in March 1978 when a fire erupted in the Surrogate's chambers. It destroyed the chambers and Surrogate's courtroom, but left the records room and the rest of the building unscathed.

A separate jail in 1932 relieved the ever-increasing need for space, but threatened a crisis. The heirs of Jacobus Van den Bogart brought to the county's attention that the original deed specified that the land must be used for a courthouse and jail or revert to them. The county responded by constructing a couple of vestigial jail cells in the basement, now used by Department of Public Works employees as a lounge.

The county called upon Beardsley again in 1933, a year before his death, to redesign the former jail on the third floor and to create a fourth story. He made new foundations and added columns through the building to support the extra floor.

During the 1980's the courthouse received necessary modifications and repairs, including ramps for handicapped access. A grant from the McCann Foundation, a local charity, substantially augmented county funds to repair and refurbish the exterior, including the fashioning of new cornices.

To relieve crowding, the county built a new County Office Building next to the courthouse in 1965 to accommodate all county offices except for those related to the courts. In 1996, the District Attorney's office moved to the historic Poughkeepsie Trust Building adjacent to the courthouse. In the same year, the Family Court moved to a new building on Market Street south of the County Office Building. Bit by bit, the west side of the street has become a government center, while the 1903 courthouse continues to serve the courts.

The county's prominent judicial and legal history goes back over two centuries. Morgan Lewis (1754-1844) was a Revolutionary War soldier and General in the War of 1812. He was Attorney

General in 1791 and Chief Justice of the (old) Supreme Court in 1792 and then Governor (1804-1807). He built and lived in what is now Mills Mansion in Staatsburgh, Dutchess County and is buried in Hyde Park. Lewis County is named after him. James Kent (1763-1847), the father of American law, practiced in Poughkeepsie in the 1780's. Egbert Benson (1746-1833), New York's first Attorney General, was from Red Hook. George Clinton (1739-1812), New York's first Governor, lived in Poughkeepsie for many years. Clinton House State Historic Site is on Main Street in Poughkeepsie. Smith Thompson (1768-1843) was a Justice of the United States Supreme Court from 1823 to 1843, after having served on New York's (old) Supreme Court and as its Chief Judge. Franklin Delano Roosevelt (1882-1945) and Thomas E. Dewey (1902-1971) were two of Dutchess County's most prominent lawyers. In 1944, they ran against one another for President.

Among Dutchess County's Judges, Charles Ruggles (1789-1865) served on the New York Court of Appeals from 1847 to 1855 and was Chief Judge from 1851 to 1853. Albert M. Rosenblatt (1936-) served on the New York State Court of Appeals from 1999 through 2006. Serving on the court, ex officio, were Gilbert Dean (1819-1870) of Pleasant Valley in 1855; James Emott (1823-1884) in 1863; and Josiah Sutherland (1804-1877) in 1862.

Thanks to Joyce Ghee, Eileen Hayden, Stephanie Mauri, and the Dutchess County Historical Society and Dutchess County Historian Stanley Mersand.

Court House, Poughkeepsie, N. Y.   72

In 1933, William J. Beardsley redesigned the Dutchess County Courthouse to make it a four-story building.

When Erie County built a new courthouse in 1876, the old one was demolished to make way for the Public Library.

Erie County

Eighth Judicial District

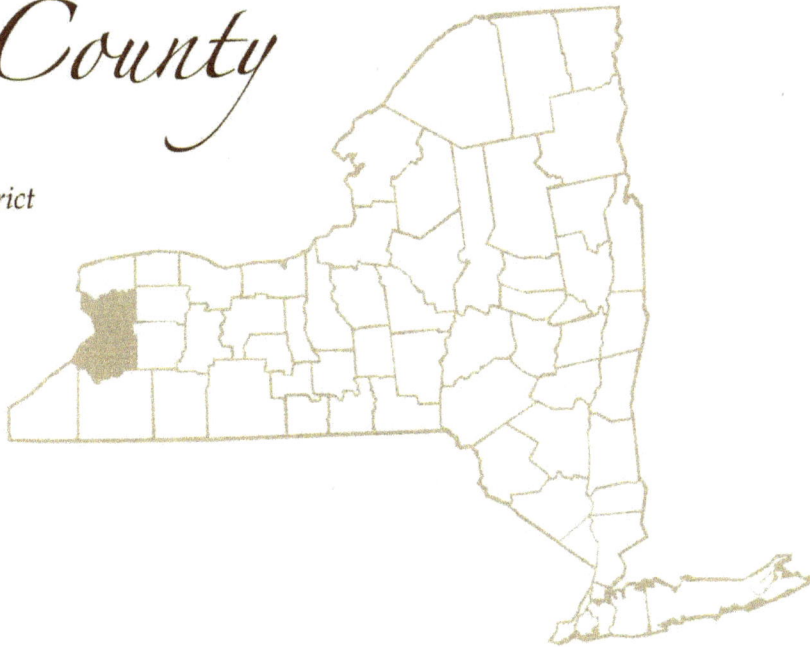

Erie County evokes the Canal, the culmination of the journey to western New York, and the names of Presidents Fillmore, Cleveland, and McKinley. Erie's courts figure in all these events, beginning with the origins of the county in 1821.

In that year, Erie became separated from Niagara County and inherited the county seat at Buffalo. The first courthouse had been built there in 1806-1809 by the Holland Land Company, which owned much of western New York and was selling land to settlers. During the War of 1812, the British burned the Village of Buffalo, destroying the courthouse and leaving only the stone jail intact.

In 1816, the Legislature authorized Niagara County to raise $4000 to rebuild the courthouse. Completed in 1817, the brick structure rose two stories high with a front porch and large pillars. Erie County inherited this courthouse. In the early 1830's, Millard Fillmore practiced law in Buffalo and surely would have frequented the courthouse several years before he became the 13th President of the United States.

In the late 1840's, the county put up an additional courthouse nearby, a three-story brick building bounded by Washington, Batavia, Ellicott, and Clinton Streets. The county outgrew both these buildings 25 years later. After the county replaced and abandoned them in 1876, they were razed to make way for the Buffalo and Erie County Public Library.

The city and county joined forces and commissioned Rochester architect Andrew Jackson Warner to design a new City and County Hall, laying the cornerstone on June 14, 1872. The building, which opened March 13, 1876, cost approximately $1,200,000. The Norman Gothic structure features a 268-foot bell tower with a clock designed after the style of Big Ben. It had four faces, each 19 feet in diameter, and a pendulum 15 feet long. The faces were translucent and illuminated at night. The courthouse bell weighed 4400 pounds. There were four 16-foot-tall granite statues of women, representing Justice, Mechanic Arts, Agriculture, and Commerce, each guarding a corner of the tower. Sculpted by Giovanni F. Sala, each statue cost $22,000. Grover Cleveland had his office in this building, in 1881, when he was Mayor of Buffalo. President William McKinley lay in state there after his assassination.

At the beginning of the 20th Century, the nation's eyes turned to the courthouse for one of the most famous trials in American history. On September 6, 1901, Leon Czolgosz, a self-proclaimed anarchist, shot President William McKinley at the Pan American Exposition in Delaware Park. McKinley died on September 14 at the Delaware Avenue home of John G. Millburn, President of the Exposition, and Theodore Roosevelt was sworn in at the Wilcox Mansion in Buffalo.

After indictment by an Erie County Grand Jury, Czolgosz was tried on September 23, 1901 in Buffalo at City and County Hall, Part III of the Criminal Term of State Supreme Court, with Hon. Truman C. White presiding. At the conclusion of a two-day trial, the 12-man jury deliberated for just over a half-hour and found Czolgosz guilty of first-degree murder. Three days later the Judge sentenced Czolgosz to death, and on October 29, 1901, he was executed at Auburn State Prison. So ended one of Buffalo's most closely followed proceedings.

Eventually, the needs of both city and county government outgrew the building. The county bought out the city's interest, and expanded the building in 1929. The city built a new Buffalo City Hall. The courthouse was expanded once more in 1936, when un-der a federally assisted WPA project, the county converted the attic into useable space.

The county built a $7 million, eight-story annex in 1963, adjacent to the County Hall. In 1999, the county embarked on a $52 million project that included a new $35.3 million, seven-story courthouse as well as the renovation of the three existing structures.

Not surprisingly, Erie County has produced an array of distinguished jurists who served on the New York Court of Appeals. Henry E. Davies (1805-1881) was on the Court from 1860 to 1867 and was Chief Judge in 1866 to 1867. William H. Cuddeback (1852-1919) served from 1913 to 1919; Albert Haight (1842-1926) from 1895 to 1912; Charles Sears (1870-1950) in 1940; Charles S. Desmond (1896-1987) from 1941 to 1966, and as Chief Judge from 1960 to 1966; Matthew Jasen (1915-2006) from 1969 to 1985. Eugene Piggot (1946-), who joined the Court in October 2006, hails from Buffalo.

James Mullett (1784-1858) served ex officio in 1851. Charles Daniels (1825-1897) founded Buffalo Law School and served on the Court of Appeals ex officio in 1869.

Thanks to Senior Law Librarian Jeannine E. Lee, Presiding Justice (now Court of Appeals Judge) Eugene F. Pigott, Administrative Judge Sharon Townsend, District Attorney Frank Clark, attorney Michael Powers, and Judge Sheila A. DiTullio.

City & County Hall.   Buffalo, N. Y.

Erie County and the City of Buffalo shared this building until 1929 when the city moved out.

This Colonial style Essex County Courthouse was built in 1825 and modified in 1843 and 1880. It is now used by the Essex County Board of Supervisors.

Essex County

Fourth Judicial District

Essex County was formed in 1799 from land taken from Clinton County. The first county seat was in the town of Essex. Daniel Ross, the first County Judge held court and confined prisoners in a little blockhouse built in 1797 for protection from Indians.

In 1807, commissioners appointed to select a site for a courthouse chose Elizabethtown village, but it took another seven years until the courthouse was furnished. Not long thereafter it burned, but it was quickly rebuilt. It burned again in 1823.

Officials then decided to build something more substantial and allocated $15,000 for a one-story Colonial style brick structure. In between the fire and the completion of the courthouse in 1826, court was held at the Brick Tavern in Elizabethtown.

In 1843, the county added a second story, which became the courtroom. Further construction in the 1880's enlarged the main section and added a wing for county offices. As a result, the year "1880" appeared over the main entrance of the courthouse. In 1973,

at the request of the Essex County Historical Society, the date was changed to "1825 – 1880," reflecting the date the courthouse construction actually began.

In the 1990's, the county built a new $4.7 million courthouse. The Board of Supervisors has taken over the old courthouse for its chambers and offices. The old courtroom is lined with portraits of judges and lawyers from the past 100 years and two paintings by D.C. Lithgow, commissioned by the Board in 1923. One depicts Samuel De Champlain. The other shows John Brown speaking at his trial. John Brown's body lay in the courthouse, guarded by local citizens, while it was on its way to his family's home in North Alba.

Although small in population, Essex County has contributed greatly to our legal history. It gave us the Hand family, one of the most notable in our American legal constellation. Augustus Cincinnatus Hand (1803-1878) served as Essex County Surrogate (1831-1839), member of Congress (1839-1841), State Senator (1844-

1848), and State Supreme Court Justice (1847-1855). He sat on the State's highest court, the Court of Appeals, in 1855. He was the father of Samuel Hand (1833-1886) who was born in Elizabethtown, Essex County and served on the Court of Appeals in 1878.

In 1869, Samuel Hand was named Official Reporter of the Court of Appeals and served for three years. In 1876, Governor Tilden, then running for President, wanted Samuel Hand to be nominated for Governor. It is likely that Samuel Hand argued more cases before the New York Court of Appeals than any other lawyer in its history. In 1853, he married Lydia Learned Hand, daughter of Billings P. Learned. The couple had two children one of whom, Learned Hand (1872-1961), became one of America's most renowned jurists. Samuel Hand is buried in Riverside Cemetery in Essex County.

The Hand house on River Street in Elizabethtown is currently owned and maintained by the Bruce L. Crary Foundation and can be visited by appointment. The Hand papers are in the Cornell University Library, Division of Rare and Manuscript collections.

Chester B. McLaughlin (1856-1929) was born in Moriah, Essex County, attended Sherman Academy there, and later practiced law in Port Henry. He was a delegate to the State Constitutional Convention in 1894, and was an advocate for a constitutional amendment to help improve New York's canals. He served on the New York Court of Appeals from 1917-1926 and is buried in Moriah Cemetery.

The portraits of several prominent sons of Essex County are hanging in the Old County Courthouse. They include August Noble Hand (1869-1954), who served on the Second Circuit Court of Appeals; his father, Richard Lockhart Hand, a President of the New York State Bar; O. Byron Brewster (1886 -1935), who served on the Supreme Court, Appellate Division, Third Department from 1945-1949; Members of Congress George A. Simmons (1791-1857); Orlando Kellogg (1809-1865); and Robert S. Hale (1822-1881).

Thanks to Susan Doolittle, Assistant Director, Adirondack History Center.

From another angle, a more recent picture of the Essex County Courthouse, shown on a bright, sunny day.

Malone, N.Y. Franklin County Buildings.

The Franklin County buildings as they appeared at the turn of the 20th century. The building to the left was the sheriff's residence and jail. The small center building housed the county clerk's office. The building with the steeple was the courthouse. All three were demolished to make way for a new courthouse. The building to the far right, not a county building, can be discerned in later photographs.

Franklin County

Fourth Judicial District

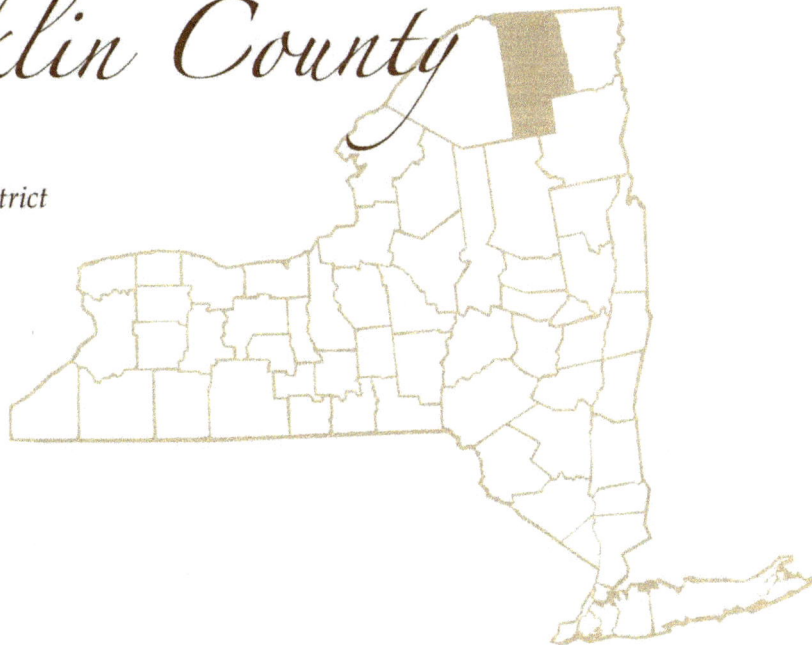

Franklin County was formed in 1808 from part of Clinton County. Before the county had a courthouse, court was held in a school building, the Harison Academy. A room in that building also served as a temporary jail. Noah Moody built the county's first courthouse, which included the jail, on a parcel of land in Malone where he made his home.

A separate, fireproof, county clerk's office was built in 1819. This was the very year that Franklin County's William Wheeler was born in Malone. He practiced law in Franklin County, serving as its district attorney from 1846-1849. Wheeler was Vice President of the United States from 1877-1881. He is interred in Morningside Cemetery in Malone.

As was common in the early 19th Century, various religious denominations met in the courthouse. In 1824, the Board of Supervisors published a notice that, unless these organizations cleaned the courthouse after use, the building would be closed to all but public and governmental functions. Bickering among these groups caused the sheriff to publish a notice a year later apportioning the time allotted to each denomination according to population. Rather than enforce the Supervisors' resolution about cleaning the courthouse, the sheriff offered to have the courthouse cleaned at this own expense, if the groups failed to do so.

Further construction in 1892 and 1893 resulted in a trio of buildings of brick and stone, providing separate buildings for the jail and sheriff's residence, general offices, including the county clerk's office, and the courthouse. These buildings were demolished to make way for a new courthouse.

The present courthouse was proposed as a WPA project in 1930, designed by architect William J. Beardsley of Poughkeepsie. The *Malone Evening Telegram* of March 27, 1930 described it as "drawn on practical lines as approved in modern public building construction with attractive front elevation – a building which gives an imposing effect upon the large lot fronting West Main Street." The courthouse had some moments on the national scene with the trial of mobster Arthur "Dutch Schultz" Flegenheimer in 1935.

When the courthouse opened, the courts occupied the second floor and now have expanded to most of the third floor as well. A county office building located behind the courthouse, erected in 1987-1988, houses most of the county offices.

Thanks to Robert G. Main, Jr. County Judge, Surrogate, and Family Court Judge of Franklin County and to Franklin County's Jan H. Plumadore, Deputy Chief Administrative Judge for the Courts Outside New York City.

COURT HOUSE, MALONE, N. Y.

The Franklin County Courthouse was designed by Architect William J. Beardsley of Poughkeepsie and built in 1930 as a WPA project.

The Franklin County Courthouse, shown on Main Street in Malone in the mid-20th Century. The building to the right of the courthouse also appears in the photo of the earlier county buildings.

Built in 1772, the Fulton County courthouse is one of the oldest in the United States.

Fulton County

Fourth Judicial District

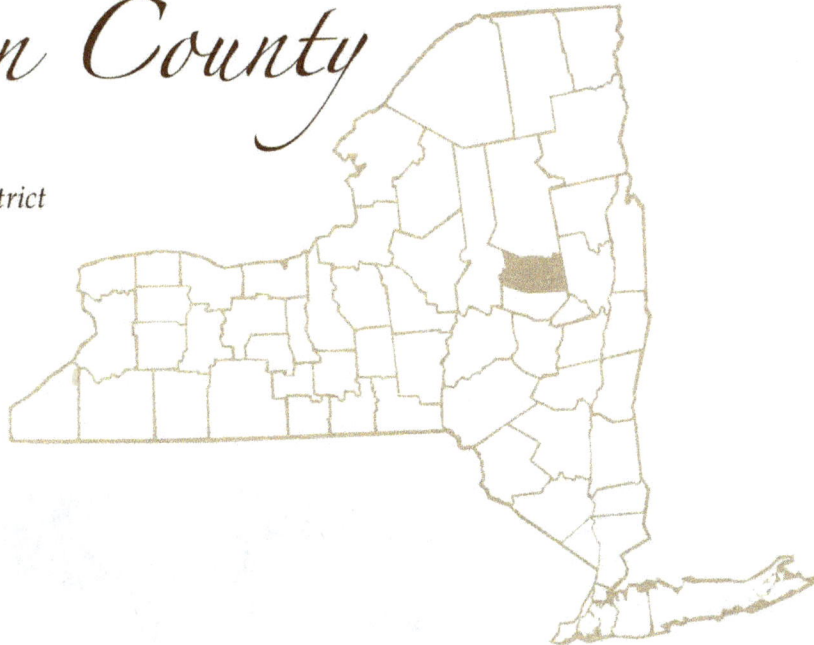

Fulton County's courthouse, the oldest in New York State, brings us back to our colonial roots. Dating from 1772, it is the only colonial courthouse still in use in New York and one of only about five in the nation.

The story began when Sir William Johnson grew tired of having to make frequent trips to Albany for court or to gain access to county records. Of the ten original 1683 counties, Albany comprised all of northern and western New York. Johnson used his influence to advance a proposal already before the Provincial government to split Albany County. Under this proposal, much of the northeastern portion would become one county, to be called Charlotte, after the wife of George III. Another portion, all the land to the as yet undetermined western border, would be a new county named Tryon, for the Colonial governor, William Tryon. The Provincial government erected Tryon County on March 12, 1772.

Sir William further proposed that the county seat be located in Johnstown, conveniently near for him. In order to secure the county seat where he wanted it, Sir William immediately set about to provide a courthouse, contributing some of his own money as well as 25 gallons of rum for the workers, in order to speed up the process. By the following September, the unfinished building was sufficiently well along to open court.

Sir William died in 1774 before the courthouse was completed. In 1775, his son, Sir John Johnson inherited the estate, succeeded his father as Trustee for the courthouse, and served as a judge. He claimed ownership of the buildings, pending payment of the funds his father advanced. The county claimed otherwise. The matter might have been settled for sure in court, but it became moot on May 1, 1776. Patriot sentiment dominated the region. Johnson, a confirmed Tory, along with 170 of his friends and tenants, fled to St. Regis, Canada, and his entire estate was confiscated.

The one-story brick courthouse with gabled roof and cupola was much more substantially built than other courthouses of its day. It had a bell, a triangular piece of wrought iron, which still rings. It was rung when the news of the signing of the Declaration of Independence came to Johnstown and with the news of the victory at the battle of Yorktown. It rang for the signing of the U.S. Constitution as well as for its 200th anniversary.

In the late 18th Century, most counties built an all-purpose courthouse cum jail. Johnstown, perhaps more forward looking, built a separate jail at the same time as the courthouse, a substantial stone building with walls four feet thick. Sir William would not have foreseen that the patriots would use it as a fort. George Washington visited Fort Johnstown during his tour of the Mohawk Valley in 1783.

The patriots despised Governor Tryon. After independence, the county lost little time in ridding itself of his name. On April 2, 1884, the State Legislature renamed it Montgomery County, in memory of Gen. Richard Montgomery who was killed during the battle of Quebec.

Montgomery County did not remain New York's largest county for long. In 1789, Ontario County was carved out of it, to encompass the sparsely settled western part of the state. The creation of Tioga, Otsego, and Herkimer counties, further reduced Montgomery's size. Fulton County, yet to come, would shrink Montgomery even more.

With the building of the Erie Canal in 1817, population within the county was redistributed. Johnstown was no longer a center of population. Travel over roads remained difficult. The people who settled along the Mohawk Valley wanted the county seat moved to Fonda, a more convenient location. The Legislature granted this

OLD COURTHOUSE, ERECTED IN 1772, JOHNSTOWN, N. Y.   17

90640

request in 1836. With that, the county sold its courthouse and jail to private individuals.

This greatly angered the folks in the northern towns who did not want to lose their county seat at Johnstown, to say nothing of their excellent courthouse. They petitioned for secession, and in 1838, the Legislature granted it. The Legislature also directed the owners of the courthouse and jail to sell the buildings to the newly formed county for the original purchase price.

The influence of Judge Daniel Cady (1773-1859) helped the legislature decide in favor of the new county and probably contributed toward its being named in honor of Robert Fulton, the inventor of the steamboat. Judge Cady's wife, Margaret Livingston, was a relative of Fulton's.

Judge Cady was a State Supreme Court Justice who served ex officio on the New York Court of Appeals in 1849. He was the father of Elizabeth Cady Stanton (1815-1902), an American leader in the women's rights movement, who was born and raised in Johnstown.

In 1849, a fire destroyed all the woodwork in the jail, but the sturdy building was rebuilt and afterward received only minor repairs until 1904 when the county engaged the Cummings firm of Troy to design a major modernization at a cost of $25,800. The jail, receiving some necessary repairs and updates, confined prisoners well into the latter part of the 20th Century. It now houses the County Personnel and Payroll Office. To accommodate the further needs of county government, the county constructed a County Office Building in 1961-62.

There comes a time in the life of almost every courthouse when it faces the possibility of demolition to make way for something completely modern and up-to-date. This happened in Fulton County as recently as 25 years ago. State Supreme Court Judge Robert Best headed up those who wanted to save the courthouse. In 1989, the Board of Supervisors began planning a project to expand court facilities and, at the same time, preserve the historic courthouse. It took 13 years and $1.38 million, but the project was completed in 2002. After the building was preserved and renovated, those who used it on a regular basis unanimously praised the building's acoustics, appearance, and space.

Thanks to County Historian William G. Loveday, Jr.

Right: This real photo card shows the Fulton County Courthouse from another angle.

Left: The Fulton County Courthouse, still in use, as seen in 1937.

Ellicott Hall, County Clerks Office & Court House, Batavia, N. Y.

The Town of Batavia took over the original Genesee County Courthouse in 1849 and renamed it Ellicott Hall. The building burned in 1918.

Genesee County

Eighth Judicial District

Joseph Ellicott believed that the founding of Genesee County was essential to the settlement of western New York. Ellicott (1760-1826) was the resident land agent for the Holland Land Company, a group of Dutch investors who had acquired more than three million acres of land with plans to sell it at a profit. Ellicott made his headquarters in Batavia, in what was then Ontario County. Roads to the county seat at Canandaigua, some 45 miles away, were little more than footpaths. Travel to file deeds took an inordinate amount of time. However, county taxes were even more troubling to Elliott than the transportation problems. Ontario County's land taxes largely benefited the more populated eastern section of the county. Moreover, taxes paid by the Holland Land Company far exceeded its revenues from land sales.

In 1802, Ellicott got his wish when Genesee County was split from Ontario County. The Holland Land Company built the courthouse, employing architects Isaac Sutherland and Samuel F. Gerber. It was built of heavy oak timbers, causing its builders to take three days to raise the frame. The first courthouse west of the Genesee River was ready for use in 1803. The north half consisted of the courtroom on the second floor, county offices on the first floor, and a jail in the basement. The south half was rented out as a tavern until 1820 when it became the sheriff's residence. In 1819, a separate jail was built to the south of the courthouse.

The New York State Legislature authorized a new courthouse in 1840, and the building was completed in 1843. It is built of Onondaga limestone, quarried nearby. The Greek Revival building has five bays on each façade with a slate and copper roof and wooden cupola. Originally, a porch supported by six heavy stone pillars extended across the front. In 1931, the porch area was filled in to provide additional office space when the entire building was renovated and repaired. The project cost $58,073.

In 1849, the Town of Batavia took over the original courthouse and renamed it Ellicott Hall. The old structure burned in January 1918 leaving only the bell that had hung in the original courthouse. That bell was moved to the new courthouse, where it remains.

In 1975, the courthouse received further repairs and renovations to the tune of $155,000. These improvements included a sprinkler system, fire alarm, new roof, new windows, new wood trim, and the restoration of the exterior stone. The timbers supporting the bell in the cupola were replaced, and an electrical system installed replacing the ropes that had been used to toll the bell. The building was added to the National Register of Historic Places on June 18, 1974 and is within the Genesee County Courthouse Historic District.

After the New York State Legislature passed the Court Facilities Act in 1987 and the Federal Government enacted the Americans with Disabilities Act in 1990, it became evident that the historic courthouse could not be retrofitted to meet the specific requirements. The county engaged the architect and engineering firm of MRB Group of Rochester to design a new two-story court facility building. Completed in 1997, it houses a Law Library; the County, Supreme, Surrogate, and City Courts; the Grand Jury; Community Dispute Settlement office; the Commissioner of Jurors; District Attorney; Law Guardian, and the Public Defender. The historic courthouse remains a focal point in Batavia and houses offices for the County Legislature and County Manager.

Moses Taggart (1799-1883) of Genesee County served ex officio on the Court of Appeals in 1853.

Thanks to Genesee County Historian Susan L. Conklin.

9710. Genesee County Court House, Batavia, N. Y.

Genesee County Court House
Batavia, N. Y.

2C29-N

Above: Although the courts have moved to a new Court Facility Building, the 1843 Genesee County Courthouse remains a focal point in Batavia and houses various county departments.

Left: Originally, the 1843 Genesee County Courthouse had a porch running the length of one side. During a 1931 renovation, the porch was filled in to provide more office space.

COURT HOUSE & PRESBYTERIAN CHURCH, CATSKILL, N. Y.

After construction of Greene County's 1910 courthouse, the Masonic Order bought the old one, shown on the right.

Greene County

Third Judicial District

When Greene County was formed in 1801, Abraham Van Vechten was 39 years old. Born in Catskill in 1762, he was the first lawyer admitted to the Bar under New York's earliest constitution, and was known as "the Father of the Bar in New York State."

Greene County, named after General Nathaniel Greene (1742-1786), was created by an Act of the New York State Legislature, the very year in which Thomas Cole was born. Cole (1801-1848) is synonymous with the Hudson River School of landscape painting that has enthralled the world since he began painting in the Catskills in 1825, returning summers to paint his unforgettable scenes. He took up residence in the Catskills in the 1830's. While Cole was maturing as an artist, the history of jurisprudence in Greene County was developing.

From 1801 to 1812, Greene County hosted court in a schoolhouse called the academy. In March 1903, the county set about building a jail. It was built of stone and outlasted, by far, the courthouse built in 1812, which burned soon thereafter. The following year, the county built a brick courthouse on the corner of Bridge and Franklin Streets. The lot cost $600, and for a century, this courthouse gave Catskill a large auditorium for all manner of events, including church functions, lectures, and fairs.

In 1908, the Greene County Grand Jury instigated a new courthouse. The timing was right: The old building was proving inadequate, and the county had paid its final installment on its Civil War debt.

A Citizens Advisory committee, which included Emory A. Chase, who served on the New York Court of Appeals from 1906-1921, furthered the proposal. County officials engaged William J.

GREENE COUNTY COURT HOUSE, CATSKILL, N. Y.

1

Opened in 1910, the Greene County Courthouse was designed by William J. Beardsley of Poughkeepsie. The fountain on the lawn, "Justice with Scales" no longer exists.

Beardsley of Poughkeepsie to design a two-story structure, 65 feet wide, underwritten by a bond issue of $170,000.

The cornerstone ceremony on November 12, 1908 drew an audience of 2500. The cornerstone includes a copper box containing, among other items, a copy of the *Catskill Packet* of 1792. The cornerstone stone was consecrated by pouring wine, corn, and oil on it.

The old courthouse was sold at auction for $5,810. Soon thereafter, the Masonic Order bought it at that price.

The new courthouse, which serves today, is made of Ohio sandstone. Four Ionic columns support a cornice, frieze, and architrave. The bas relief on the pediment symbolizes the advance of civilization under law, with Justice as the central figure. It is an apt contrast to Thomas Cole's "The Course of an Empire," which he painted in the 1830's.

Beyond Emory A. Chase, Greene County boasts a number of eminent legal and judicial figures, including Washington Hunt (1811-1867) who served as Governor of New York, 1851-1853; Lyman Tremaine (1819-1878), New York's Attorney General, 1858-1859; Thurlow Weed (1797-1882), an influential 19th Century political leader, and Malbone Watson (1804-1857) who served on the New York Court of Appeals in 1852.

Thanks to Greene County Historian Raymond Beecher and to Eric Mauer, Chief Clerk, Surrogate's Court, Greene County.

Green County Court House, Catskill, N. Y.

The Greene County Courthouse as an artist's conception.

Lake Pleasant, N. Y.

The Hamilton County Courthouse was completed in 1930. In the 1970's it was augmented by an annex connected by an elevated walkway. It was listed on both the State and National Register of Historic Places in 1992.

Hamilton County

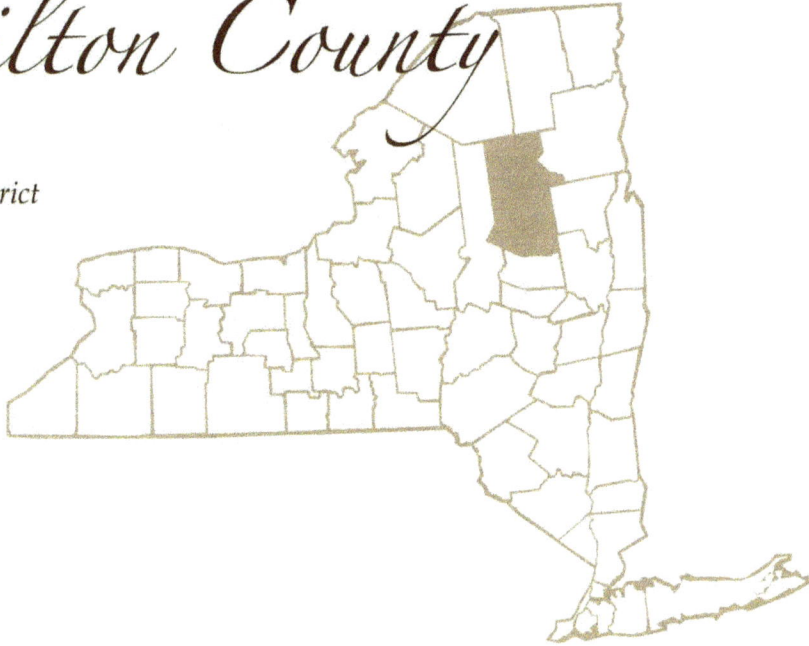

Although the third largest county in New York by size, Hamilton County has the smallest population. It lies in the heart of the Adirondacks. Much of the county falls within the Adirondack State Park, and is therefore not open to development. Today Hamilton County draws many summer travelers, attracted by its wilderness. In the early days, this wilderness quality gave the impression that the land was uninhabitable.

In 1816, land was split off from Montgomery County to form a provisional county named for Alexander Hamilton. It would receive full county status when it had 1,288 taxable residents who qualified to vote. This took about two decades. The township of Lake Pleasant was to be the county seat. In 1817, Philip Rhinelander, a large and politically active landowner, sold the fledgling county a scenic plot of land for the courthouse where the community of Speculator now lies.

There was no need to build a courthouse right away so long as the county was only provisional. The Supervisors of Hamilton County continued to be part of the Board of Supervisors of Montgomery County and, until 1836, met at the courthouse in Johnstown.

The prospective county grew slowly. Population growth picked up a little in the 1830's. An 1835 census identified 1,654 qualified inhabitants. With Hamilton County having met its requirement, the State legislature granted it full-fledged status, but reserved the right to revoke it. For decades, Hamilton County stood in danger of being annulled, and to have its lands divided among its neighbors.

Because the County had no courthouse in 1836, court convened at the home of Elijah Scidmore in Lake Pleasant. Prisoners continued to go to Montgomery County, pending construction of the jail.

As to the county seat, the only point agreed upon was to reject the originally proposed site. No community had yet formed there, and the roads did not go that far. Furthermore, Rhinelander was no longer around to defend the choice, having moved back to New York City after the tragic death of his wife. After several months of wrangling, the county chose a site in the Village of Lake Pleasant, overlooking both Lake Pleasant and Sacandaga Lake. Construction began in 1839. The community where the courthouse lay was renamed Sageville in the 1840's, a name it kept until 1897.

The courthouse was a white frame Colonial-style building with a foundation of stone quarried in Lake Pleasant. The county postponed building a jail until 1847, when they constructed one of fieldstone. Later, the county built a brick building to house the county clerk's records.

In the 1890's the courthouse received repairs. The county clerk's building was expanded, and the jail improved. By the beginning of the 20th Century, however, the old buildings were becoming increasingly inadequate. By November 1927, the Board of Supervisors was ready to plan a new courthouse. Scott Conroy won the bid to build it and began work in 1928. By 1930, the new courthouse and county clerk's office were completed.

In 1931, Cecilia D. Patten, Commissioner of the State Commission of Corrections informed the county that the jail did not live up to 1930's standards. The Hamilton County citizens, in the midst of the Depression, were in no mood to pay for a new jail when they were struggling just to provide themselves the necessities of life. The state persisted, and the county eventually built the new jail, which was opened August 1, 1940.

Hamilton County may not be densely populated, but its population has grown and, with it, the needs of county government. By the 1970's it needed more space. An annex was begun in 1975 and finished in 1976 to the west of the old courthouse connected by an elevated walkway. The courthouse complex was added to the State Register of Historic Sites on August 5, 1992 and to the National Register on September 24, 1992.

Thanks to Hamilton County Historian Paul Wilbur and Judge S. Peter Feldstein.

HAMILTON CO. COURT HOUSE, LAKE PLEASANT, N. Y. B101

The Hamilton County Courthouse in black and white.

Herkimer Co. Court House, Herkimer, N. Y.

The Herkimer County Courthouse, built in 1873, has been on the National Register of Historic Places since 1972.

Herkimer County

Fifth Judicial District

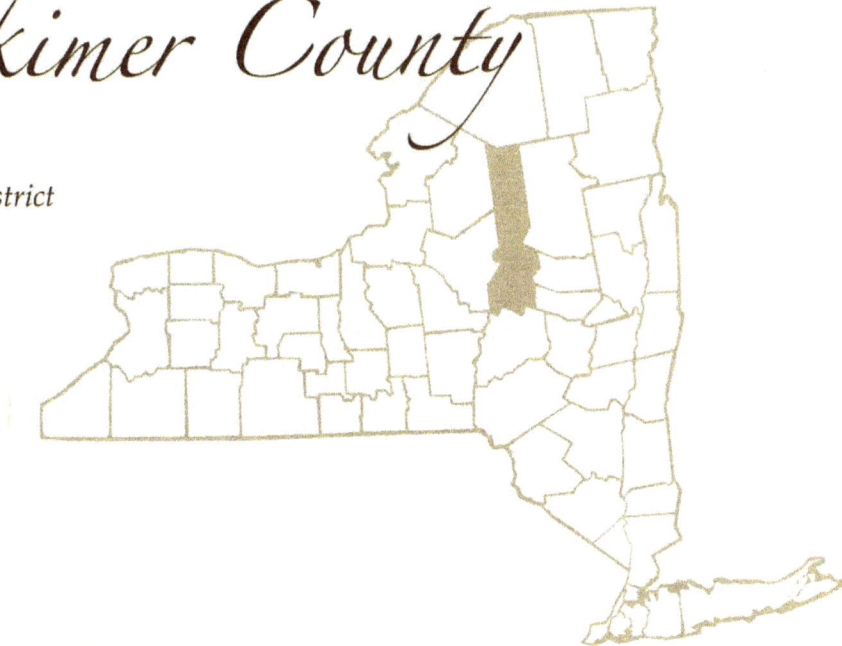

In 2006, Herkimer County observed the centennial of its most famous murder trial, that of Chester Gillette who murdered his pregnant girlfriend, Grace Brown, by drowning her in Big Moose Lake. The trial began in November 1906 before Judge Irving R. Devendorf and a jury. After hearing evidence of poignant letters that Grace Brown wrote to Gillette, and his evasive and inconsistent accounts of the event, the jury convicted him on December 12, 1906. In a decision written by Judge Frank H. Hiscock, the Court of Appeals affirmed the conviction on February 18, 1908. [*People v. Gillette* 191 NY 107 (1908)] The following month, Gillette's mother appealed unsuccessfully to Governor Charles Evans Hughes, who was said to be moved and tearful but resolute. Gillette was executed on March 31, 1908, admitting his guilt.

The event became part of America's literary scene with the 1925 publication of *An American Tragedy* by Theodore Dreiser. Cinema followed, including the 1951 movie *A Place in the Sun*, starring Elizabeth Taylor, Montgomery Clift, and Shelley Winters. Recently the Metropolitan Opera commissioned an opera entitled *An American Tragedy* with music by Tobias Picker and libretto by Gene Scheer.

With the creation of Herkimer County in 1791, court was held in Whitestown, but when Oneida County was founded in 1798, Whitestown went with it. The Village of Herkimer became the county seat, and the Herkimer community lost little time in building a plain two-story courthouse. When this building burned in 1834, the county responded with a brick structure, which served for almost 40 years. The county also built a jail next to the courthouse in 1835.

In 1871, the *Herkimer County Democrat and Gazette* denounced the courthouse as "insufficient and unsuitable." Apparently the county officials agreed because they set about to replace it. After the old courthouse was demolished, court moved into temporary quarters at Fox Hall. Construction began in 1872. The *Herkimer Democrat and Gazette* couldn't resist a partisan jibe: "The Old Court House has been taken down and the work of clearing the site for the new building is rapidly going on. The old one cost, originally $5,400. The new one at a cost of $35,000 will be much better, but owing to the Republican war prices we cannot get as much for our money as when the old one was put up."

The building was completed in 1873 at a final cost of $46,471. In the ensuing years, the building received some minor repairs and remodeling. It was wired for electricity in 1902. When a judges' restroom was installed in 1890, a staircase leading to three upstairs rooms was removed. In 1933, the County Building Committee discovered the rooms along with a law library, exhibits, and records that were in one of the sealed rooms.

In 1935, the Building Committee proposed that the county build a new building to house all the county offices as well as the courts. The Supervisors soundly defeated this recommendation. The following year, the county embarked on a courthouse renovation. The work included connecting the county clerk's office with the courthouse with a ramp and tunnel. The remodeled courthouse was dedicated on July 12, 1939, and it was placed on the National Register January 14, 1972.

In 1998, Herkimer County put up a new County Offices and Court Facilities building. Court is held on the fifth floor of the new building. The Sheriff's Department and the Rural Health Network occupy the old courthouse.

Three men from Herkimer County served on the State's highest court: Robert Earl, Charles Gray, and Celora Martin. Robert Earl was born in Herkimer in 1824 and attended Herkimer Academy. He served on the Court of Appeals for an extraordinarily long time – from 1869 to 1894, and was Chief Judge in 1870 and 1892, writing over 1000 opinions in all. Judge Earl was part of a group that formed the Herkimer (National) Bank and the Herkimer Historical Society. His love of community was so great that he bequeathed his home to the Herkimer Free Library.

Charles Gray (1796-1871) entered a Herkimer law firm in 1819 and after being admitted to the Bar, settled in Herkimer and practiced law there. He was named Herkimer County Jail Commissioner in 1832 and was elected a member of the State Assembly in 1835. He held the office of master in Chancery in Herkimer County for a number of years and in 1847 was elected a Justice of the State Supreme Court. In that capacity he served ex officio on the Court of Appeals during 1847-1848. He died in Herkimer on February 21, 1871. Celora E. Martin (1834-1909) was born in Newport, Herkimer County. Elected to the Court of Appeals in 1895, he served from 1896 through 1904.

Thanks to Susan R. Perkins, Executive Director, Herkimer County Historical Society.

Library, Herkimer, N. Y.

Judge Robert Earl bequeathed his home to the Herkimer Free Library.

County Buildings, Watertown, N. Y.

Horatio Nelson White designed this Anglo Norman Courthouse for Jefferson County. It was completed in 1862 and has been on the National Register of Historic Places since 1974.

efferson County

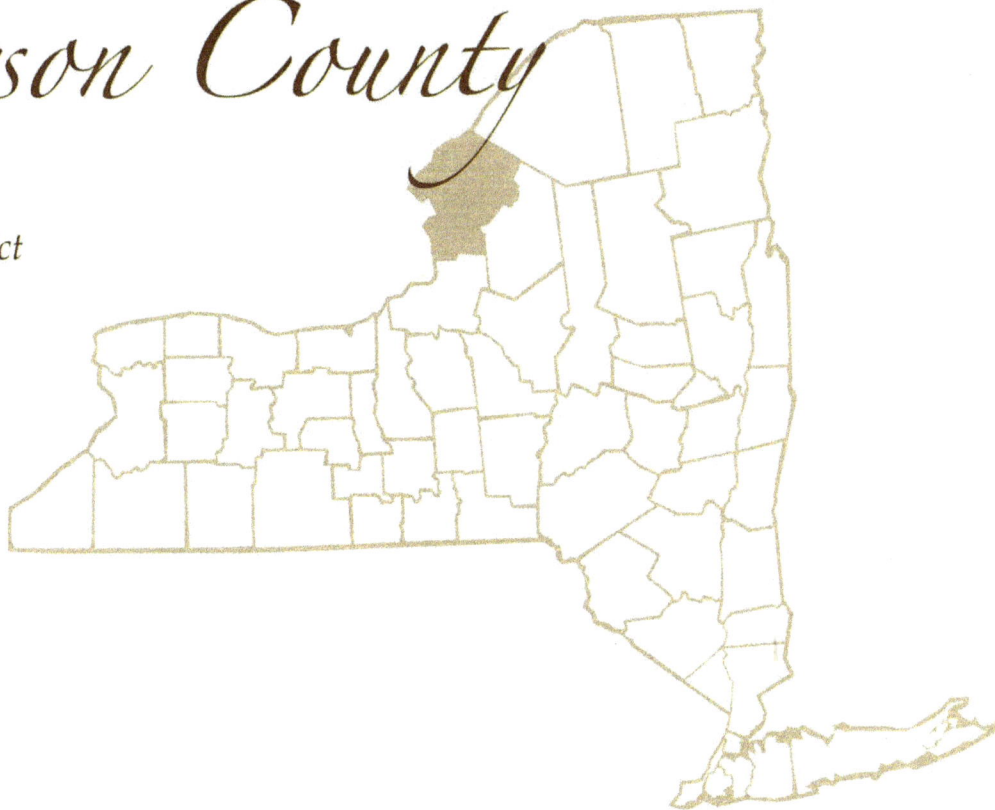

the days when debtors were imprisoned, counties frequently
signated "jail limits" or "jail liberties," an area in which the
soners could walk freely. If they stepped over the line, this
n would be taken away, and they'd be confined to their cells.
cause debtors were not considered dangerous, most counties
de a plot of ground near the jail for this purpose. Jefferson
y set the jail limits in a novel fashion. They included a set
ways 4 to 8 feet wide, which would allow access to almost
building in the village. It inadvertently turned out to be a
r the unwary. If a wagon or a mud puddle blocked the path-
ne hapless debtor might try to walk around the obstruction,
ver the line, and end up losing his privilege. In 1821, this was
ied when a rectangular area round the village was made the
its.

fferson County had its origins in Oneida County, where in
rly 1800's settlement had proceeded rapidly. In 1805, the

Oneida County: Lewis and Jefferson. Several towns in Jefferson
County sought to become the county seat. The commissioners appointed to make the decision compromised on Watertown, and the
people accepted the choice fairly well.

The county built its first courthouse in 1807-1808 with a jail on
the first floor. The building included a tower and a tin-covered cupola, which held a bell and a lightening rod.

In 1816, the county built a separate fire-resistant county clerk's
office. As it turned out, it was just in time. The combined court-
house/jail was damaged by fire in December 1817, repaired, and
then completely destroyed by fire in 1821. The legislature authorized a new courthouse and separate jail. While the new buildings
were under construction, prisoners were sent to Lewis County, and
court met in a school building. The county clerk's office was replaced in 1831.

Although the courthouse was substantial, measuring 45 by 48

In 1858, a grand jury declared the courthouse a public nuisance, and steps were taken to build a new one. The county chose architect Horatio Nelson White, of Syracuse, who had already designed courthouses for Onondaga County and Chemung County. John Hose served as contractor.

The Anglo-Norman style brick and stone structure used limestone blocks quarried nearby, in which marine fossils can be seen. The grand interior featured two wooden staircases on each side of the vestibule. Ornate woodwork and marble fireplaces graced several of the first floor offices. The structure was completed in 1862 at a cost of $25,000. For years, the bell in the courthouse tower served as Watertown's only fire alarm.

At first, the county clerk moved the county's records to the new courthouse. Eventually, needs of the courts for more space and concern for the safety of the records prompted the county to build a separate clerk's office in 1884.

The county was less swift to deal with the jail, which had been declared unfit for habitation. In 1893, the county renovated the interior of the jail to bring it up to code and built a new residence for the sheriff. The project cost more than $13,000.

The courthouse was listed on the National Register of Historic Places in 1974 and is part of a Locally Designated Historic District. Despite its grandeur, the needs of the courts outstripped the building's capacity. The county opened a new court facility in 2004 and has yet to designate the next use for the old courthouse.

Denis O'Brien (1837-1909) was born in Ogdensburg but made his adult home in Watertown. After serving as Alderman and then Mayor of Watertown, O'Brien was elected New York State Attorney General in 1883 and again in 1887. He joined the New York Court of Appeals in 1890, serving until 1907. His son, John F. O'Brien (1874-1939), who was born in Watertown, also served on the Court of Appeals.

Other noted jurists from Jefferson County are John W. Hogan (1853-1926), Frederick W. Hubbard (1815-1882), and Joseph Mullin (1811-1882). Hogan served on the Court of Appeals from 1913 to 1923. Hubbard, who served ex officio on the New York Court of Appeals in 1856, was born in Champion, Jefferson County, the son of Judge Noadiah Hubbard, and one of the first settlers of Champion in 1798. Mullin, of Watertown, served ex officio on the Court in 1864.

Thanks to Susan Drake Jenne, County Court Law Assistant and to Hon. Kim Martusewicz, Jefferson County Judge.

Post Office, Watertown, N. Y.

213674

Jefferson County based its new courthouse on another historic building. The former post office, shown here in 1912, was thoroughly renovated and expanded, incorporating state-of-the-art technology. The new facility opened in October 2004.

COURT HOUSE - Brooklyn, New York.

ILLUSTRATED POST CARD CO., N. Y.

Come up and see us
ag uin soon.
Aunt Mamie

Designed by King and Tackritz of Brooklyn, the 1865 Kings County Courthouse was
demolished in 1961, having been replaced two years earlier by a modern building.

Kings County

Second Judicial District

When the Brooklyn Dodgers and the New York Giants held their classic pennant race in 1951 ("The shot heard round the world"), the Kings County court system was 283 years old. As far as is known, the first court of record held in Kings County was convened in Gravesend (Amersfoort) in 1668, some 32 years after planters settled along the shore of Gowanus Bay in 1636. A second courthouse was built in Flatbush in 1686 and these two buildings conducted the county's legal affairs for over 70 years.

The name Brooklyn, now coterminous with Kings County, came from the Dutch. It appears variously as Breucklyn, Breukland, Brouklyn, and the like, meaning marshland, reminiscent, perhaps of Breuckelen, Holland.

After barely escaping a fire in 1757, the Flatbush Courthouse was razed and a new building erected in its place. The third courthouse was built in 1792 at a cost of $2,944.71.

Until the beginning of the 19th Century, there were almost no lawyers living in Kings County. By 1821, there was talk of moving the courthouse from Flatbush to Brooklyn. Both towns later united to form what would become Brooklyn. In 1832, the Flatbush building caught fire and Flatbush ceased to be the county seat. Business was transferred to Brooklyn, where a courthouse went up in the late 1830's.

By the middle of the 19th Century, there was talk of a new courthouse, which came to fruition when the cornerstone was laid on May 20, 1862, at the corner of Fulton and Joralemon Streets. The structure followed a plan by King and Tackritz of Brooklyn, and was made of Westchester marble with Corinthian columns, and a dome rising to 104 feet. On May 21, 1862, the *New York Times* reported that 8,000 people witnessed the ceremony. In 1865, the building opened, housing the full panoply of courts.

The 1865 courthouse, demolished in 1961, had been replaced by a new building in 1959. The needs of the courts continued, and in November 2005, Mayor Michael R. Bloomberg and New York

State Chief Judge Judith S. Kaye cut the ribbon for a new Criminal, Supreme, and Family court complex. The $670 million facility, 32 stories high, provides 84 courtrooms and includes a large parking garage for court personnel. The old building will not be razed. It will submit to a $42 million renovation to bring it up to state-of-the-art capability.

Formerly known as "the City of Churches," Brooklyn became part of New York City in 1898. Shortly after that, the Supreme Court Appellate Division, Second Department, used the Common Council Chamber in Brooklyn's City Hall. In 1938, after leaving that location, the Appellate Division moved to its present location at Monroe Place in Brooklyn. Architect Robert H. Bryson, who died 18 days before the court held its opening session there on September 28, 1938, designed this handsome structure.

Brooklyn has produced a considerable number of esteemed jurists, including four Chief Judges of the New York Court of Appeals: Edgar M. Cullen (1843-1922), Frederick E. Crane (1869-1947), Willard Bartlett (1846-1925), and Albert Conway (1889-1969). Benjamin F. Tracy (1830-1915) served on the Court of Appeals, as did John A. Lott (1806-1878). Nathan B. Morse (1799-1886) served on the Court, ex officio, in 1853.

Thanks to James Pelzer, Clerk of the Supreme Court, Appellate Division, Second Department.

The Brooklyn City Hall, now Borough Hall, housed the Supreme Court Appellate Division from 1903 to 1938. The 1865 Kings County Courthouse can be seen behind it.

The Supreme Court, Appellate Division, Second Department on Monroe Place in Brooklyn. Designed by Robert H. Bryson, the building appears now much the same as it did when it opened in 1938.

Trinity Church, Court House and County Clerks Office, Lowville, N. Y.

Hoping to become the Lewis County seat, Lowville built this building in 1852. Unsuccessful at first, Lowville used it as the town hall. When Lowville became the county seat in 1864, the town turned the building over to the county for a courthouse.

Lewis County

Fifth Judicial District

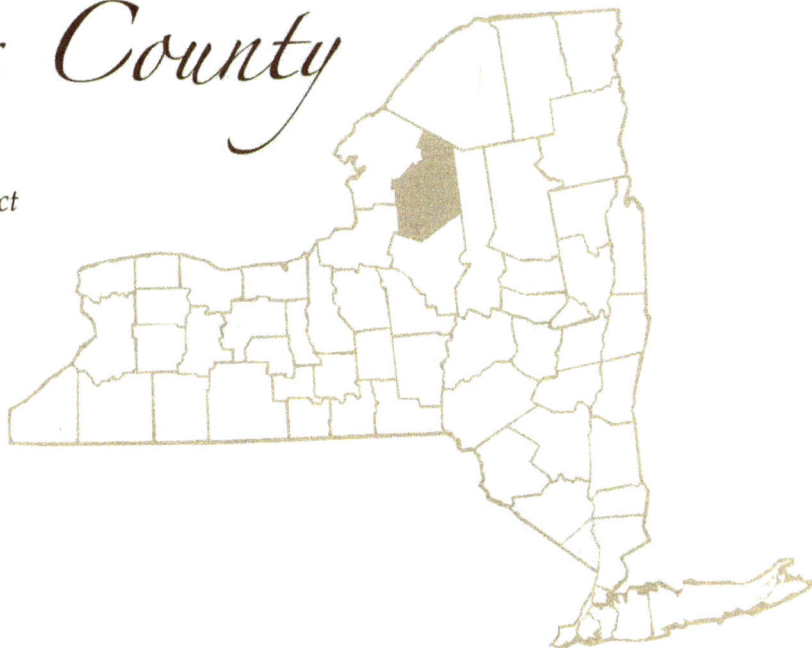

Lewis County lies in northern New York State, with a large part in the Adirondack State Park. It remains one of the few counties that has "three-hatters," judges who serve as County Judge, Surrogate, and Family Court Judges.

When the Duke of York established counties in New York in 1683, the land that comprises Lewis County was part of Albany County. After a series of incarnations, it became part of Oneida and, like Jefferson County, was split off from Oneida in 1805.

Lewis County was named for Morgan Lewis, a Dutchess County Revolutionary War soldier and General in the War of 1812. He served as State Attorney General in 1791, as Chief Justice of the (old) New York State Supreme Court in 1792 and New York's third Governor from 1804 to 1807. He built what is now Mills Mansion in Staatsburgh, New York. He is buried in St. James Cemetery, Hyde Park, New York.

Pending the building of a courthouse and jail, Lewis County prisoners were confined in Rome, Oneida County; court was held at the inn of Chillus Doty in Martinsburg. Both Lowville and Martinsburg campaigned for designation as county seat. Martinsburg had the advantage of one General Walter Martin who commanded a great deal of influence and swung the decision to Martinsburg.

The courthouse-jail building was ready by January 1812. It was a large frame building with the courtroom on the second floor and jail cells, sheriff's office, and housing for the jailer's family on the first.

Lowville never gave up the fight for county seat. When after 50 years, the question of a new courthouse came up, the contest renewed with three localities as candidates: Lowville, Martinsburg, and New Bremen. Lowville even went so far as to build a new courthouse in 1852, hoping this would clinch the decision. It didn't, and the would-be courthouse became the town hall.

But in 1864, Lowville finally prevailed, and the town gave its town hall to the county, an imposing building with an Ionic portico, reminiscent of classical architecture. This courthouse was enlarged in 1875, a county clerks' office added next door in 1902, and additional expansion in 1939. In November 1947, the courthouse burned, destroying many of the county records, parts of the building, and the law library. The county leaders decided to repair the damage with fire-resistant materials and to further expand the building, adding a third floor. The courthouse reopened November 3, 1949.

In order to provide additional space, increased security, and handicapped accessibility, the county had to either build a new courthouse or renovate the present one. It has stirred up a heated debate whether to built an additional building behind the present courthouse or to build an entirely new courthouse at the outskirts of town.

Among Lewis County's most prominent judges was Fred Young who served as Chief Judge of the New York State Court of Claims. He died in 1973 at age 69. Another prominent judge, Edgar S. Merrell, served on the Supreme Court, Appellate Division. He died at age 77 in 1942.

Thanks to Judge George R. Davis and Lewis County Historian Lisa Becker.

After a fire in 1947, Lewis County repaired the courthouse and added a third floor.

LEWIS CO. COURT HOUSE AND CLERK'S OFFICE, LOWVILLE, N. Y.

The Lewis County Courthouse as it looked in the 1920's.

Livingston County Court House. GENESEO, N. Y.

The core of the Livingston County Courthouse dates to 1823. In 1898, this façade was added. The building received at $3.3 million renovation in 1995 to bring it up to present-day standards.

Livingston County

Seventh Judicial District

A historical marker notes the first settlement in Williamsburg in 1792, in what is today Livingston County. In 1797, in the Town of Geneseo, the Seneca Indians released title to 3,600,000 acres of land in the Treaty of Big Tree (7 Stat 601), making it possible for a group of Dutch investors, known as the Holland Land Company to sell parcels of land to settlers. The western part of the state experienced rapid growth in the early 1800's. This increased the need for land transfers and access to public records. Roads were poor and travel difficult. Residents of the more outlying portions of Ontario County and Genesee County experienced hardship in getting to Canandaigua or Batavia. A transaction that should be concluded within a day would often take as much as three or four days to complete. They petitioned to have those counties divided, and the Legislature complied.

In 1821, Livingston County was formed out of parts of Ontario and Genesee Counties. Several towns declared their candidacy for county seat. The commissioners selected Geneseo because the town

of 6,500 was near the geographical center of the county. Pending the building of a courthouse and jail, court was held in a school building in Geneseo, and prisoners were sent to Canandaigua, Ontario County. James and William Wadsworth gave the county approximately four acres for a courthouse, jail, and a public square. The courthouse, completed May 1823, cost $11,000, $2000 more than estimated.

Two years later, in 1825, Daniel Shays (of Shay's Rebellion fame) died and is buried in Springwater, Livingston County. Twelve years later in the Town of York, just northwest of Geneseo, President Chester A. Arthur attended school from 1837 to 1842.

The building received its first expansion in 1866 and in1898 got a major overhaul. Architect Claude Bragdon of Rochester was called upon to provide plans. Parts of the building were demolished, and a new façade added. At that time, America's Pledge of Allegiance was six years old, having been written by Francis Bellamy in 1892. Bellamy was born in Mount Morris, Livingston County in 1855.

In 1914, the Livingston County Courthouse was a center of national attention after the trial of New York City "Merchant Prince," Henry Siegel, head of a chain of department stores in New York, Boston, and Chicago, was transferred there. The indictment charged Siegel with theft. New York County District Attorney Arthur Train (author of the Mr. Tutt series) represented the prosecution along with Livingston County District Attorney Frank K. Cook. A Livingston County jury convicted Siegel.

The next courthouse expansion took place in 1957. When New York State issued specifications for all courthouses in 1989, the officials of Livingston County took that as an opportunity to correct problems they had already observed as well as to fulfill the state mandate. They responded with a $3.3 million repair and remodeling project that was completed in 1995. Transformed in several stages since 1823, the Livingston County courthouse now has air conditioning, handicapped access, improved security as well as a new roof, new windows, and new mechanical, plumbing and electrical systems.

Northeast of Geneseo in the Town of Lima, Kenneth B. Keating (1900-1975) was born. Keating was admitted to practice in 1923 and elected United States Senator in 1958, serving until 1965. He served on the New York Court of Appeals from 1964 to 1969.

Richard C. Wesley (1949-) of Livonia, Livingston County, after serving in the New York State Assembly representing Livingston, Allegany, and Ontario Counties, joined the judiciary and rose to a seat on the New York Court of Appeals, where he served from 1997 to 2003. He now is a Judge of the United States Court of Appeals for the Second Circuit.

Thanks to Deputy County Historian Aime Alden.

The writer of this card was in Geneseo on July 4, 1908. She describes the noise as "fearful," but she is having a good time.

Court House   Geneseo, N. Y.

The Livingston County Courthouse as it looked in the mid-20th Century.

NEW YORK STATE AGRICULTURAL BUILDINGS, MORRISVILLE, N.Y.

When Wampsville became the county seat, the New York State Agricultural School at Morrisville took over the 1865 courthouse, the white building in the center. It is now known as Madison Hall at Morrisville State College.

Madison County

Sixth Judicial District

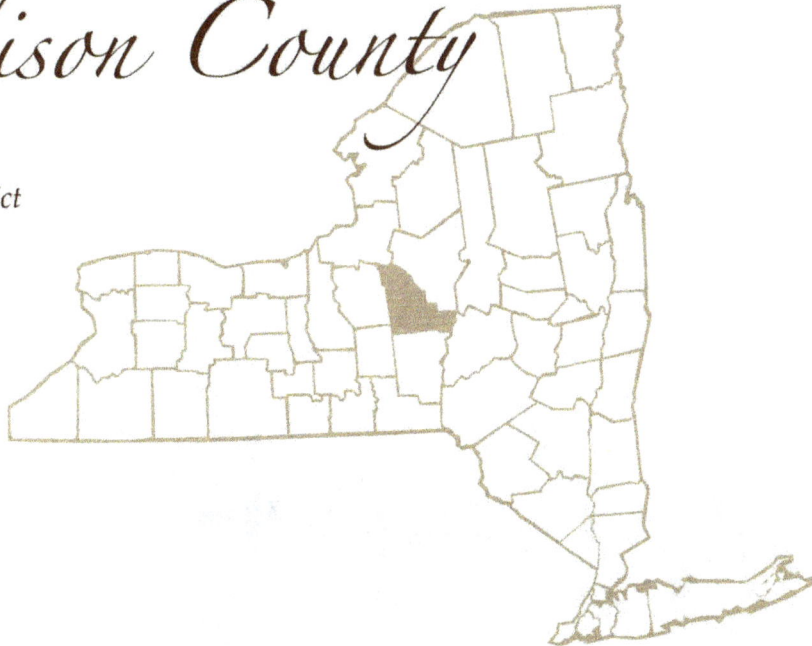

Madison County has had several county seats since it was set off from Chenango County in 1806. At first, court was held in schoolhouses in two towns; Hamilton, which had been one of the two county seats of Chenango, and Sullivan. When the time came to build a real courthouse in 1810, the county built a courthouse in Cazenovia at the cost of approximately $4000. It was a brick copy of the first Oneida County Courthouse in Whitesboro. Cazenovia was not centrally located, and its choice is generally attributed to the influence of land developer John Lincklaen. It helped that it was also located on a good road, the Cherry Valley Turnpike, now US Route 20.

By 1817, there was a campaign to have the county seat moved to a more central location. Smithfield, Eaton, and Morrisville all made bids. Morrisville won. The Methodist Episcopal Church bought the Cazenovia courthouse and used it as a place of worship and later a seminary. Until it burned down in 1959, the building remained part of the seminary, now Cazenovia College.

The county built a courthouse in Morrisville in 1817. The courthouse lasted until 1847, when it was condemned as unsafe and subsequently replaced. The 1847 courthouse burned in 1864 while court was in session. Court proceedings moved across the street to the Exchange Hotel, and the county constructed a new courthouse the following year. This was a two-story frame building with a courtroom, gallery, jury rooms, and library. It was located across from a small park near a reservoir, which could provide plenty of water in case of fire. The county built an addition to the courthouse in 1877.

By the beginning of the 20th Century, Morrisville was considered too isolated to remain the county seat. The 1872 jail at Morrisville had been condemned, and the county was looking at an estimated price tag of $30,000 to build a new one. The Village of Canastota and the City of Oneida competed fiercely with each other for the honor. Eventually Wampsville, a tiny hamlet located between the two rival cities, came up as a compromise. When the matter first arose, no municipality could get enough votes to supplant Morrisville, but in 1907, Wampsville won.

For one dollar, John Coe granted the land for the new courthouse and jail. James Reilly Gordon of New York City was the architect. The cornerstone was laid on January 7, 1909, and the courthouse finished by 1910.

Morrisville's third courthouse, however, still stands. When the county seat moved to Wampsville, the Morrisville courthouse was taken over by the New York State Agricultural School at Morrisville, now Morrisville State College. The building, now named Madison Hall, was listed on the National Register of Historic Places on June 15, 1978.

The Wampsville courthouse does not face the street. It is said that it was placed on the bias so that the back door would not be turned toward the City of Oneida. The building faces a rail route, and the county anticipated that a boulevard would eventually run parallel to it. That never happened.

Madison County has had several notable jurists. Charles Mason (1810-1879) served on the New York Court of Appeals in 1861, 1868, and 1869. Philo Gridley (1796-1864) sat on the Court, ex officio, in 1852 as did Erasmus D. Smith (1806-1882) in 1862.

Thanks to Madison County Historian Sarah Davies.

The County Clerk's Office in Morrisville was part of the county court complex before the county seat moved to Wampsville.

Madison County Court House and Jail, Wampsville, N. Y.

Above: The need to build a new jail was one factor prompting Madison County to move its county seat to Wampsville. Here, the jail was built close to the courthouse, the domed building in the background.

Right: The Madison County Courthouse, designed by James Reilly Gordon of New York City, opened in 1910.

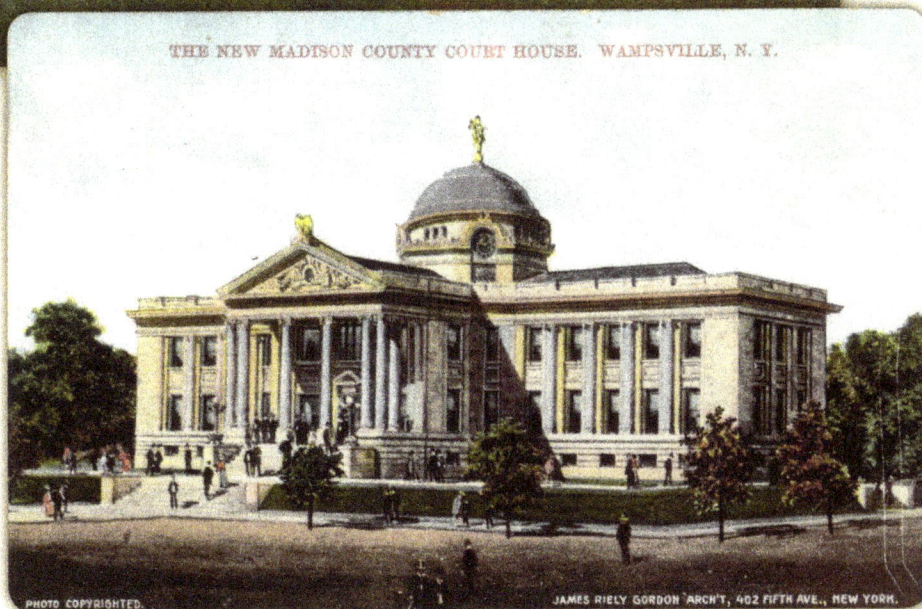

THE NEW MADISON COUNTY COURT HOUSE. WAMPSVILLE, N. Y.

PHOTO COPYRIGHTED.

JAMES RIELY GORDON ARCH'T, 402 FIFTH AVE., NEW YORK.

Historic Court House Overlooking Early Rochester Village

This 1934 postcard shows the first Monroe County Courthouse (1822-1850).

Monroe County

Seventh Judicial District

To meet the needs of an expanding New York State in the early 1800's, it was obvious that Ontario and Genesee Counties would have to be divided. Colonel Nathaniel Rochester (1752-1831) wanted to make sure that his namesake location, where he owned land, was made the seat of one of the new counties. After an unsuccessful try, he led a delegation to Albany, traveling by sleigh, to lobby for it. The Legislature approved Monroe County, and the Governor DeWitt Clinton signed the bill on February 23, 1821. The new county consisted of more than 600 square miles, which made it slightly larger than the other new counties of the time.

There was little controversy about the choice of Rochester as county seat, but the location within Rochester was an issue. Rochester had become a thriving community ever since Ebeneezer Allan had built gristmills on the Genesee River in 1789. The commissioners chose a site at the center of Colonel Nathaniel Rochester's 100-acre tract because of its central location. The three-story stone courthouse cost $7000 and was ready by September 1822. It was expected to last a century, but it served for less than 30 years.

The first courthouse was replaced at the same site by a second one, begun in 1850 and completed in 1851. The building was originally designed to be two stories, but the City of Rochester prevailed on the County to add a third story and paid more than half the cost of the building. Built of brick with a foundation of Onondaga limestone, it had a portico, supported by four columns and two domes, the upper one supporting a figure of Justice. It was used jointly by the City and County until 1874 when the City built a City Hall. The dome of this courthouse was a favorite site from which to view the city until 1873 when a taller building called the Powers Block Tower provided a superior vantage point.

By 1894 this courthouse had become too small, and work began on a new one. It was a period of economic hard times, and the project provided much-needed jobs for the distressed community.

The laying of the cornerstone during a Fourth of July ceremony prompted much celebration.

Designed by J. Foster Warner, it is of Italianate design and built of New Hampshire granite with a heavy cornice. It extends four stories above a high basement. Four polished columns grace the north front. The vestibule opens into an atrium with a skylight 92 feet above. An impressive marble staircase leads to the second floor where the original millstones from Allan's mill are on display.

In 1964, Monroe County built a Hall of Justice, which houses all the courts. The Old Courthouse is alive and well as the County Office Building.

A large number of jurists who served on the New York Court of Appeals were born or resided in Monroe County. Addison Gardiner (1797-1883) was on the first bench of the newly established 1847 Court, serving from 1847 to 1855, and as Chief Judge in 1854 and 1855. Samuel L. Selden (1800-1876) served on the Court of Appeals, ex officio, in 1854, as a member from 1856 to 1862, and as Chief Judge in 1862. His brother Henry R. Selden (1805-1885) served on the Court from 1862 to 1864.

George F. Danforth (1819-1899) served from 1879 to 1889; William E. Werner (1855-1916) from 1901 to 1916; Harlan Rippey (1874-1946) from 1937 to 1944; Marvin Dye (1895-1997) from 1945 to 1965, and Kenneth B. Keating (1900-1975) from 1966 to 1969. Erasmus D. Smith (1806-1882) served on the Court, ex officio, in 1862.

Thanks to Judge John J. Connell.

ROCHESTER, N. Y. Court House and City Hall,

Designed by J. Foster Warner and built in 1894, the Old Monroe County Courthouse now functions as the County Office Building.

Left: The 1894 courthouse's striking interior is shown in this 1909 card.

Below: A grand marble staircase greets visitors to Monroe County's third courthouse (1894), now the County Office Building.

In 1964, Monroe County built a Hall of Justice to accommodate all the courts.

Old Montgomery Co. Court House, built 1836, Fonda, N.Y.

Montgomery County's elegant "Old Courthouse," built in 1836, is still used for county offices.

Montgomery County

Fourth Judicial District

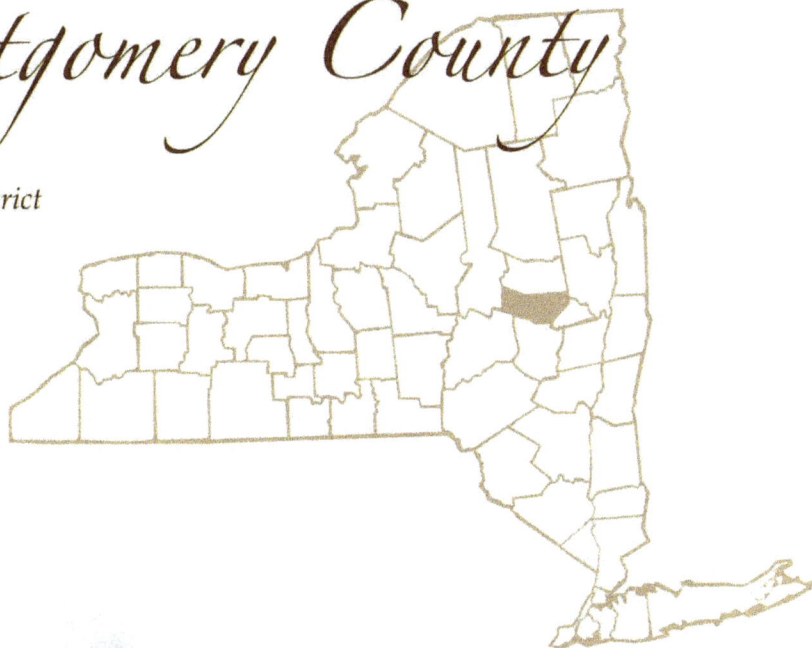

Montgomery County entered the scene in 1772 as one of the 12 colonial counties. During colonial days it was called Tryon County, named for the Provincial Governor William Tryon (1729-1788). Johnstown was the county seat. Tryon County was taken from Albany County, which it replaced as the county with the largest land mass and yet undefined borders. Theoretically, the western border of Tryon/Montgomery County could have extended all the way to the Pacific Ocean. Only after the 1786 Treaty of Hartford settled the conflicting land claims of Connecticut and Massachusetts, did New York's western boundary become what we know it today. In 1784, after the Revolutionary War, the county succeeded in discarding the name of the detested Governor Tryon, in favor of General Richard Montgomery's who had lost his life in the battle for Quebec.

As New York's population expanded westward into new territory, the Legislature created new counties for the convenience of the settlers. In 1798, Ontario County replaced Montgomery as the large rest-of-New-York county. Tioga, Otsego, and Herkimer were carved out of Montgomery's territory soon thereafter. When the Erie Canal and the Utica-Schenectady Railroad brought improved transportation to the Mohawk Valley, the population centers shifted toward these arteries. Poor roads still prevailed, and the county seat at Johnstown became inconvenient for most of the county's residents. By 1836, the New York State Legislature was ready to move the county seat from Johnstown to Fonda. Johnstown was not without political influence, however, and the Legislature went along with the demand from the northern townships to secede and form Fulton County.

For its new courthouse, Montgomery County chose the site of Colonial Sheriff Joseph White's home in Fonda. Carpenter Lawrence Marcellus and mason Henry Holmes built the courthouse and nearby jail for $30,000. Built in 1836, it was an elegant building with Ionic columns supporting a portico leading to a double-door entrance to the first floor. An outside staircase led to the courtroom on the second floor.

This courthouse had only one major flaw, its proximity to the railroad. For 60 years, noise and tremors from the passing trains disrupted court proceedings. Finally, in 1892, the Board of Supervisors decided to build a courthouse far enough from the tracks that court could be held in peace.

Fuller and Wheeler of Albany designed the Renaissance Revival building. Owen Canna of Amsterdam constructed it at a cost of $13,961. After the courts moved to the new building, several county offices moved into the old building. It was expanded and an interior staircase installed for access to the second floor. At that time a New York State seal was added to the pediment above the portico.

For more than a century, Fonda has had its "Old Courthouse" and "New Courthouse," both receiving constant use. In 1940 two wings were added to the north end of the New Courthouse. J.L. Finlay of Amsterdam was awarded the $21,000 contract. A 1962 extension of the two wings cost $125,000 adding a law library, additional Judges' chambers, and more space for jurors.

A couple of decades later, the courthouse received another courtroom for the Family Court and Surrogate's offices, which had been located in the County Office Building. The 13,000 square foot addition was finished in 1988 and dedicated in 1989. The New Courthouse was listed on both the State and National Registers of Historic Places in 1982.

Students of the law will recognize Hill's Reports (1841-1844). State Reporter Nicholas Hill (1805-1859) was a practitioner in Amsterdam, as was Robert J. Sise, who served as New York State's Chief Administrative Judge in 1983 and 1984.

Thanks to County Historian Kelly A. Yacobucci Farquhar.

Court House, Fonda, N. Y.

200,501. JV

This building has been Montgomery County's "New Courthouse" since 1892. It has seen several expansions since this photo was taken, and it still houses the courts.

NASSAU COUNTY COURT HOUSE, MINEOLA, L. I.

1801 ILLUSTRATED POST CARD CO., N. Y.

Dear Margaret:- Your Postal rec'd all O.K. I attended the Fair at Mineola yesterday & to-day. Louise.

When a woman named Louise wrote this card showing the Nassau County Courthouse to her friend Margaret in 1906, she said she had attended the fair in Mineola. Little did she (or anyone else) know that the fairgrounds would be the next site for court buildings.

Nassau County

Tenth Judicial District

Nassau County, the second youngest in the state, was created in 1899 out of land taken from Queens County. Wrangling over the county seat began at least a year before the county became official. Both Hempstead and Mineola wanted it. The Long Island Railroad had become a major artery of transportation, and the specifications for county seat required a courthouse near a railroad station. Hempstead negotiated with the heirs of Austin Corbin, the late president of the railroad, for eight acres near the Hempstead railroad station. Mineola secured a grant from the Garden City Corporation for four acres not far from the railroad station. The Garden City Corporation, apparently neutral in the matter, also reportedly offered land in Hempstead. The question was put to referendum, and the voters chose Mineola.

Not long after Nassau County's creation, pursuant to Chapter 588 of the Laws of 1898, litigation broke out over the constitutionality of the enactment. The point was settled by the Supreme Court Appellate Division in a suit over the election of Nassau County officers [*In re Noble* 34 App. Div. 55 (1898)]. Daniel Noble was a candidate for Queens County Surrogate. When the Legislature created Nassau County, it carved out the towns of Oyster Bay, North Hempstead, and Hempstead from Queens County. Noble learned that the Queens County Clerk printed the ballots for the election in those three towns to include the names of not only Nassau County candidates but Queens County candidates as well. The court ruled that Queens candidates should not be placed on the ballots of the voters in the three newly created Long Island towns. The voters in the three towns, the court held, were to vote only for Nassau County officials, not Queens County officials. It further held that Nassau County was constitutionally created.

The county was created, the county seat determined. Next came the courthouse. On July 13, 1900, then-Governor Theodore Roosevelt, who was born in Oyster Bay, Long Island, laid the cornerstone for the Nassau County Courthouse. Roosevelt was an obvious choice. He had lived at Sagamore Hill. Architect William G.

Tubby designed the Classic Revival structure. The plans, selected in a competition, called for reinforced concrete using a system patented by Ernest L. Ransome. The two-story building is topped by a white dome, and is graced by a grand entrance portico, supported by Ionic columns.

Nassau County grew rapidly, and the need for more space prompted the county to call upon Tubby in 1916 to supervise the addition of north and south wings, connected by arcades. The courthouse was further enlarged in 1926 with additions to the rear, supervised by architect William J. Beardsley. A WPA art project added four murals in the central rotunda stairwells, painted by Robert Gaston Herbert, depicting events of local history.

In the late 1930's the County built a new court complex on the site of the old Mineola Fairgrounds, and all judicial functions moved there. The old courthouse was reserved for county offices. After World War II, changes were made to the old courthouse, without disturbing the major architectural features, in order to accommodate the County Executive and Legislative offices as well as various county departments.

Today, court is held in a modern multi-storied building. The old courthouse was listed on the National Register of Historic Places in 1978. On July 13, 2002, Nassau County announced that the old county courthouse was renamed the Theodore Roosevelt Executive and Legislative Building, in memory of the man who had laid the cornerstone 102 years earlier. Roosevelt is buried in Oyster Bay.

Beyond Theodore Roosevelt, other notables figured in the history of Nassau County. Samuel Jones (1734-1819) was a delegate to the Constitutional Ratification Convention in Poughkeepsie in 1788. His motion that New York ratify the Constitution "in full confidence" rather than "on condition" of the addition of a Bill of Rights was instrumental in New York State's joining the Union. He was known as the "Father of the New York Bar."

Also from Nassau County, William T. McCoun (1786-1878) was the first vice-chancellor of New York State (1831). He served on the New York Court of Appeals in 1851.

Sol Wachtler (1930-) of Manhasset was New York's Chief Judge (1985-1992). Bernard S. Meyer (1916-2005) served on the Court of Appeals from 1979 to 1987.

Thanks to County Historian Edward J. Smits.

Nassau Co, Court House, Mineola, N. Y.

The Nassau County Courthouse in 1913.

TOMBS, (CITY PRISON) N.Y. CITY.

"The Tombs," the second New York County prison to be known by that name, housed prisoners from 1900 until 1941. The red building on the right was the courthouse, connected to the Tombs by the "Bridge of Sighs".

New York County

First Judicial District

New York County courthouses have had an uncommonly interesting history. One postcard shows an artist's rendering of the courthouse that never was, in which the writer, "Aunt Lizzie," some time around 1915, says "Haven't seen this." Indeed she hadn't; no one ever had, or ever would. The cost was too high and the plans were reconfigured.

Another landmark was the multi-million dollar courthouse that grew out of the excesses of William "Boss" Tweed in the 1860's. Ironically, it is referred to as the "Tweed Courthouse," a testament to his corruption. Today it is occupied by the Board of Education. And then there is the "Tombs," the exotic Criminal Court building – attached to "The Bridge of Sighs" that held forth in the 19th and early 20th Century. More about these later.

In 1623, when the Dutch settled the colony they called Nieuw Amsterdam, they brought their jurisprudence directly from Holland. In 1642, they converted a tavern into the Stadt Huys on Pearl Street in Manhattan. In 1664, the English took the colony from the Dutch, adding their judicial system.

In the 17th Century, New York had a confusing array of courts derived from both European traditions. A major event occurred on May 6, 1691 when the New York Assembly passed an act establishing a Supreme Court of Judicature. City Hall, completed in 1811 in Manhattan, housed the New York City terms of the Supreme Court of Judicature.

In 1893, the City of New York completed its new Criminal Courts building on the site of the old New York and Harlem freight depot, bounded by Centre, Elm, White, and Franklin Streets. In an August 26, 1894 article, the *New York Times* described the $1,800,000 fire-proof structure as of Renaissance style with a façade "of tender rufous materials," an almost parallelogram, filling an entire city block. Above its tall granite foundation, red brick, terra cotta, brownstone, and niches for statues gave the building's exterior a striking appearance. The interior

For 39 years, some 500,000 prisoners crossed this "Bridge of Sighs" from prison to their court proceedings.

rotunda formed "a vast air and light shaft, surrounded by galleries circling the various offices. The article concluded "The interior adornments of balustrades, columns, and metal work, are not too lavish for a municipal headquarters destined to outlive many generations."

The building was constructed on the plans of James W. Wilson and connected to the "Tombs" prison, the second facility to bear that name. The first Tombs was built in 1838, designed by architect John Haviland, in a briefly popular style known as Egyptian Revival. The name Tombs is credited to John A. Stevens, an engineer and philanthropist, who when touring Egypt in 1830, studied the tombs along the Nile. Later, his photographs were used for the design and name of the prison.

The Tombs was connected to the Criminal Court by a raised passageway, known as the "Bridge of Sighs" that extended across Franklin Street. This passageway was constructed three years after the old Tombs prison was built in 1900 on the site of the original 1838 Tombs prison.

The *New York Times* may have thought the Criminal Courts building "destined to outlive many generations," but its life proved much shorter. By 1936, officials began to feel pressured to build a new Criminal Courts building. The Grand Jury issued a report declaring the Criminal Courts building unfit and urging that a new courthouse be built. Mayor Fiorello La Guardia supported the project and on June 29, 1940, laid the cornerstone. He wrote a letter to posterity and placed it in a metal box under the cornerstone in what was said to be the largest building in the country to be constructed with the help of Federal public works funds.

At the time, New York City – and the rest of the nation – was witnessing criminal prosecutions brought by Thomas E. Dewey, who had been appointed Special Prosecutor in 1938. In June 1941, the new Criminal Courts building was dedicated, and the exodus from the old buildings began. On November 10, 1941, 723 prisoners were shifted from the Old Tombs to the new without public notice. A week before, Frank S. Hogan was elected and would begin a three-decade tenure as Mr. District Attorney in the new Criminal Courts building that became almost synonymous with his name. The DA's entrance to the building is now known officially as Hogan Place.

The City was, at first, uncertain of what would become of the old Tombs and Criminal Courts building and for a time used it as a "fire college" to train firefighters. The building had lots of steel; after all, it was the lock-up for some of the City's most dangerous criminals for four decades. The City arranged to remove 100 tons of steel for the government as scrap for manufacture of munitions to keep the Germans and Japanese at bay.

In July 1942, the City declared that the Bridge of Sighs would sigh no more, as a force of WPA workers dismantled it. The *Times* reported that "in the 39 years since the bridge was built, 500,000 men and women accused of felonies and misdemeanors, from murderers down to peddling, were led from the tombs cells across the structure for trials in the Magistrate's Court, Special Sessions, or General Sessions."

As buildings go, the old Criminal courts building did not have a long or happy life. Built in 1894, on wooden piles sunk in the marshland, it drew complaints not only from prisoners, but also from jurists. In 1946, it was razed.

The "Tweed" chapter is another fascinating part of New York's history. In 1861, John Kellum was chosen to build a new courthouse on Chambers Street in Manhattan. The structure, now known as the Tweed courthouse, is associated with appalling graft and corruption, by which William "Boss" Tweed and his companions bilked the City out of millions – in today's money said to be billions – of dollars in inflated costs. In 1873, Tweed was tried in a courtroom in the then-unfinished building and was eventually convicted and jailed. On April 12, 1878, Tweed died as a debtor in the Ludlow Street prison. The following day, the *Times* said that Tweed "has passed the custody of the New York Sheriff, and gone to an assize where Justice is less halting than here below." After the Tweed ring was broken, construction con-

No. 150—COUNTY COURT HOUSE, CHAMBERS ST., N. Y.

The corrupt administration of William "Boss" Tweed built this edifice, and it has been known as "The Tweed Courthouse" ever since. It now houses the New York City Board of Education.

tinued until the building was completed in 1881, a testament both to thievery and to beauty.

Grandeur does not necessarily guarantee long-term utility. In 1903, the City created a Court House Board to plan a new courthouse. Architect Guy Lowell originally proposed a magnificent circular design. The cost estimate for this 1913 design fell within a range of 20 to 30 million dollars. The City decided to exchange the notion of a magnificent Palace of Justice for a more modest Temple of Justice and asked Lowell to go back to the drawing board. He complied, presenting plans for a hexagonal building with a cost estimate of $7 million. The City agreed. In 1927, the courthouse was opened, but Guy Lowell did not live to see the dedication. He passed away only two weeks before the event. The building is still in use. Its inscription reads, "The true administration of justice is the firmest pillar of good government."

Shortly after the close of the Tweed administration, New York City built another new courthouse at 425 Avenue of the Americas in the Jefferson Market region of Greenwich Village. Built from 1874 to 1877, the building was designed by Frederick Clarke Withers and Calvert Vaux. On June 20, 1885, the *New York Times* reported that, according to the *American Architect*, the Jefferson Market Courthouse was one of the ten finest in the country. The City renovated the building in 1967, and it is now a branch of the New York Public Library

The New York State Supreme Court, Appellate Division was created by the Constitution of 1894. In 1896, four Appellate Division branches replaced what had been called General Terms. The First Department, covering Manhattan and the Bronx, began to conduct its business in rented office space on Fifth Avenue and 19th Street. In June 1896, the justices approved plans for a courthouse on Madison Avenue and 25th Street, at a cost of $700,000. The building is still in use today as the court's home. Architect James Brown Lord designed the Beaux-Arts structure with columned porches and statues, drawing on the style of Andrea Palladio. Among the most impressive features are the stained glass windows designed by Orange County attorney David Maitland Armstrong (1836-1918).

Thanks to Norman Goodman, New York County Clerk.

The New Court House, New York City.

Above: Architect Guy Lowell designed this magnificent circular Palace of Justice for New York County. The post card lives, but the building never went up. Officials rejected it as too costly.

Right: After his original circular design was rejected, Guy Lowell proposed a hexagonal courthouse. The building opened in 1927 and is still in use.

THE NEW YORK COUNTY COURT HOUSE, NEW YORK CITY

COPYRIGHT BY IRVING UNDERHILL, INC., N. Y. C.

New Court House. New York.

Above: This Beaux-Arts courthouse, designed by James Brown Lord, still houses the Supreme Court, Appellate Division, First Department, on 25th Street and Madison Avenue in Manhattan.

Right: The Jefferson Market Courthouse, built in 1875, is now a branch of the New York City Public Library.

COURT HOUSE, LOCKPORT, N.Y.

Niagara County's 1886 courthouse featured a tower
topped by a large statue of the Goddess of Justice.

Niagara County

Eighth Judicial District

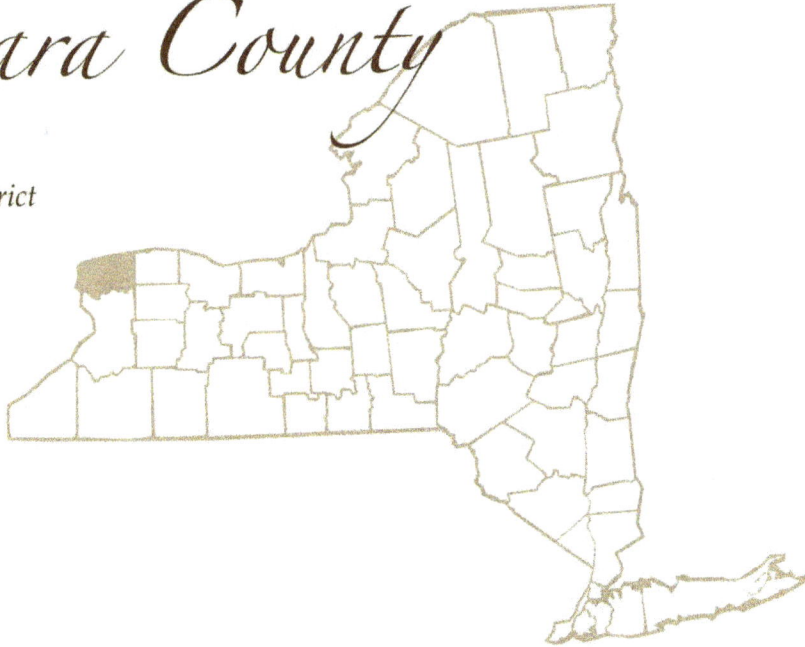

Niagara County represents a milestone in the westward expansion of law in New York State. Before its creation in 1808, when Niagara was split off from Genesee County, no court had been held in New York west of Batavia. The British burned the first courthouse, a frame structure, in 1813. The stone jail next to it was only slightly damaged, and was repaired.

The Legislature authorized a new courthouse in 1816, but Niagara County did not use it for long. When Erie County was taken from Niagara County in 1821, Buffalo, which had been the county seat of Niagara County, became the seat of Erie County.

Niagara had to designate a new county seat. For a couple years, a schoolhouse in Lewiston served as a courthouse. In 1822, Lockport became the permanent site. Colonel William M. Bond donated two acres, and the construction of the courthouse began. The structure, completed in 1825, served for 60 years. It was a square stone building, covered with white plaster, with chimneys on each corner and a cupola in the middle. On the ground floor were four jail cells, quarters for the sheriff, an office for the district attorney, a grand jury room, a waiting room, and a hallway. The courtroom occupied the second floor.

Levi Bowen (1808-1889) was one of the County Judges serving in this first courthouse. He was a delegate to the 1867 State Constitutional Convention and in 1857 served ex officio on the New York Court of Appeals.

The jail on the ground floor of the courthouse proved insecure, and there was no separate cell reserved for debtors. The courtroom was too small, and the courthouse provided no space for the County Treasurer or Board of Supervisors. After several grand juries called for a new jail, the process of building one began in 1839. It was finished in 1844.

The removal of the jail and subsequent remodeling temporarily provided more space, but by 1874 there was much talk of the need for a new courthouse. Niagara Falls put in a bid to become the new county seat, but the suggestion never took.

Although the Board of Supervisors could meet in the courtroom, they usually met in a hotel or tavern. When, in 1885, the need for a new courthouse became more pressing, they were meeting in the Hodge Opera House. They chose William J. Blackley of Lockport as builder, specifying that the building be built of Lockport Stone. The building was completed by December 13, 1886 at a final cost of $70,466. When it was finished, it was large enough to accommodate all county offices.

A tower with a large statue of the Goddess of Justice on top crowned the building. She wielded a large sword in her right hand and held the Scales of Justice in her left. The Goddess fell prey to the vicissitudes of weather. In 1909, she lost her left arm, the one holding the Scales of Justice. County employees, considering this a bad omen, tried unsuccessfully to repair it. A new twelve-foot replica made of copper replaced her.

Between 1913 and 1915, the county responded to the need for more space by building a large addition on the south and west portions of the courthouse. In 1914, the copper Goddess was taken down from the dome and placed on the front lawn. When the renovations were completed, she was not put back on the dome, but placed in the basement. Sometime in the 1930's, it was discovered that she was missing. No one knows of her fate, but surmise has it that a county employee stole her and sold her for the value of the 450 pounds of copper.

In the early 1950's, the county needed much more space, and officials contracted with the firm of Albert Elia of Niagara Falls to build an addition. The result is a three-story office building to the west of the historic courthouse. Its typically mid-20th-Century modern style contrasts sharply with the 1886 portion.

In the 1980's, the old courthouse was restored to its former grandeur. The construction crew replicated the original appearance of the courthouse using modern materials such as energy efficient windows and fiberglass to reinforce the moldings. The project cost $118,000.

Portraits of some of Niagara County's distinguished judges hang in the Supreme Court chambers. One portrait is of Cuthbert W. Pound (1864-1935), a renowned son of Lockport. He was born in 1864, the son of a Lockport factory owner. He served as Lockport City Attorney (1888-1890) and as State Senator (1894-1895) where he sponsored a proposal extending suffrage to women. In 1895, he joined the Cornell Law School faculty as a professor, a position he held until 1904.

After returning to practice in Lockport, Pound was elected to the Court of Appeals, serving from 1915-1934 and as Chief Judge from 1932 to 1934. While he was on the court, no judge was a more ardent supporter of the people's right to criticize the government. He was eminent enough to be considered for the United States Supreme Court in 1922. Pound died in 1935 and is buried in Cold Springs Cemetery in Lockport.

Thanks to Judge Peter L. Broderick, Sr., Lockport, NY and Niagara County Historian Christine Derby-Cuadro.

NIAGARA COUNTY COURT HOUSE, LOCKPORT, N. Y.

In 1914, during courthouse renovations, the copper statue of the Goddess of Justice was placed on the front lawn. Afterward, she was consigned to the basement and later disappeared, presumably sold by some unknown county employee for the value of her copper.

NIAGARA COUNTY COURT HOUSE. LOCKPORT, N. Y.

The Niagara County Courthouse as it appeared before the 1957 addition. The county retained the façade and the short dome of the courthouse and attached a sharply contrasting 3-story modern office building.

EAST PARK, GANSEVOORT MONUMENT AND COURT HOUSE, ROME, N. Y.

Court proceedings still take place in the 1851 Rome courthouse.

Oneida County

Fifth Judicial District

Most of the counties that were half shired, with more than one courthouse, have now consolidated their court activities to one. Oneida County still maintains two active courthouses, one in Utica, and the second in Rome. The Utica Courthouse houses the Family Courts and County Courts and the offices of three Supreme Court Justices. The Family Court regularly uses the Rome courthouse, and two Supreme Court Justices maintain their offices there.

Oneida County's history began in 1798 when it was formed from part of Herkimer County. The county subsequently was reduced in size by the creation of St. Lawrence County, Jefferson County, and Lewis County, but that did not affect the county seats or the courthouses for Oneida. Two citizens donated land for courthouses: Dominick Lynch in Rome and Hugh White in Whitesboro, part of the Township of Whitestown. In January 1802, the county constructed its first jail in Whitestown, and the Rome jail followed soon thereafter.

The Rome and Whitestown courthouses were built in 1806-1808 with court to be held alternately in the two towns. A courthouse was built in Utica in 1818, but Whitestown remained the half-shire town.

In 1847, a new courthouse opened in Rome. The following year, a fire started in the jail and spread to the courthouse, destroying both buildings. Using columns salvaged from the remains of the courthouse, the county replaced the Rome courthouse and jail at a cost of $12,000. The building, still in use, was expanded in 1897 and 1903.

Utica was designated the half-shire town in 1848, but court continued to be held in Whitestown until 1852 when the new Utica courthouse was ready. After the Whitestown courthouse was abandoned, the property reverted to the heirs of Hugh White, according to the provisions of the original deed. Philo White, grandson of Hugh White, conveyed the courthouse to the town for use as a town hall, which it remains today.

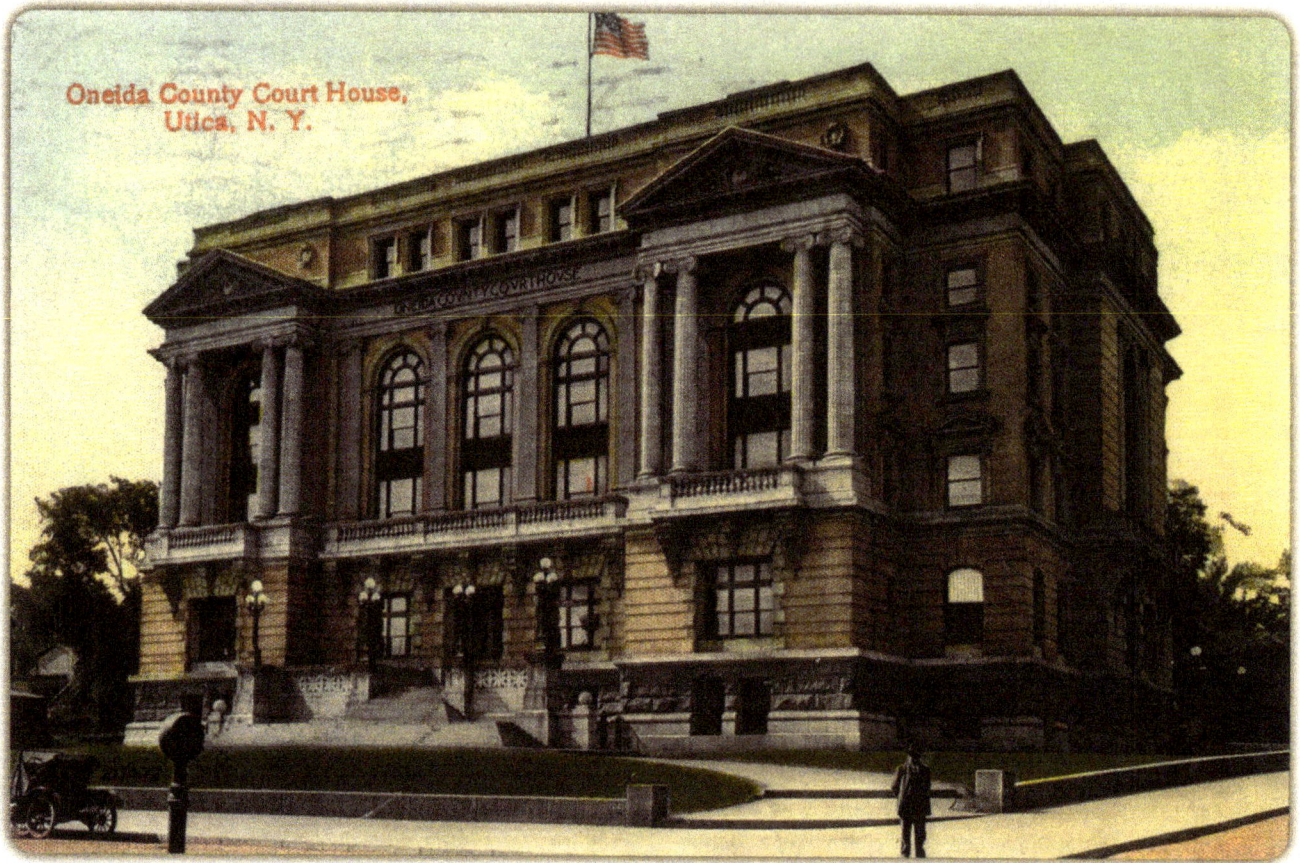

Olin W. Cutter of Boston designed the Utica courthouse, completed in 1909.

The first Utica courthouse served for half a century and was home to some of the great judicial figures of the day, including Hiram Denio (1799-1868), who served on the Court of Appeals from 1853 to 1865 and as its Chief Judge from 1856 to 1857 and from 1862 to 1865. Samuel Beardsley (1790-1860) was District Attorney of Oneida County from 1821 to 1825 and was the last Chief Justice of the (old) Supreme Court.

Ward Hunt (1810-1886) would also have frequented the 1851 courthouse. He was Mayor of Utica in 1844, a Judge of the New York Court of Appeals in 1865, Chief Judge from 1868 to 1869, and a Justice of the United States Supreme Court from 1873 to 1883.

William J. Bacon (1803-1889) served ex officio on the Court of Appeals in 1860 and 1868. Greene Bronson (1789-1863) was Oneida

Surrogate in 1819 and Attorney General from 1829 to 1836. He later became Chief Justice of the (old) Supreme Court in 1845 and was on the first bench of the new Court of Appeals in 1847, where he served as Chief Judge in 1850 and 1851.

Another eminent judge of the era, Henry A. Foster (1800-1889), was Oneida County Surrogate and Supreme Court Justice before serving on the Court of Appeals, ex officio, in 1870. He was also United States Senator and President of the Board of Trustees of Hamilton College.

Oneida County was also home to Roscoe Conkling (1829-1888) United States Senator from 1867 to 1881, who sponsored key anti-slavery legislation. He declined President Ulysses S. Grant's offer to be Chief Justice of the United States Supreme Court (preferring, perhaps, the Oneida Courthouse). Charles Mason (1810-1879) practiced in Oneida County before joining the Court of Appeals from 1868 to 1869. George F. Comstock (1811-1892), as a schoolteacher in Oneida County, studied law and eventually served on the Court of Appeals from 1856 to 1861 and as Chief Judge in 1860 and 1861.

By 1900, the Utica courthouse had deteriorated, and the Board of Supervisors voted to build a new one. They chose a design submitted by Olin W. Cutter of Boston. The courthouse was ready for occupancy in 1909 at a final cost of $924,366, far greater than most courthouses of that day. Its size and stateliness reflects grandeur. The building is now undergoing extensive renovation to restore it to its architectural beauty, including the main courtroom with its magnificent coffered ceiling. Originally it housed both county government and the courts. Now the courts, except City Court, use it.

William Ruger (1824-1892), Alexander S. Johnson (1817-1878), and Philo Gridley (1796-1864) were born in Oneida County. Judge Ruger, born in Bridgewater, served as Chief Judge of the New York Court of Appeals from 1883 to 1892. Judge Johnson served on the Court from 1852 to 1859, as Chief Judge from 1858 to 1859, and as Associate Judge again in 1874. Judge Gridley served ex officio on the Court in 1852.

In later years, Oneida County was represented on the Court of Appeals by Richard Simons (1927-) of Rome, who served from 1983 to 1997 and as Acting Chief Judge 1992 to 1993, and by Hugh R. Jones (1914-2001) of Utica who served on the Court from 1973 to 1984.

Thanks to County Historian Donald F. White and Judge Barry M. Donalty.

County offices occupy the modern County Office Building behind the Utica courthouse. The 1909 courthouse houses the courts, except for City Court.

Old County Court House, Syracuse

Horatio Nelson White designed this Anglo-Norman courthouse for Onondaga County, located in Clinton Square, Syracuse. It preceded the present (1907) courthouse.

Onondaga County

Fifth Judicial District

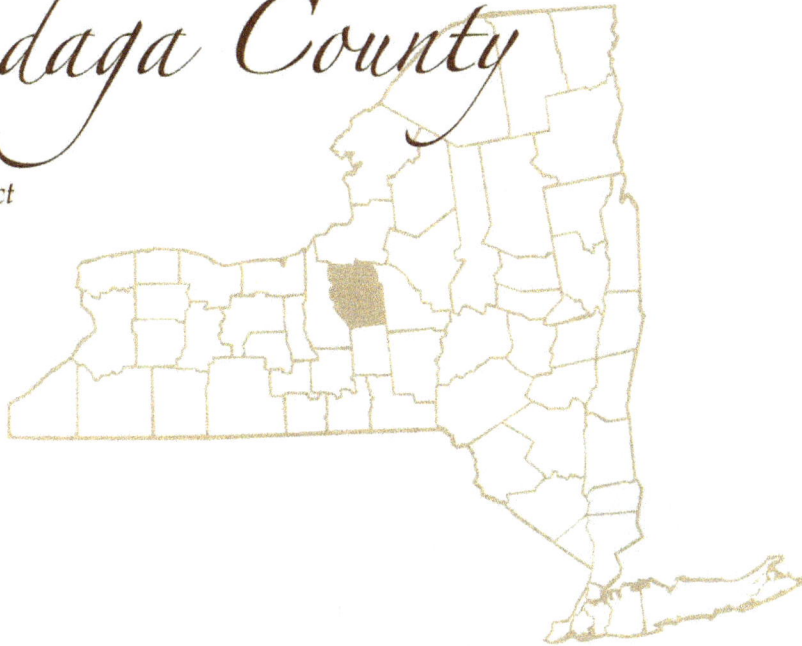

Onondaga County has contributed well to the New York State's judiciary, particularly to its high court. In 1882, both candidates for the State's Chief Judgeship – Charles Andrews (1827-1918) and William Ruger (1824-1892) – came from Onondaga County. Both eventually served as Chief Judge.

Others from Onondaga who served on the New York Court of Appeals were Chief Judge Edmund H. Lewis (1884-1971), Chief Judge George F. Comstock (1811-1892), Chief Judge Frank H. Hiscock (1856-1946), Chief Judge Freeborn G. Jewett (1791-1858), and Judges Edward T. Bartlett (1841-1910), William S. Andrews (1858-1936), John W. Hogan (1853-1923), and the estimable Stewart F. Hancock, Jr. (1923-), now actively practicing in Syracuse.

Onondaga became a county in 1794. Court convened in several places, including the corn house of Asa Danforth in Onondaga Hollow (now called "the valley"), before a courthouse was built. It was a battle between Onondaga Hill and Onondaga Hollow for the location of the courthouse. Onondaga Hill, less marshy and less

malaria-prone, won. Progress on the courthouse depended on the availability of money for construction. It took nine years to complete the two-story square building with cupola. Meanwhile, a temporary floor was put within the enclosed frame and seats installed so that the unfinished building could be used when weather permitted. The building served until 1829.

In the years that followed, there was considerable growth in the villages along the Erie Canal. Syracuse rapidly became the largest village in the county and wanted to be the county seat, claiming to be a convenient location for more people. Salina, which had prospered from the salt industry, also made a good case. A compromise ignored shrinking Onondaga Hill and authorized a courthouse right between Salina and Syracuse. The new two-story brick courthouse provided a little more room than the old one, and the separate stone jail freed up even more space.

Compromises do not always work. No community grew up around the county's second courthouse. The site turned out to inconvenience everyone, and nobody mourned the unfortunate building when it burned to the ground.

Syracuse became a city in 1848 and had little competition as a site for Onondaga's third courthouse. The building committee chose architect Horatio Nelson White, who designed the courthouse in the Anglo-Norman style to be built of Onondaga limestone. The first floor provided offices and jury rooms on either side of a central hall. On the second floor, the courtroom measured 52 by 72 feet with high ceilings and tall windows.

It was a grand building, more spacious than its predecessors, but growth soon demanded more room. In the 1880's the county built two more buildings in Clinton Square, designed by Archimedes Russell who made them in an ornate Queen Anne style.

When in 1901, the county decided it must have a new courthouse, it chose Russell to design it. He and the building committee looked at public buildings in other states. They particularly liked the Rhode Island State Capitol in Providence, which had been designed by McKim, Mead and White. Russell and his draftsman, Melvin King, used this as their inspiration for the fourth – and present – Onandaga courthouse, in a style labeled "Beaux Arts." Originally intended for Clinton Square, the site was shifted to Columbus Circle, a quiet residential neighborhood. Four residential buildings were demolished to make way for the courthouse. Indiana limestone covers a steel frame and gives the illusion of marble. Its granite base gives it a sense of solidity, when if fact the building floats on a concrete raft because of its swampy location.

70:—Court House, Syracuse, N. Y.

15915

Onondaga County chose Archimedes Russell to design this 1901 courthouse. He took his inspiration from the Rhode Island State Capitol in Providence.

The interior of the Onondaga County Courthouse features marble floors, wainscoting, and tall columns.

The local firm of Allewelt and Brothers received the contract to finish the interior. They chose William D. L. Dodge to paint four murals depicting events in Onondaga County's history for the lobby, a light filled atrium. Three murals in the hallway leading to the ornate courtrooms on the third floor, painted by Gustav Gutgemon, symbolized the power of law and justice. The decor featured marble floors, wainscoting, and tall columns.

Completed in 1907, the building provided the modern conveniences of the day. It had elevators, a ventilation and steam-heating system, and concealed wiring. The powerhouse to run them was placed in the jail across the street so that the people in the courthouse would not be bothered by the noise and soot coming from it. The original estimate for the building was $1 million. It cost $400,000 more than that, but most citizens considered it worth it.

After 99 years, this magnificent building needs major repairs. The architectural firm of Klepper Hahn and Hyatt reviewed the condition of the structure and recommended approximately $6.7 million in repairs to the exterior in order to keep the building sound, including new copper cladding for the domes, new roof tiles, and re-pointing and cleaning of the limestone block. The county is seeking funding and plans the work to take place in 2007 and 2008.

George B. Vashon, the first African-American to pass the New York bar, lived in Syracuse. He had an office in a building located at the corner of Warren and Water Streets. Vashon also ran for New York State Attorney General, the first African-American to run for a statewide office in New York.

Thanks to Michael P. Martin of the Onondaga Historical Association Research Center.

Town Hall, Canandaigua, N Y

Before building its 1857 courthouse, Ontario County sold the 1824 courthouse (above) to the Town of Canandaigua. It is still used by the municipality.

Ontario County

Seventh Judicial District

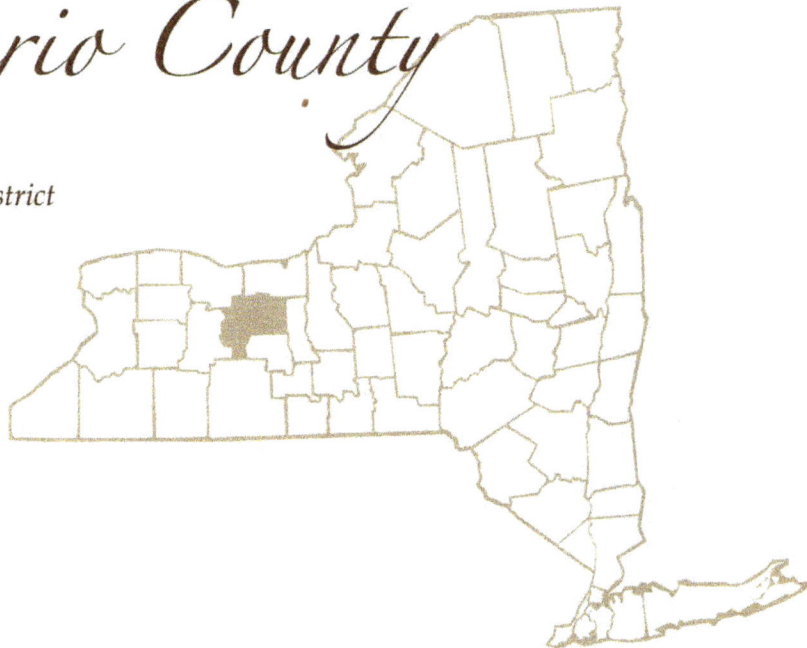

Ontario County's present courthouse was the site of one of the nation's most famous trials. The building has since been renovated and expanded but will always be remembered as the site of the trial of Susan B. Anthony in June 1873. She was prosecuted for having voted, in violation of Federal law, which barred women from the election process.

Although she had voted in Monroe County where she lived, the trial was held in Ontario County, on a change of venue owing to pre-trial publicity. Newly appointed United States Supreme Court Justice Ward Hunt, sitting as a trial judge, directed the jury to render a guilty verdict, following which he imposed a fine. She never paid it.

Ontario County has been nicknamed "Mother of Counties." The State Legislature erected Ontario County in 1789 from Montgomery County, comprising all the land west of Seneca Lake. Since then the rest of the counties in central and western New York have been formed from land taken from Ontario. When created, Ontario County was wilderness with, perhaps, fewer than 1000 people.

There is no record of court proceedings of any kind until 1792 when the Court of Common Pleas and General Sessions met in Sanborn's Tavern in Canandaigua. Dr. Moses Atwater, pioneer physician and judge, later bought this building. The following year Ontario's first court of Oyer and Terminer took place in Patterson's Tavern in Geneva. Although Geneva might have had hopes of hosting court permanently, Canandaigua has always been Ontario's county seat.

In 1794, construction began on Ontario's first courthouse. Land developer Oliver Phelps contributed the site and paid for some of the embellishments with his own funds. The two-story frame building with cupola built by Elijah Murray cost the county $1500. The county did well with this expenditure. The building survived, even after it was no longer the courthouse. It was moved in 1860, and served other public functions until 1899, when it was razed.

The county grew rapidly in the early 19th Century. The Legislature carved out new counties in western New York in response to demand for convenient access to county services. In 1823, Ontario shrank to its present boundaries, but its population increased. The county had outgrown its first courthouse.

In 1824, the Board of Supervisors asked permission of the State Legislature to levy a $6000 tax to build a new courthouse. The Legislature granted the request. Construction began during the summer of 1824 and finished the following summer. It was a brick two-story building of Federal Style with a cupola and a broad portico supported by heavy columns. In 1831, the county built two small brick buildings to house the surrogate and the county clerk.

By 1853, the old courthouse had become too small for the county's needs. Concerned with the cost of building a new one, the Supervisors entered into a novel agreement with the federal government. By contributing $12,000 toward the construction costs, the Federal government could have a courtroom and a post office in the new building. It also received some money from the Auburn and Rochester Railroad in a settlement for the railroad's having encroached on a corner of the Public Square when it laid its tracks.

To further finance the new structure, the county sold the old courthouse to the Town and Village of Canandaigua for $4000. This building is still used as a Village Hall.

The Building Committee chose Rochester architect Henry Searle, who also designed a new courthouse for Wayne County at about the same time. For Ontario County, he designed a two-story brick building surmounted by a dome, which housed a bell. On top of the dome stood a 12-foot statue of Lady Justice with a sword in her left hand, scales in her right. The brick was faced with a plaster-like substance called mastic.

This mastic coating caused perennial problems. During a $10,000 renovation project in 1894, an outer layer of brick and a layer of light-colored pressed brick replaced the mastic. That same year, the building received running water and flush toilets. Steam heat and electricity were probably introduced about this time. The roof, dome, statue, several rooms, walls, and staircases saw repairs.

This is how the Ontario County Courthouse appeared during the Susan B. Anthony trial in 1873. Renovations in 1908-1909 added wings on each side, doubling the size of the building.

Several monuments adorn the courthouse grounds. Among them, a large granite rock marks the spot where the 1794 Treaty of Canandaigua, also known as the "Pickering Treaty," was signed.

The county had to address the need for more space after the turn of the 20th Century. The Committee on County Buildings debated whether to demolish and start over or to expand and renovate the courthouse. Architect J. Foster Warner recommended expansion and reconstruction, and the county accepted his plan in 1908. The success of the plan depended on moving the post office out of the building. The federal government was unresponsive at first, but eventually agreed to build a separate post office.

Warner's renovation in 1908-1909 added wings on both sides of the courthouse and a partial third floor, doubling the building's size. In 1923, a full third floor added still more office space. As space needs increased, some offices moved out of the courthouse into other buildings. As the century progressed, means of communication changed. In 1942, the county removed the bell from the dome to make way for the sheriff's radio.

By the 1980's, the courthouse needed major work. which began in 1986 and reached completion in 1988, under architect John Waite, a specialist in historic renovations. The original two-story building now has five stories. The work preserved the historic character of the building while outfitting it for the needs of the 21st Century.

The original statue of Lady Justice stood on top of the court-

COURT HOUSE, CANANDAIGUA, N.Y.

house from 1858 to 1951, when it had to be removed because the wood had rotted to the point of unsightliness, and possibly danger. It took a decade before it was replaced by a 15-foot wooden statue, carved by William J. Eddy of Geneva, incorporating the sword and scales from the original. Alas, this statue soon deteriorated, probably because it had not received the necessary wood preservative, and was taken down in 1981. Dexter N. Benedict fashioned its replacement of cast aluminum, which was covered with gold leaf and hoisted to the top of the dome in August 1983.

In 1834, philanthropist William A. Wood established a portrait gallery of notable individuals with ties to Ontario County. The collection, expanded with new portraits over the years, has been displayed in the courthouse ever since. Among the many figures are Charles J. Folger (1818-1884), Samuel A. Foot (1791-1878), James Cosslett Smith (1817-1900), Henry Wyllys Taylor (1796-1888), and Susan B. Anthony (1820-1906).

Folger, born on Nantucket, MA, moved to Geneva, Ontario County in 1830. One of New York's most eminent public figures, he was elected to the New York Court of Appeals in 1870 and served until 1881, having been Chief Judge from 1880 to 1881. Before sitting on the Court of Appeals, Folger had been Ontario County Judge (1851-1855) and State Senator (1861-1869). He resigned from the Court of Appeals in 1881, to become United States Secretary of the Treasury. In 1862, he was Republican candidate for Governor but was defeated by Grover Cleveland. Foot, of Geneva, served on the New York Court of Appeals in 1851. Smith was born in Phelps, Ontario County and served ex officio on the New York Court of Appeals in 1866. Taylor, an Ontario County Judge, served on the Court ex officio in 1850.

Another interesting piece of Canandaigua history relates to Henry W. Johnson. In 1864, Johnson was the first African-American to pass the Bar in the Seventh Judicial District. He lived in Canandaigua in the mid-19th Century and read law in the office of Henry O. Cheseboro. He emigrated from the United States to Liberia in 1885.

Thanks to Dr. Preston E. Pierce, Ontario County Historian.

Right: In 1901, when Dr. Dwight Burrell donated the boulder commemorating the 1794 Treaty of Canandaigua, he specified that no shrubbery be planted near it. Clearly, this provision has not always been honored. The courthouse appears today much as it does in this photo.

Below: The view from the courthouse dome affords a wide vista of Canandaigua as shown in this postcard, mailed in 1909.

ORANGE COUNTY COURT HOUSE, GOSHEN, N. Y.

The 1841 Goshen courthouse was designed by Thornton Niven. Court proceedings were held there until 2000. It now houses the office of the Orange County Historian.

Orange County

Ninth Judicial District

Orange County boasts twin Neo-Classical courthouses in Goshen and Newburgh, both designed by Thornton R. Niven. Both are standing and in good condition, although neither hosts court sessions any more. They represent the interplay of Newburgh, the port city on the Hudson River, and centrally located Goshen as county seats. The Goshen Courthouse, now the office of Orange County Historian Theodore Sly, was built in 1841. The Newburgh Courthouse, which houses various legal service agencies as well as the Newburgh City Historian, was built in 1842.

Orange County, named after William of Orange (King William III, 1650-1702) was one of the ten original colonial counties designated by the Duke of York in 1683. It included what is now Rockland County. Before 1703, when the first court of record was held in Orangetown, the county was administered from New York County. In 1737, the legislature authorized a courthouse in Goshen, and the building was completed in 1740. Court was also held in Newburgh on the upper floor of the academy building.

In 1795, when the county was reorganized, Goshen became the county seat. Thereafter, the residents of Newburgh and of the northeastern towns continually agitated for the division of the county. In late 1833, discussions began about replacing the Goshen courthouse. At first, there was talk of repair, but the condition of the courthouse was so bad that the Grand Jury charged the Board of Supervisors with neglect of duty in allowing the facility to become unfit for use. The Board was slow to respond. After years of inaction, the Supervisors agreed to the two courthouses, one in Goshen at a cost of $17,000 and one in Newburgh, at a cost of $13,000. Instead of borrowing from the State, the county obtained funds from private lenders, including banks. The Goshen 1841 courthouse was built first, followed by the 1842 Newburgh courthouse. The facades of the twin courthouses are nearly identical. Newburgh's courthouse originally had a jail in the basement. The county built a separate jail in Goshen.

The Orange County Historian has a gruesome newspaper article describing the execution of William Schweitzer, a/k/a William Saunders, or Sanders, inside the Goshen courtroom. Some years later, people discovered part of the gallows, high in the courtroom attic, just above the ventilator. They saw a pulley, over which the rope had passed. At the upper side it held a heavy weight, which "jerked the defendant to his fate," as he stood on a low platform in the courtroom.

In the late 1960's as space needs increased, the county commissioned noted architect Paul Rudolph to design a new Orange County Government Center in Goshen, which opened in 1970. Typical of 1960's architecture, the structure features 87 different flat roofs and 127 windows. A center courtyard leads to the government and court wings of the building.

Every courthouse goes through a period of crisis when it needs repairs. Is it worth saving? Should it be demolished to make way for a fresh start? On the one hand, the Orange County Government Center is a striking example of mid-20th Century style, designed by a historically significant architect. On the other hand, the 87 flat roofs leak; and the multi-level building does not lend itself well to handicapped accessibility. Designed before the 1973 energy crisis, the building's 127 single-paned windows need to be replaced by ones with greater energy efficiency. The debate about the building's fate continues.

Meanwhile, Orange County built a new courthouse in 2000, a brick building of a different style adjacent to the Government Center in Goshen. Before then, some court sessions were held regularly in the town's 1841 courthouse.

William B. Wright ((1806-1868) who was born in Newburgh, served on the Court of Appeals from 1862 to 1868 and as its Chief Judge in 1868. William H. Cuddeback (1852-1919) of Orange County served as a Judge of the New York Court of Appeals from 1913 to 1919. Charles F. Brown of Newburgh served on the New York Court of Appeals, Second Division from 1889 to 1892 and as the first Presiding Justice of the Appellate Division, Second Department when it was formed in 1896. He died in 1929 at the age of 84. John W. Brown (1796-1875), a Newburgh lawyer, served ex officio on the Court of Appeals in 1857 and 1865.

Thanks to Hon. Jeffrey G. Berry and Orange County Historian Theodore Sly.

Court House, Newburgh, N. Y.
Hoping to see you o

The Newburgh courthouse, a twin of the one in Goshen, was designed by Thornton Niven and built in 1842. It occupies the center of a park established for it by the City of Newburgh. It houses the Newburgh City Historian and various legal service agencies.

ORANGE COUNTY COURT HOUSE, GOSHEN, N. Y.

The Goshen 1841 Courthouse, Newburgh's twin, as shown in the 1940's.

Thursday Evening.

COURT HOUSE AND COUNTY OFFICES, ALBION, N. Y.

A group of girls posed in front of the Orleans County Courthouse in 1919.

Orleans County

Eighth Judicial District

Orleans County's 1859 courthouse has kept its historical character although it has grown larger over the years. The county recently built an addition on the back of the courthouse, and this project won an award from the New York State Preservation League in 2003. The courthouse has been on the National Register since 1979.

When Orleans became a county in 1824, two towns had good credentials to become county seat, and each wanted the honor. Gaines may have had a slight advantage. It was the largest village in the county, on the Ridge Road, and well established. Albion, known as Newport until 1828, was near the geographical center of the county and, for accessibility, had the Erie Canal and the Oak Orchard Road. In order to prevail, it had to demonstrate economic viability. Its chief asset was the Sandy Creek, on which there were two saw mills, but the commissioners who would choose the county seat were slated to visit these two communities during the dry season when the mills were idled. The people of Albion/Newport

knew this would not look good. They patched a couple of dams and held back the water until shortly before the commissioners were due to arrive. They sent teams to haul logs and lumber around the sawmill and mill yard, so that it would look as though there was a thriving business there. They wined and dined the commissioners and took them on a tour of the town including, of course, the busily working sawmill. The commissioners were so impressed by the fine waterpower that they granted the county seat to Albion before the ponds gave out.

The first courthouse was a brick structure, built in 1827, with the county clerk's office on the first floor. In 1857, this building was torn down and replaced by the present courthouse at a cost of $20,000. It was built in 1857-1858, and celebrated its opening at the beginning of 1859. W.V.N. Barlow was the architect. The present courthouse is a red brick building with 50-foot high Greek columns and white trim. Its silver dome is 36 feet high and can be seen from miles away. A trap door on the dome allows access to the roof, and provides a vantage point to see Lake Ontario 12 miles away. In the past, musicians played Christmas carols from the roof during the Holiday Season. The courthouse has a bell, which used to signal that court was in session. Later, the bell was reserved for special occasions, such as Armistice Day on November 18, 1918 and the 100th anniversary of the courthouse on January 19, 1959.

In 1957, during the excavation for a $62,000 brick two-story addition to the courthouse, workers unearthed the skeleton of a woman. Although the discovery was a surprise, there was no hint of foul play. It was probably that of Mrs. William McAllister, the first woman to live in Albion, and the wife of the man who had cleared the land that is now Court House Square. He had built a cabin there in 1812.

William J. Beardsley designed the third jail to be erected in the Court House Square. It cost $54,000, and was completed in 1904. It replaced an 1838 jail that had been built at a cost of $4000. The State Corrections Commission condemned the jail in 1967, noting that while the exterior was sound, the interior was a firetrap with inad-equate security. The county considered alternatives and eventually built a new jail, beginning work in 1970. Completed at a cost of 1.5 million dollars, it was ready for occupancy in 1972. In the interim, male prisoners were confined in the Niagara County jail.

Sanford E. Church, who had been District Attorney of Orleans County in 1845, was the first elected Chief Judge of the New York Court of Appeals after the 1869 Constitutional Amendment. He served as Chief Judge from 1870 to 1880.

Orleans County has contributed to the State's jurisprudence, as well. Few researchers of New York law are unaware of Sickels' Reports. Born in Albion, Hiram Sickles (1827-1895) was New York's 13th official reporter, publishing 101 volumes of New York Reports, more than any other reporter. He interrupted his law practice to serve as a Captain in the Civil War.

Thanks to C. W. Lattin, Orleans County Historian and to Hon. James Punch, Orleans County Judge.

ORLEANS COUNTY BUILDINGS, ALBION, NEW YORK

46464

The Orleans County Courthouse, seen from a different angle in this photo, looked much the same in 1942 as it did in the 1919 photo.

9447, Court House and County Clerk's Office, Albion, N. Y.

This photo was taken close in time to the black and white version that showed the group of girls in 1919. The awnings are different, but everything else looks much the same, including even the trees.

Oswego County Court House, Oswego, N. Y.

The Oswego courthouse was designed by Horatio Nelson White of Syracuse. Lightning destroyed the statue on the main cupola. The statues on the other two cupolas were also lost.

Oswego County

Fifth Judicial District

Oswego County has always had two courthouses, one in Pulaski, the other in Oswego. When the county was formed in 1816 from Oneida and Onondaga Counties, Oswego was named the county seat. Pulaski made a successful bid to make Oswego a half-shire county. Building began on both courthouses in 1818.

The Pulaski courthouse, which included the jail, was a brick structure, built in the Federal style. An 1859 addition made the building both longer and wider. In 1887, a two-story annex, designed by local Architect Zina D. Stevens, greatly altered the building's façade. It features a Florentine window above the entrance and tall columns modeled after the Tower of the Winds in Athens.

Unlike the Pulaski courthouse, the original frame courthouse in Oswego housed only the courts. It soon became inadequate, and the courts moved into other buildings, first to the Supreme Court room in the Old City Hall. The Board of Supervisors failed to replace the abandoned courthouse, and in 1857, the General Term of the Supreme Court ordered the Supervisors to take action. In July of that year, the Board authorized the leasing of a building known as Mead's Hall. In the autumn, the Board appropriated $30,000 to build a new courthouse in Oswego as well as $5,000 for the expansion of the Pulaski courthouse.

Horatio Nelson White of Syracuse designed the Oswego courthouse, constructed of Onondaga limestone, two stories high. The building had three cupolas, a large one in the center, and two smaller ones on each side. Originally, each cupola supported a statue. Lightning destroyed the one on the main cupola, and no one knows what happened to the other two. The interior woodwork was of pine, meticulously "hand grained" to give the appearance of oak. In those days, hardwoods were more expensive than the labor of skilled artisans. Among the amenities included in the building were a law library and 60 spittoons. The building was completed in 1859 at a cost of $29,390, $610 under budget.

By the 1880's the courts needed more space. As before, the

Supervisors did nothing about it. John C. Churchill, who as District Attorney in 1857 delivered the court order to the Board, had become a Supreme Court Justice. He issued an order directing the enlargement of the Oswego courthouse in accordance with recommendations made by the Oswego County Bar Association. In 1891, the county expanded the Oswego courthouse, and in 1895 built a county clerk's office next to it, which has been used for court proceedings as well, serving Family Court until the late 1970's.

Although the exterior of the Oswego courthouse retained its stately appearance, the inside fell into disrepair. By the 1990's, plaster and paint had begun to crumble; water had stained the ceilings and walls. Furthermore, the building did not meet the requirements the state had mandated in 1987.

In 1992, the Oswego County Legislature renovated the interior of the Oswego courthouse. They issued a $1.1 million bond and, in 1994, budgeted another $100,000 for the project. James Schug of JCM Architectural Associated of Syracuse designed the renovations. The work brought the building into compliance with state and federal codes and enhanced its appearance in a style appropriate to the Victorian era of the building's origin.

Judge Irving Hubbs (1870-1952), who served on the New York Court of Appeals from 1929 to 1939 was born in Oswego County.

William F. Allen (1808-1878) was a judge of the Court of Appeals from 1870 to 1878 after having practiced law in Oswego, and having served as a State Assemblyman from Oswego in 1843 and 1844.

Thanks to Barbara Dix, Oswego County Historian and to Hon. Walter W. Hafner, Jr.

PULASKI COURT HOUSE, PULASKI, N. Y.

9-2337

The dramatically tall pillars at the entrance of the Pulaski courthouse were modeled after the Tower of Winds in Athens. The original building dates to 1918.

EAST SIDE PARK AND COURT HOUSE, OSWEGO, N. Y.

Shown here on a flowery summer day, the Oswego courthouse, since renovated, is still in use.

County Clerk's Office. Oswego, N. Y.

Court proceedings took place in the county clerk's building until the late 1970's. The center cupola of the courthouse can be seen beyond it to the right.

Otsego Co. Court House
Cooperstown, N.Y.

The 1881 Otsego County Courthouse, designed by Archimedes Russell of Syracuse, escaped demolition in 1982 by the narrowest of margins. A $1.7 million project restored the grandeur of this Victorian building and brought it up to modern standards.

Otsego County

Sixth Judicial District

Mention Cooperstown, the county seat of Otsego County, and most Americans will say "baseball," because Cooperstown is the home of the Baseball Hall of Fame. Some, of a literary bent, might also think of the author James Fenimore Cooper and that, too, would be entirely appropriate. Cooperstown was named for the author's father, William Cooper, who bought a large tract of land on Lake Otsego, established a village, and sold lots to prospective settlers. When Otsego County was split off from Montgomery County in 1791, William Cooper became its first judge.

Otsego County's first courthouse was a simple log and frame structure, housing only a courtroom and a jail. The jailer lived across the street in Griffen's Tavern, where the jurors deliberated. In the early 19th Century, the county built a larger courthouse, with a jail on the first floor. This burned in 1840, and was replaced the following year by a Greek Revival courthouse and a separate jail. By 1880, the county's third courthouse had de-

teriorated. The Board of Supervisors deemed it unsafe and not worth repairing.

Because the county was starting over with a new building, Oneonta made a bid to become the county seat. After some debate, the Board of Supervisors defeated that move. The Board designated a five-man committee, chaired by Luther Burditt from the Town of Otsego, to oversee the building of the new courthouse. They selected Archimedes Russell, a Syracuse architect who had apprenticed with the noted Horatio Nelson White. The committee accepted his plans in 1879 and chose McCabe Brothers of Cooperstown and S. R. Barnes of Milford to build it.

Russell designed an imposing asymmetrical brick building with contrasting limestone stonework. It featured a large tower, a dramatic Gothic window, blue stained glass windows, and gargoyles. Cost overruns above the original $25,000 estimate caused some concern, but eventually the Board of Supervisors approved the additional funds. When the building was ready for occupancy in 1881, it became a community focal point.

The story of a courthouse only begins with victory over construction obstacles. It suffered ordinary wear and tear, such as a leaking roof, and constantly needed modernization. The courtroom received new carpeting in 1887. The building was wired for electricity in 1888. Antiquated plumbing constantly needed attention, and in 1939, a women's rest room had to be installed to accommodate female jurors. Members of the County Bar Association complained about the cold drafty interior and poor acoustics. A dropped ceiling was installed as an attempt to correct those problems.

As the county grew, and the need for more judicial services increased, the pressure for space multiplied. The county built a county office building in 1969 to relieve the strain. Finally, concern about fire safety put the future of the courthouse in jeopardy.

Louis C. Jones and Frederick Rath succeeded in having the structure listed on the National Register of Historic Places in 1972. The National Trust for Historic Preservation gave a matching grant to repair the serious leaking tower. In 1980, Thomas Campbell, a student in the Cooperstown Graduate Program, prepared a detailed structural analysis and plan for restoration and renovation. The county engaged the Albany architectural firm of Mendel, Mesick, Cohen, and Waite to draw up plans.

These measures did not ensure the survival of the courthouse. By 1982, some members of the County Board strongly advocated demolition and rebuilding. When the matter came to vote, the historic courthouse won by only one vote.

The firm of Homer Gow and Sons of Binghamton, who restored the Chenango County Courthouse, was chosen as general contractor for this 1.7 million-dollar project. Robert Sammis was Clerk of the works for the county. The restoration brought back the grandeur of the 19th Century while bringing it up to present-day standards. The high-vaulted ceiling was once again visible. The stained glass windows were uncovered. New chandeliers look like they belong to the Victorian era but provide sufficient light. Tiled floors, oak furnishings, and ornate woodwork all evoke the era of the building's origins.

Visitors to the Farmers' Museum will encounter a two-room law office, which Samuel Nelson (1792-1873) built while practicing law in Cooperstown in the late 1820's. Nelson went on the State Supreme Court bench in 1831. In 1845, he took a seat on the United States Supreme Court, on which he served for 27 years.

Other notable figures from Otsego County include Martin Grover (1811-1875) who was born in Hartwick and served on the New York Court of Appeals from 1868 to 1875. Sanford Church (1815-1880), born in Milford, NY was the New York Court of Appeals Chief Judge from 1870 to 1880. Schuyler Crippen (1794-1872), born in Tusculum (Worcester) served ex officio on the Court of Appeals in 1855, and William H. Shankland (1804-1883) born in Cherry Valley served ex officio on the Court of Appeals in 1849.

Thanks to Nancy Green Milavic, Otsego County Historian and Judge Brian D. Burns.

As seen from the air, the Otsego County Courthouse spire rises high.

Court House and County Clerks Office, Cooperstown, N. Y.

The Otsego County Courthouse still stands, but a modern brick county office building replaced the stone clerk's office in 1969.

Built in 1914, the Putnam County Courthouse is still in use.

Putnam County

Ninth Judicial District

Putnam County's courthouse is one of the oldest in the state, having been built two years after the county was formed in 1812. Putnam was originally part of Dutchess County, but the difficulty of travel to the county seat at Poughkeepsie prompted the residents of the southernmost towns to petition for separation. The county took the name to honor Israel Putnam (1718-1790), a Revolutionary War General and Bunker Hill hero.

Dr. Robert Weeks donated the land in the Town of Carmel for the courthouse, and John Townsend completed the building for the sum of $3882, well under the $6000 budgeted by the State Legislature. During construction, the county held court at the Baptist Meeting House. The courthouse was ready by October 1914, for the first session of the Court of Common Pleas.

By 1840, the county had outgrown the simple two-story structure, which included the jail, courtroom, and county clerk's office. Plans to build a new courthouse elsewhere were scuttled when it was discovered that the deed from Dr. Weeks was conditioned on its use for a courthouse and for no other purpose. Instead, the county built a separate jail, enlarged the courthouse and added a new façade, a Greek Revival portico with Corinthian columns.

In 1859, the Board of Supervisors authorized a new, brick jail at the back of the courthouse. This building was repaired in the 1880s, and the county added new cells in 1907.

Fire swept through Carmel in 1924, destroying many buildings and seriously damaging the courthouse. Once again the fate of the historic structure was held in the balance. Public opinion strongly favored preservation. By a close vote, the Board of Supervisors decided to repair it rather than construct a new courthouse elsewhere.

The period between 1980 and 1993 represents the only time court was not held in the historic courthouse. During that time it was closed for extensive renovation and restoration. The building has been on the National Register of Historic Places since 1976.

Putnam County broke ground for a new courthouse in 2005 to meet contemporary needs. The 1814 courthouse will still be used by the Surrogate and for ceremonial purposes.

In legal history, James Kent (1763-1847) of Putnam County stands out as one of this country's leading figures, known as a father of American jurisprudence. Born in Fredricksburg, New York, he studied law under Egbert Benson, New York's first Attorney General, and was elected to the State Assembly in 1796-1797. He gained eminence as a Justice of the (old) New York State Supreme Court, to which he was appointed in 1798 and then as Chief Justice in 1804. He was New York's Chancellor from 1814 to 1823, and as "Chancellor Kent" made an enduring reputation as one of the country's leading jurists. He was the first Professor of Law at Columbia University and the author of Kent's commentaries, which served generations of lawyers and judges.

Thanks to Deputy Putnam County Historian Sallie S. Sypher.

The Putnam County Courthouse at about age 140, shown in a card mailed in 1955.

The County Court House
Carmel, New York

County clerk's office and Court House, Carmel, N. Y.

This card was mailed in 1915 when the Putnam County 1814 Courthouse was a century old.

Queens County Court House,
Long Island City, N. Y.

216338

Built in 1872 and redesigned after a 1904 fire, the Long Island City courthouse was used as the setting for Cecil B. DeMille's *Manslaughter* and Alfred Hitchcock's *The Wrong Man*. It has been on the National Register of Historic Places since 1983.

Queens County

Eleventh Judicial District

As Queens grew to be one of New York's most populous counties, with a comparably high level of litigation, finding space for court proceedings often has been improvisational. Queens County's population, over two million people, outnumbers Maine and Vermont's combined. Public buildings dot the landscape in Queens communities, including various municipal courthouses.

One of the original 10 in New York, Queens County was organized in 1683, while Charles II (1630-1685) was on the English throne. Queens County then included what would eventually become Nassau County. Proceedings date back to 1666 in Jamaica, which had a sessions house and jail. During the Revolutionary War, the British tore down the courthouse and carried off its marble to construct barracks for soldiers in and around Jamaica.

After the war, the old stone Presbyterian Church in Jamaica was used as a courthouse, but by 1785, the Legislature ordered that a Queens County Courthouse be built in North Hempstead. The courthouse's first capital trial was held in 1790, with State Supreme Court Judge Robert Yates presiding. This two-story building, which included the jail, continued in use for close to a century, long after it became woefully inadequate.

In 1872, the State Legislature decided that Long Island City was to be the county seat, and in 1876 the county courthouse was built there at the junction of Thomson and Jackson Avenues, at a cost of $276,000. The building, designed by Massachusetts architect George Hathorne, was made of brick and granite in French Second Empire style. It was gutted by fire in 1904. Redesigned by Peter M. Coco, the rebuilt structure opened in 1909. It still functions as a courthouse, and was used as the setting for Cecil B. DeMille's *Manslaughter* and Alfred Hitchcock's *The Wrong Man*. It has been on the National Register of Historic Places since 1983.

When Queens stretched from New York to Suffolk County, its eastern and western residents fought over the location of its courthouse. The point was finally settled when Nassau County was carved out of Queens in 1898, the same year that Queens County became a Borough of New York City.

In 1936, the City broke ground for what today is the largest courthouse serving Queens County. The Sutphin Boulevard, Jamaica building, designed by Alfred E. Eccles and W.W. Knowles and faced with white Alabama limestone, was a $5,685,400 project, financed in part by a federal grant authorized by President Franklin D. Roosevelt. The contract went to John J. Kennedy and Co. The dedication of the building by Mayor Fiorello La Guardia on March 1, 1939 represented a high point of Queens County court facilities.

Following the La Guardia years, Queens County continued to grow rapidly, but the court facilities did not. The need for more space prompted two Grand Jury investigations, one in 1949 and one in 1959, but little action came of them. Every so often, plans were announced, then abandoned.

Eventually Queens received expanded facilities, some located at Kew Gardens. A new Criminal Court wing opened there in 1996. A new Civil Court building went up in 1999, and a new Family Court building opened in 2001.

Two Queens County residents served on the New York Court of Appeals. Charles W. Froessel (1892-1982) sat on the Court from 1950 to 1962; John F. Scileppi (1902-1987) served from 1963 to 1972.

Thanks to Paul E. Kerson and Justice Sidney F. Strauss.

405   General Court House, Jamaica, Long Island, N. Y.

8A-H1148

The dedication of the courthouse in Jamaica by Mayor Fiorello La Guardia on March 1, 1939 represented a high point of Queens County court facilities.

COUNTY HOUSE, JAMAICA, N. Y.

Jamaica, the county seat of Queens, was settled in 1656 and in 1683 became part of Queens County. Egbert Benson, New York State's first Attorney General is buried there in Prospect Cemetery. These two post cards show the Jamaica courthouse. The one on top (with car and people) was mailed in 1915. The other, printed on Kodak postcard photo paper, is undated.

1528—Rensselaer County Court House, corner 2nd and Congress Sts., Troy, N. Y.

The present Rensselaer County Courthouse was designed by Marcus and Frederick Cummings of Troy and completed in 1898.

Rensselaer County

Third Judicial District

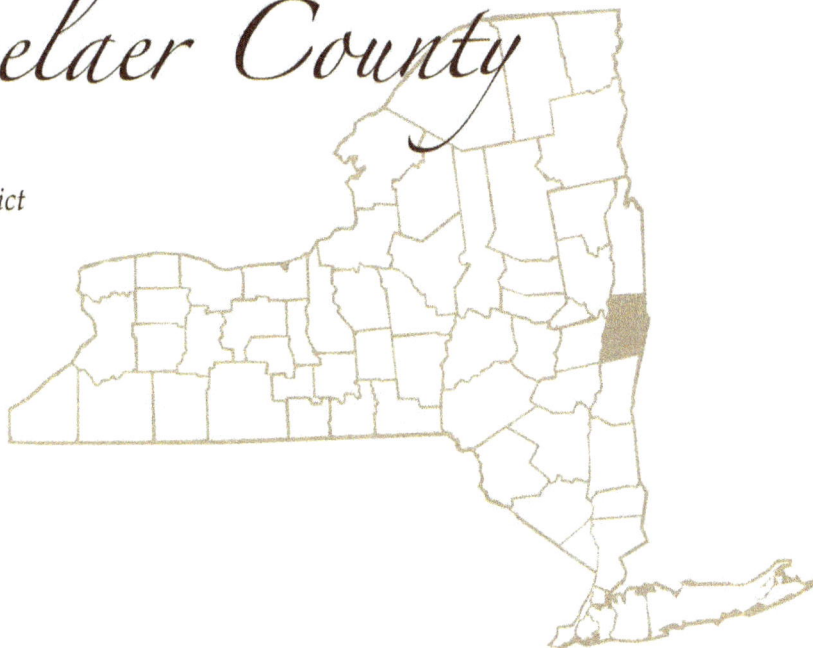

In a move described as an effort to "crush the underworld," Governor Franklin D. Roosevelt ordered an extraordinary and special term to be held in Rensselaer County, and in 1931, all eyes settled on Troy for the trial of notorious racketeer Jack "Legs" Diamond. The *New York Times* reported that the trial promised to be "one of the sensations of the Summer season."

Diamond had been indicted for torturing a Greene County farmer who declined to answer questions about the location of a cider still. The farmer told authorities that he had been overtaken while driving a truck on a lonely mountain road and was beaten by the Legs Diamond gang and burned about the soles of his feet when he refused to reveal anything about his applejack sales. The trial, conducted in Troy because of a change in venue, lasted less than two days, and a jury acquitted Diamond after deliberating for an hour and 52 minutes. Events followed. Authorities arrested an alibi witness for perjury. Diamond was sentenced in New York City on other charges. He was indicted again in Troy for kidnapping, and on December 18, 1931, a jury again acquitted him, this time after deliberating for five and a half hours, including an hour for lunch.

Diamond was murdered eight hours later at a ten-dollar-a-week lodging house on Dove Street in Albany. He had been celebrating acquittal and left a speakeasy to bed down in a drunken stupor. This gave his enemies the chance they were waiting for. After several earlier attempts, rival gangsters finally caught up with him and rubbed him out. He had been shot on so many previous occasions that police had a full time job investigating shootings that over the years rendered him a walking ammunition dump. Diamond's wife met a similar fate in Brooklyn 18 months later.

Rensselaer County's history goes back long before the Legs Diamond episodes. Named for the Dutch patroons, the VanRensselaers, it was created in 1791 from Albany County. The first session of court was held July 5, 1791 at the Platt Tavern in Lansingburgh. Until a courthouse was built, county court was held alternately between Platt Tavern and the public house of Steven Ashley in Troy. From the beginning, Lansingburgh and Troy competed for the county seat. Troy won by raising $5000 to built a courthouse and jail. The first Court of Common Pleas convened there June 1794.

By 1826, the county needed a new courthouse. Troy agreed to pay two-fifths of the cost of the new building provided the municipality could use space in it. The old courthouse was torn down and, while the new one was being built, court was held in the Methodist Meeting House. The courthouse was modeled after the Temple of Theseus in Athens.

Rensselaer County's third, and present, courthouse was designed by Troy architect Marcus F. Cummings and his son Frederick. The gray granite building was completed in 1898 at a cost of $346,000.

In 1912, the county purchased the adjacent Second Street Presbyterian Church and between then and 1914 renovated it to provide more space, including a grand ceremonial courtroom in what was the nave of the church. In 1915, the two buildings were united by a cupola-covered passageway.

The expansion project of 1912-1915 sufficed for another 50 years. In 1967, the county built another annex to the rear and east of the buildings.

In 1996, officials engaged restoration architect John G. Waite of Albany to restore, renovate, and further expand the courthouse. The $20 million project included moving the Family Court into what had been the Rensselaer County jail. The old jail building was transformed from a vacant and badly deteriorating building into a spacious state-of-the-art facility. Architect Waite has received several awards for this project.

In November 2002, the courthouse complex was named in memory of the late Judge Con G. Cholakis. The main ceremonial courtroom was named in honor of retired Appellate Division Justice John T. Casey. The Supreme Court Library has been named in memory of the late Supreme Court Justice F. Warren Travers.

Rensselaer County has had other notable judges. Samuel Beardsley (1790-1860), born in Hoosic, NY was the last Chief Judge to serve under the old constitution before the Court of Appeals was formed in 1846. John W. Hogan (1853-1926) was born in Troy and served on the New York Court of Appeals from 1913 to 1923.

Alonzo C. Paige (1797-1868), born in Schaghticoke, compiled eleven volumes of the Court of Chancery Reports from 1830 to 1848. He served ex officio on the Court of Appeals in 1851 and 1857.

Several other Rensselaer County people served ex officio on the Court of Appeals, including Amaziah B. James (1812-1883), Cornelius L. Allen (1800-1878), George Gould (1807-1868), and Charles R. Ingalls (1819-1908). Judge James served in 1861 and 1869, Judge Allen in 1859, Judge Gould in 1862, and Judge Ingalls in 1870.

At present, Susan Phillips Read (1947-), of Rensselaer County, serves on the New York Court of Appeals. Before that she had been Presiding Judge of the New York State Court of Claims.

Thanks to Judge Edward O. Spain.

U. S. Series 135/1.   First Presbyterian Church, Emma Willard School and Court House, Troy, N. Y.

Right: Before the 1914 renovation, the courthouse is pictured next to the red brick Presbyterian Church and the Emma Willard School.

Below: In an expansion completed in 1914, Rensselaer County purchased and remodeled the adjacent Second Street Presbyterian Church. The following year the county connected the two buildings with a cupola-covered passageway.

Rensselaer County Court House and Annex, Troy, N. Y.

219316

Court House and County Clerk's Office.   Richmond, Staten Island.

Richmond County's 1837 courthouse in Richmondtown now serves as the Visitor Center for the Richmondtown Restoration.

Richmond County

Second Judicial District

The history of Richmond County's courthouses is a fiery one. Much of Richmond County's early history was lost during the Revolutionary War, when the British occupied the island and the courthouse. Anticipating the occupation, Richmond County patriots took precautions, with mixed success. For weeks, people went to the courthouse and carried away armloads of papers to be kept in their homes and restored in less perilous times, but they were not able to save all of them. The British showed no respect for the documents, and when the courthouse burned, all remaining records perished in the flames. Fire also consumed that courthouse's replacement and the county clerk's office.

Otherwise known as Staten Island, Richmond was one of the original New York counties, established in 1683. According to the Staten Island Chamber of Commerce, Richmond is named after the Duke of Richmond, son of King Charles II of England. The name Staten Island comes from the Dutch "Staaten Eyland," after Staten-Generaal, the Dutch parliament, and was allegedly given to the is-land by Henry Hudson.

Richmond County's earliest court and jail facilities were primitive. The first colonial county seat, at Stony Brook, provided a small two-room building. One of the rooms, roughly built of logs, served as the jail. Its door, swinging outward on rawhide hinges and secured with rawhide, was ill-suited to the task of confining prisoners. The courtroom portion was too small, and court frequently took place elsewhere on the island. The building ceased operation when the county seat moved in 1729, but portions of its foundations remained visible until about 1850.

In 1729, Richmondtown, then quaintly known as Cuckholdstowne, became the county seat and remained so until 1920. The 1724 courthouse was the one occupied by the British and burned during the Rebellion. In 1794, the county replaced its burned-out courthouse with a shingled two-story building with a belfry. It had a courtroom on the second floor, and on the first floor, offices and a large public room.

When it came time to build a structure to house the county clerk and surrogate in 1827, the county was acutely aware of the danger of fire. A debate on the subject resulted in a new two-story, allegedly fireproof building, which ironically burned.

The county sold the 1794 courthouse (which remained in private hands until it, too, burned in 1944), and replaced it with a Greek Revival style courthouse in Richmondtown in 1837. Richmondtown's central location was an asset in the 19th Century when life and commerce could stay relatively insular. After Staten Island became annexed to New York City in 1898, connection with and transportation to Manhattan and Brooklyn became increasingly important. St. George, with its ferry access, became a logical choice for a Civic Center encompassing all public buildings.

Staten Island's first Borough President, George Cromwell, envisioned a large plaza encompassing Borough Hall, the Richmond County Courthouse, a Federal building, post office, and Staten Island Museum. John Merven Carrere and Thomas Hastings, noted Beaux Arts architects, who also designed the New York Public Library and the Manhattan Bridge Approach, designed the first two. The latter three were never built.

Borough Hall went up first, completed in 1906. Construction on the courthouse began in 1913. Although Paris-educated Carrere and Hastings preferred French-inspired architecture, they designed the L-shaped courthouse in neo-Classical, Roman-inspired style, honoring the historical roots of our legal system.

The front façade, facing the harbor, features a long flight of stairs leading to a portico, surmounted by a pediment and supported by six Corinthian columns. For practical purposes, the main entrance to the building is on the opposite side. The lobby features a grand marble staircase and a marble colonnade. The courtrooms are finished with marble or wood paneling and decorative ceilings.

A three-tiered formal garden with stairs and fountains between the courthouse and Borough Hall was refurbished in a recent project, which also provided handicapped access and repaired the masonry. The building is listed on both the New York State and National Registers of Historic Places, and was designated a New York City Landmark on March 23, 1982.

Construction of the St. George courthouse was completed in 1919. The courts moved in the following year. The Richmondtown 1837 courthouse building survives as the Visitor's Center of the Richmondtown Restoration.

After close to a century, the courthouse has become cramped. Plans are afoot for an additional $20 million renovation of the courthouse to house the Criminal and Family Courts as well as a new $114 million building for the Supreme Court and Surrogate's Court. If the plans proceed as projected, the new facility may be ready in 2009.

New York Court of Appeals Judge Vito J. Titone (1929-2005), who served from 1985 to 1998, was a Staten Island resident, as is former District Attorney and Supreme Court Appellate Division Justice Thomas R. Sullivan.

Thanks to Surrogate John A. Fusco.

Borough Hall and Court House, St. George, Staten Island, N. Y.

Above: John Merven Carrere and Thomas Hastings designed the Staten Island Borough Hall, seen in the foreground, and the neo-Classical Richmond County Courthouse pictured beyond it.

Right: The 1837 Richmond County Courthouse is a handsome 60-year-old in this 1897 drawing.

Staten Island

Richmond County Court House.

Church in Richmond.

Copyright, 1897, by American Souvenir Card Co. 127 Duane St., New York.

COURT HOUSE AND JAIL, NEW CITY, N. Y.

Rockland County's 1873 courthouse was expanded in 1907. It was demolished to make way for the present courthouse, which opened in 1928.

Rockland County

Ninth Judicial District

Rockland County lies in one of the first regions settled by Europeans. In 1609, when Henry Hudson sailed up the river that carries his name, he stopped at what is now Haverstraw in Rockland County. A man known as Captain De Vries had purchased land from the Indians in the area of Tappan in the 17th Century. Other people soon followed in neighboring areas. Rockland became a county in 1798, after being a part of Orange County. When Orange County and Rockland County were one, officials built a courthouse in Tappan in 1691 and a second one in Goshen in the 1730's.

The Rockland region played a notable part in the Revolution as a fortification point in battles along the Hudson River. In Tappan, the trial of Major John André took place for conspiring with General Benedict Arnold to betray the plans for West Point. Because the Tappan courthouse burned in 1773 and had not been replaced, the André trial took place in the Reformed Church of Tappan, where a marker denotes the site.

After the destruction of the Tappan courthouse in 1773, the county chose New City as the site for a new courthouse. Owing to the Revolutionary War, the building remained unfinished, as New City was a military site with General Washington's Continental Army camping at or near there. By the mid 1780's, the building was completed, and an 1810 sketch of it exists, drawn by surveyor David Pye. The building was struck by lightning in 1820. A new courthouse was authorized and constructed in 1828 at a cost of $8,000. In 1873, the county built a new $23,000 courthouse, which was expanded in 1907 and served until the present courthouse was built in 1928.

Three generations of a family named Suffern figured prominently in the county's early history. After Rockland became a county, the first session of the Court of Common Pleas took place in 1798, convened at New City. The first Judge was John Suffern, appointed by Governor John Hay who served from 1798 to 1806. His son Edward Suffern, after serving a term as District Attorney, rose to the bench 1820, remaining in office until 1847. The family tradition continued, as Andrew Suffern, who like his father had become District Attorney, held the office of County Judge from 1847 until his death in 1881.

Another judge from the Suffern era, Edward Pye, served from 1856 to 1859 when he left to serve in the Union Army as a member of the 95th New York Volunteers. Colonel Pye died on June 12, 1864 from wounds sustained in the Battle of Cold Harbor, Virginia.

Listed on the National Register of Historic Places, the present 1928 Rockland County Courthouse is a Beaux Arts Art Deco limestone building in New City. The architects were Dennison and Hirons of New York City. The courthouse vestibule extends across the entire front to the two pavilions that flank the building. In the middle, a marble stairway ascends to a low platform and then in both directions to the main courtroom floor. The ceiling of the main vestibule is visible through the stair well and is embellished with designs reflecting the sources of the law.

Nearby an inscription reads, "This courthouse for the administration of the living law, whereby the peace and dignity of ordered society shall be guarded under the serene judgment of learning and humane wisdom, is erected by the people of the county of Rockland in the year one thousand nine hundred and twenty-eight."

The earlier courthouse – referred to as the 1873 courthouse – was demolished to make way for the 1928 structure, which was repaired and remodeled beginning in 2002, after the building of a $35,000,000 five-story annex the previous year.

Thanks to Judge Alfred. J Weiner and Rockland County Historian Thomas F. X. Casey.

OA5046

Designed by Dennison and Hirons of New York City, the Rockland County Courthouse opened in 1928. It was renovated in 2002 after being augmented by an annex
built in 2001.

ST. LAWRENCE COUNTY COURT HOUSE, CANTON, NEW YORK.

This 1907 postcard shows St. Lawrence County's Richardson Romanesque court-house, completed in 1895.

St. Lawrence County

Fourth Judicial District

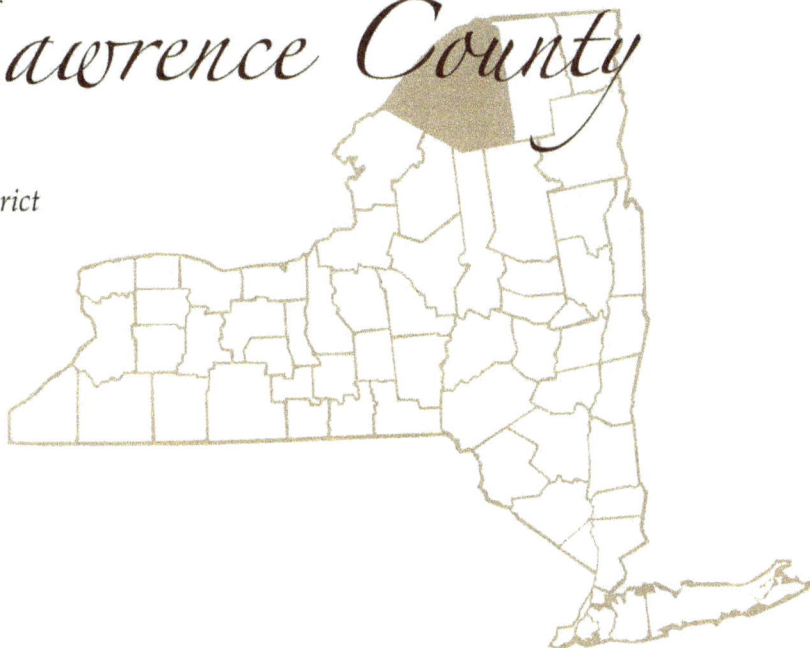

Today's St. Lawrence County Courthouse in Canton is like the Phoenix, arising out of its own ashes. The magnificent Richardson Romanesque building was opened in 1895 replacing a courthouse that had been destroyed by fire two years earlier. The architectural style was named for noted architect Henry Hobson Richardson of Brookline, Massachusetts, who has the unusual distinction of having had a style named for him. This building burned in 1925, and was rebuilt to its 1893 grandeur. It takes a keen eye to tell the post-fire building from its predecessor.

St. Lawrence County was created in 1802 to accommodate people living in that region who otherwise would have had to travel to Montgomery, Oneida, or Herkimer Counties to transact their legal business. An old barracks in the town of Oswegatchie served as a temporary courtroom, and an old stone building as a jail, awaiting more permanent accommodations.

According to Alden Chester's history, Nathan Ford, Judge of the Court of Common Pleas, brought about the building of a plain rectangular courthouse with a belfry in Ogdensburg by 1805. That year also marked the birth of Henry E. Davies (1805-1881) who was born at Black Lake in St. Lawrence County and would serve as Chief Judge of the New York Court of Appeals from 1866 to 1867.

By 1805, the county also had a good start on a jail. The courthouse did not include a county clerk's office; so Louis Hasbrouck kept the records nearby at his home. This probably preserved the young county's records when the British burned the courthouse in 1813.

Although the county was formed for the convenience of its residents, people from the more distant reaches still had difficulty getting to Ogdensburg, especially in the winter. That, and worry about invasion from Canada, prompted discussion about moving the county seat. In 1818, the State Legislature defeated the first attempt.

Some favored splitting the county into two, the eastern portion to be named Fayette, the western portion to remain St. Lawrence.

Both moving the county seat and dividing the county came before the Legislature in 1827. The Legislature defeated division but approved moving.

David Judson donated land in Canton for the courthouse, and the County Board of Supervisors approved $3,100 to build the courthouse, jail, and county clerk's office. The stone courthouse, completed in 1830, provided four rooms on the first floor and a courtroom on the upper. The total cost for the entire project came to $6,800. In 1850 the courthouse received a 24-foot addition.

In 1893, the courthouse burned, leaving nothing but bare stonewalls. The county would have to start over. Several towns – Potsdam, Norwood, Gouverneur, and Ogdensburg – put in bids to replace Canton as county seat, but the Board of Supervisors opted to remain in Canton. They chose J.P. Johnson of Ogdensburg as architect and Evans and Ackerman of Binghamton as builders.

The Richardson Romanesque courthouse was built of gray Gouverneur stone blocks and trimmed with red sandstone from Potsdam. It had a tower 120-feet tall. Two large arches framed the entrance, and scales of justice stood atop the pinnacle of the entrance. By May 1895 it was ready for a special meeting of the Board of Supervisors and was dedicated the following year. In his *Legal and Judicial History of New York*, Alden Chester described it as "one of the handsomest, most convenient, and most complete courthouses in the State."

To meet increased needs of space, the county started work on a new county clerk's office, in 1923. The supervisors specified that it be built of stone matching the courthouse. They chose Samuel. D. P. Williams of Ogdensburg as architect. Munn and Shea of Montreal, who had built Gunnison Chapel and Hepburn Hall at St. Lawrence University, were chosen as contractor.

On the evening of February 19, 1925, fire swept through the courthouse, engulfing it in flames within half an hour. The almost-finished county clerk's office got by with only minor damage.

Firemen and students from St. Lawrence University rushed in to save what they could. They salvaged some books and important papers from the law library, district attorney's office, and county treasurer's office. Three students ripped the WWI memorial plaque off the wall and carried it to safety.

The Board of Supervisors chose the same architect and contractor as they had for the new county clerk's office. Insurance paid $110,000 of the estimated $150,000 to replace the courthouse. The exterior of the building looks much the same as the old one. The tower was shortened because the fire had weakened it. The semi-circular end of the building was enlarged. Inside, the architects kept first floor much the same, but altered the floor plan of the second.

The courtroom was finished in marble and tile. The wainscoting and railing separating the audience from lawyers and officials was make of white Vermont marble with green veins. Italian marble, known as travertine, faced the walls. Marble beams supported the high ceiling. Tile decorations between the columns were designed by the architect and placed by W.P. Nelson Co. of New York. By June 1926, when the courthouse was dedicated, the price tag had risen to $226,260.

This building sufficed the county's needs for three decades. In 1957, the county built a 3-story office building for the district attorney's office, and Family Court among others.

In 1993, the county completed a $7,000,000 expansion. This has allowed the county to consolidate its services, increase security, and make the entire courthouse complex handicapped accessible.

Henry E. Davies was not the only son of St. Lawrence County to sit on the state's high court. Denis O'Brien (1837-1909) was born in Ogdensburg and served on the Court from 1892 to 1907. Amaziah James (1812-1883) served on the Court ex officio in 1861 and 1869, having practiced for a number of years in Ogdensburg.

Thanks to Trent Trulock, St. Lawrence County Historian.

COURT HOUSE AND COUNTY CLERK'S OFFICE, CANTON, NEW YORK.

The St. Lawrence County Courthouse, rebuilt after the 1925 fire, looks much the same as its predecessor. Note the shorter tower.

BALLSTON SPA, N. Y.   Saratoga County Court House

This Saratoga County Courthouse was built in 1890, replaced in 1968, and demolished in 1971.

Saratoga County

Fourth Judicial District

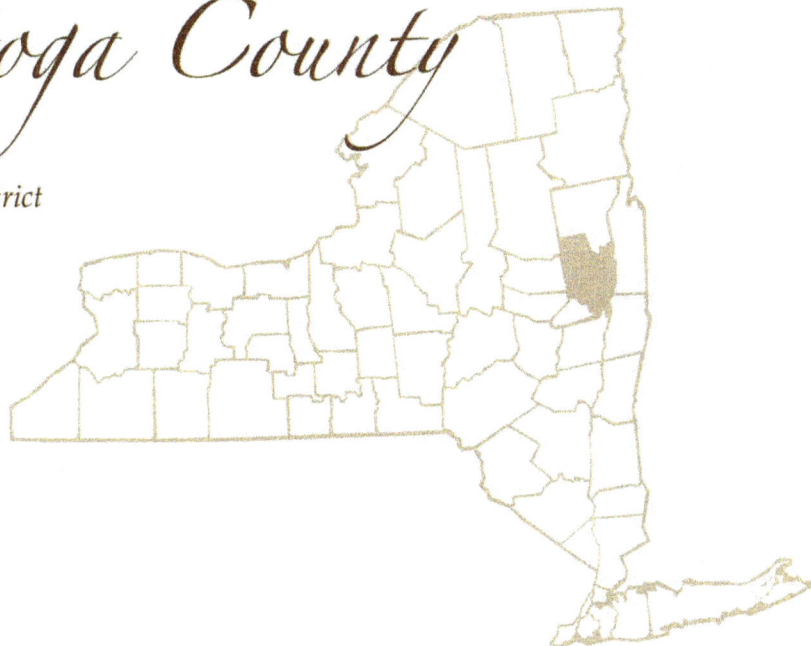

S ay "Saratoga" and, depending on their interests, people think of mineral water, racehorses, or Revolutionary War battles. The name is derived from the Native American, meaning "the place of swift water," perhaps a prescient combination of all three.

Long before the spas and the "sport of kings," Americans fought England and the policies of King George III. The defeat of England's General "Gentleman Johnny" Burgoyne at Saratoga was a decisive battle in the Revolutionary War.

The county was organized 14 years later in 1791, taken from Albany County. Milton, Waterford, and Ballston were rivals for the county seat. Ballston succeeded. At the inception, Governor George Clinton established courts, and the first session held was a Court of Common Pleas, which met on May 10, 1791 in Stillwater (now Malta), at the home of Justice of the Peace Samuel Clark. The court was presided over by several judges, who, as their first order of business, admitted 16 lawyers, including Joseph C. Yates (1768-1837) who

would serve as Governor in 1823-1824. In 1792, James Emott was admitted to practice in Saratoga. He later moved to Poughkeepsie and was elected Justice of the (old) State Supreme Court.

In 1794 the Legislature passed an act to construct a courthouse and jail. A commission chose a site since known as "Court House Hill" in Ballston and, by 1796, a structure was built costing $6,750. The two-story wood building was 50 feet square, with a one-story wing in the rear. The jailer and prisoners lived on the first floor; a courtroom and two jurors' rooms took up the second. A fire, an act of arson by two prisoners, destroyed the building in 1816, but not before it was served by such distinguished judges as Chancellor John Lansing, (1754-1829), and Chief Justices Ambrose Spencer (1765-1848), Morgan Lewis (1754-1844), who also served as Governor from 1804 to 1807, and Smith Thompson (1768-1843), who also served on the United States Supreme Court from 1823 to 1843.

After flames took the first courthouse, the county erected another in Ballston Spa, completed in 1819, at the corner of Bath and

Front Streets, at a cost of $10,000. This lasted 70 years until it gave way to the Romanesque Italianate structure that held its first session in April 1890.

In the early 1800's, Saratoga County had been home to one of the state's great Chancellors, Reuben Hyde Walworth (1788-1867) and to Nicholas Hill (1806-1859), who published seven volumes of Reports for New York's high courts from 1840 to 1845, and Esek Cowen (1787-1844), author of Cowen's Reports.

One of Saratoga County's most famous trials took place following the murder of Henrietta Wilson in Saratoga Springs, on May 13, 1892. While confined in jail, the killer, Martin Foy, Jr., overpowered the jailer and escaped to San Francisco, where he secured passage to Australia, and was set to depart. A horse race enthusiast, he could not resist a trip to the track in Oakland, where he was recognized, apprehended, and brought back to jail in Saratoga. Using a dummy revolver, he escaped again, and was captured in a pine grove just south of the Village. Foy was executed. [*People v. Foy*, 138 NY 664 (1893)].

John K. Porter (1819-1892) of Saratoga County, was one of the most eminent lawyers in America. At the behest of the White House, he was lead prosecutor in the trial of Charles Guiteau, in 1882, for the assassination of President James A. Garfield. His cross-examination of the defendant became a classic in American law. Porter also served on the New York Court of Appeals from 1865 to 1868.

Other renowned legal figures from Saratoga include Judges Augustus Bockes (1819-1907), Platt Potter (1800-1891), and Enoch H. Rosekrans (1808-1877), all of whom served ex officio on the Court of Appeals: Bockes in 1867, Potter in 1865, and Rosekrans in 1863.

The 1890 courthouse served well until the 1960's when the County Board of Supervisors approved a plan for a courthouse designed by the firm of Cadman and Droste of Troy. The new courthouse held its first proceeding and was dedicated in September 1968. It presently houses the Supreme Court, Surrogate's Court, County Court, and Commissioner of Jurors. The old courthouse was deemed beyond repair and was razed in 1971. The courthouse bell was salvaged and rests in the Saratoga County Complex. It bears the Latin inscription "nullus liber homo capitur," "let no free man be seized."

Thanks to County Judge Jerry J. Scarano, County Historian Kristina Saddlemire Reese, and Jane Meader Nye.

County Clerks Office, Jail & Court House.

April 3rd 1906

Ballston Spa, N. Y.
"A famous old watering Place"

Dear Henry. I am down street for a few minutes so thought I would send you a card I hope you got home before the show will write soon Ethel

Mailed in 1906, Ethel's card to Henry shows the Ballston Spa courthouse. Ethel revealed that she was "downstreet for a few minutes so thought I would send you a card." Ballston Spa, the card proclaims, is "a famous old watering place."

1909—Court House,
Schenectady, N. Y.

Built in 1833, this Greek Revival structure was Schenectady's courthouse for 80 years. The number 1909 at the top right of this pre-1907 postcard does not refer to the courthouse.

Schenectady County

Fourth Judicial District

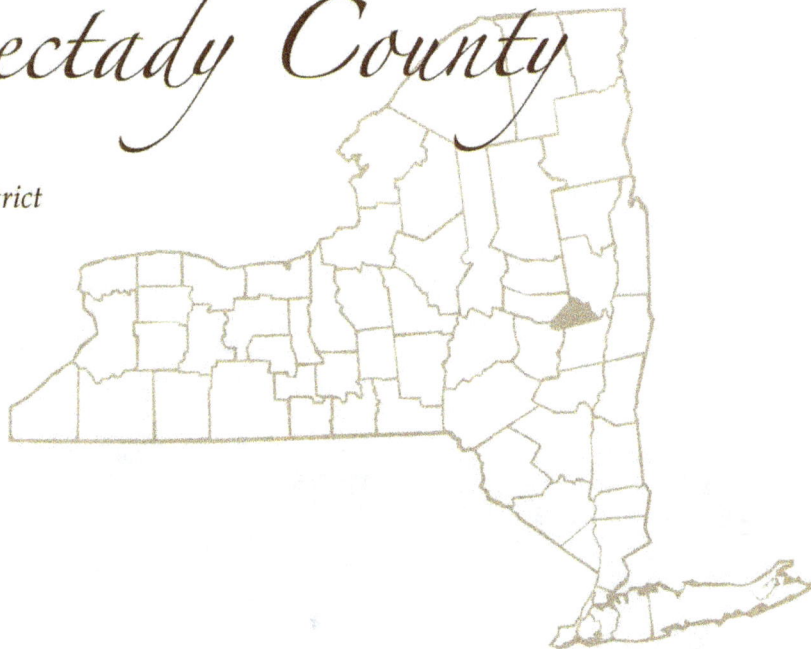

In early documents, the name Schenectady is spelled 79 different ways, but by the time it became a county in 1809, the spelling, and surely the pronunciation, had become more or less settled.

When Arendt Van Corlear first saw the region, he reported that it was "the most beautiful land that the eye of man ever beheld." One theory has it that Schenectady is a corruption of a Native American word meaning "across the pine plains."

Before 1809, Schenectady's legal history was bound up with that of Albany, from which it was taken. When the county was formed, the leading member of its judiciary was Joseph C. Yates (1768-1837), a Justice of the (old) Supreme Court from 1808 to 1822, who served as Governor from 1823 to 1824, and was a founder of Union College.

Schenectady's first Circuit Court and Court of Oyer and Terminer was held in 1810, with Justice Ambrose Spencer (1765-1848) of the (old) State Supreme Court presiding. In 1830, the Schenectady County Bar had only 12 members, including Alonzo C. Paige (1797-1868), a Williams College graduate who served ex officio on the New York Court of Appeals in 1851 and 1857. By 1840, there were 18 members including Platt Potter (1800-1891) who served ex officio on the Court in 1865.

During that era, these renowned legal figures would have held forth at the 1833 courthouse, a columned porticoed Greek Revival structure in service from 1833 until 1913, when the present courthouse was built. The 1833 structure, on Union Street, was built on land bought from Henry Delamont. The building included the jail, and from its inception until 1881 was also City Hall for Schenectady.

After its use as a courthouse ended, the 1833 building served for years as the headquarters of the Schenectady Board of Education. The building stands today, owned by the MVP health organization.

The 1913 County Courthouse is still used as such today. Construction began in May 1909 and was completed four years later at a total cost of under $500,000. The four-story granite building's exterior remains essentially unchanged.

In addition to the eminent jurists of the earlier era, two other Schenectady Judges served on the Court of Appeals. Judson S. Landon (1832-1905) served on the Court in 1900 and 1901 and was Interim President of Union College from 1884 to 1888. More recently, Howard A. Levine (1934-) was Schenectady County District Attorney, Family Court Judge, Supreme Court Justice, and Appellate Division Justice. He served on the Court of Appeals from 1993 to 2002.

Thanks to Judges Vito C. Caruso and J. David Burke.

SCHENECTADY COUNTY COURT HOUSE, SCHENECTADY, NEW YORK. 68

100264

Schenectady's present courthouse was built in 1913.

Schenectady County Court House,
Schenectady, N.Y.

Z4709

The postcard writer discloses that despite the gaiety, the courthouse was not yet completed, thus dating the card at about 1912.

SCHOHARIE COUNTY COURT HOUSE, ERECTED 1870
SCHOHARIE, N. Y.

The Schoharie County Courthouse, designed by architect John Cornelius of Albany, was built in 1870. It has been expanded since then, most recently in 1998-2002.

Schoharie County

Third Judicial District

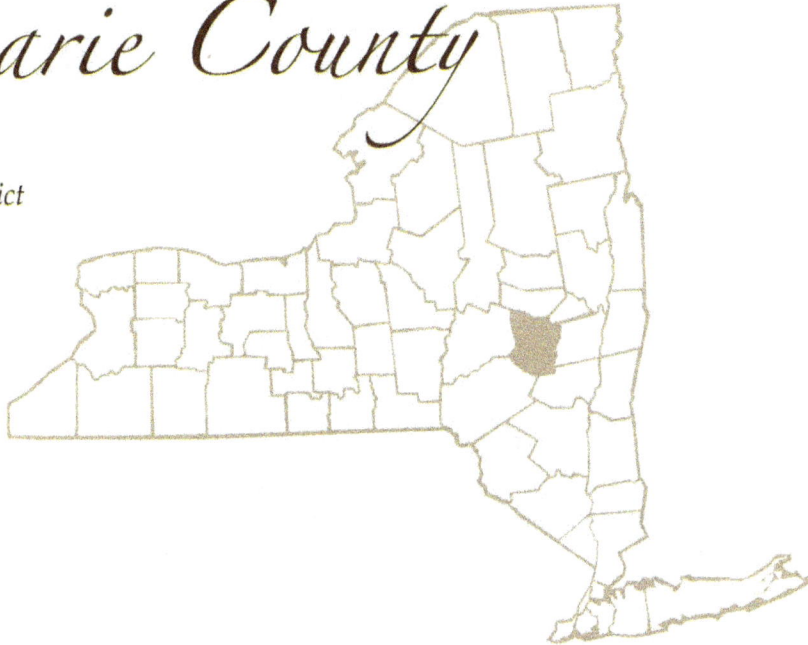

A historic marker denotes the site of Schoharie's "first court house," located on NYS Route 30 at Schoharie. William Beekman (1767-1845), whose portrait now hangs in the present courtroom, presided over the first term of court. When Schoharie became a county in 1795, the second story of a wagon house owned by tavern keeper Johannes Ingold served as a courtroom in a location just south of the present Village of Schoharie. Two tiny rooms on that floor served as cells to confine prisoners. One would hope that no one needed lengthy incarceration because the rooms were too small for a prisoner to lie down comfortably.

Planning for the county's first actual courthouse building began in 1796. The legislature raised $2,000 through a tax to do so. By 1800, court was held in the unfinished building, and the legislature authorized another $5,000 to complete it. Minutes of the first term of Oyer and Terminer in 1796 reflect that in the county's first felony prosecution, Presiding Judge John Lansing of Albany directed the jury to acquit the defendant, a Negro slave.

The simple three-story structure was built of stone with a belfry on top. The third floor comprised the jail. The sheriff had quarters on the first floor. In 1845, a prisoner named William Burton tried to escape by setting fire to the lock on the wooden door to his cell. The fire spread quickly. The frightened prisoner pounded on the floor for help. The sheriff responded to the commotion, and after having to return to his quarters to retrieve the key, he rescued the prisoner. The community responded to the alarm and prevented the fire's spread to the rest of the village and saved some of the sheriff's possessions, but the courthouse was a total loss.

In 1846, the county erected a new courthouse on the same site. It was built of stone and provided room for the court and supervisors' office. Although the building housed the sheriff as before, the jail was in a separate structure. In 1870, a fire swept through the Village of Schoharie, damaging the courthouse beyond repair but sparing the jail.

Because the county needed a new courthouse, Cobelskill put in a bid to become the county seat by offering to donate the land and pay for its construction. Schoharie kept its position by responding with a similar offer.

While building the new courthouse, the county used an array of temporary quarters. Court was held in the Methodist Church. The grand jury met in the chapel of the African Methodist Church. The Niagara Fire Engine Company and the Presbyterian Society also provided space for county government.

Architect John Cornelius of Albany designed the new courthouse built in 1870. It is of high-Victorian style, three stories high, with a footprint of 54 by 57 feet. The dressed limestone structure is decorated with cornices, pinnacles, and a dome of galvanized iron. The first floor provided room for the county clerk and surrogate, as well as a kitchen to prepare food for the prisoners in the jail. The second floor provided quarters for the sheriff and his family as well as meeting space for the board of supervisors. The court room and jury rooms occupied the third floor. The project was completed at a total cost of $20,000, considerably less than for comparable facilities of the time.

To accommodate the need for more space, the county built additions in 1960 and in 1998, began an extensive renovation and expansion of this historic building. The project, supervised by architects Mesick, Cohen, Wilson and Baker of Albany, included exterior repairs, interior renovation, and an 8,500 square-foot addition with a new court room, surrogate's record room and staff offices. The second-floor and third-floor courtrooms were completely restored. The entire complex has the modern heated, air conditioning, security, communication systems, and handicapped access required today. A spacious atrium lobby ties together the old and new. When completed in March 2002, the entire project cost approximately $8.2 million.

The first floor houses the F. Walter Bliss Supreme Court Library. Bliss was a Justice of the State Supreme Court, Appellate Division from 1933 to 1944. As a trial judge, he presided over the trial of Jack (Legs) Diamond.

The large historic courtroom was named after T. Paul Kane (1920-2002), an eminent jurist who capped his career with service on the Supreme Court, Appellate Division from 1972 to 1990. Justice Kane graduated from Yale and served in the Navy during World War II as a gunnery officer. After graduating from Albany Law School, he was elected Schoharie District Attorney before he joined the State Supreme Court in 1964.

John Lansing (1754-1829?) was a Justice of the (old) New York Supreme Court from 1790 to 1801, Chief Justice in 1801, and Chancellor from 1801 to 1814. In 1787, he went to Philadelphia as part of a New York delegation to the United States Constitutional Convention, but as an Anti-Federalist departed the scene. On December 12, 1829, he left his hotel in Manhattan to post some letters and was never more seen in this world. His mansion is in Schoharie County on Route 30 about three miles south of North Blenheim.

William C. Bouck (1796-1859), New York's "Farmer Governor," known as "Old White Hoss of Schoharie" served in the State Senate and Assembly and then as Governor (1843-1845). He was a member of the 1846 State Constitutional Convention, which created the New York Court of Appeals.

Thanks to Schoharie Town Historian Anne Hendrix, County Judge George R. Bartlett III, and Howard Zoch.

COURT HOUSE SCHOHARIE N.Y.

Sitting in front of the courthouse was a pastime, as shown in this 1910 card, sent to the writer's aunt, whose address was merely "Gilboa, Scho. Co. NY."

County Buildings, Watkins, Schuyler Co., N. Y.

The Schuyler County Courthouse in Watkins Glen was built in 1868. Although altered and expanded over the years, it is still in use.

Schuyler County

Sixth Judicial District

The creation of a county inevitably engenders some controversy over the details. Nowhere was the factionalism as prolonged or intense as it was when Schuyler County was formed from portions of Steuben, Chemung, and Tompkins Counties in 1854. There seemed to be no problem with the name of the county. It was named for General Philip Schuyler, a Revolutionary War figure and the father-in-law of Alexander Hamilton. The disputes concerned the location of the county seat and, indeed, whether it should be a county at all. The rivalry between the two principal villages, Watkins (Watkins Glen as of 1926) and Havana (now Montour Falls) persisted for 23 years, with considerable shifting of which one had the upper hand.

Havana was the first to complete the requisite buildings to state specifications. As a result, Havana was granted the honor. The county's Board of Supervisors, however, preferred to meet in Watkins, and they chose to stay.

The protracted fight took many forms over the years. Once, the sheriff was ordered to remove all official county papers to Havana within a certain period of time but was unable to find either the county clerk or the papers. This does not appear to have been willful disobedience. The county records at the time were few and highly portable. The clerk, also a local merchant, had taken the records with him to New York City in order to bring them up to date during his travels when he went to buy goods for his store. Because the time period designated for making the change expired, the removal did not take place.

Over time, the county functions tilted toward Watkins. In 1877, the matter was settled once and for all. Watkins became the county seat.

The formation of the county itself was challenged on constitutional grounds. Not everyone agreed that portions of Steuben, Chemung, and Tompkins Counties should be taken to form a new one. The matter was brought to court, not by the malcontents, but by a clever criminal defendant. In the Chemung Oyer and Terminer Court, one Rumsey was charged with assault, said to have been committed in the Town of Catherine in Chemung County. Rumsey's defense was based, not on innocence, but on his contention that he committed the offense in Schuyler County. The case reached the New York Court of Appeals, which discussed the establishment of Schuyler County [*Rumsey v. People* 19 N.Y. 41 (1859)]. The Court ruled that by an act dated April 17, 1854, the Legislature had created Schuyler County, which included the Town of Catherine, where the defendant's offense occurred. Further, another legislative action, on April 13,1857, appointed a member of the State Assembly to Schuyler County. These statutes, the Court held, confirmed Schuyler County's legitimate existence. The Court went on to hold that the defendant's conviction must be vacated because he was prosecuted in (Chemung) the wrong county. The Court recognized that if it were to annul the act creating Schuyler, the consequences would be disastrous to people and entities that had relied on Schuyler County's legitimacy. Rumsey won; but so did Schuyler County.

The Watkins Courthouse, built in 1868, has undergone alterations and expansions but is still in use. Likewise, the county clerk's office on one side of the courthouse and the jail and sheriff's residence on the other, both built at the same time, have seen considerable changes and enlargements over time.

Thanks to Barbara Bell, Schuyler County Historian and J.C. Argetsinger, County Judge.

MINNEHAHA FALLS, WATKINS GLEN, N. Y.   2A-H179

VIEW OF SENECA LAKE AND STATE HIGHWAY, NEAR WATKINS, N. Y.

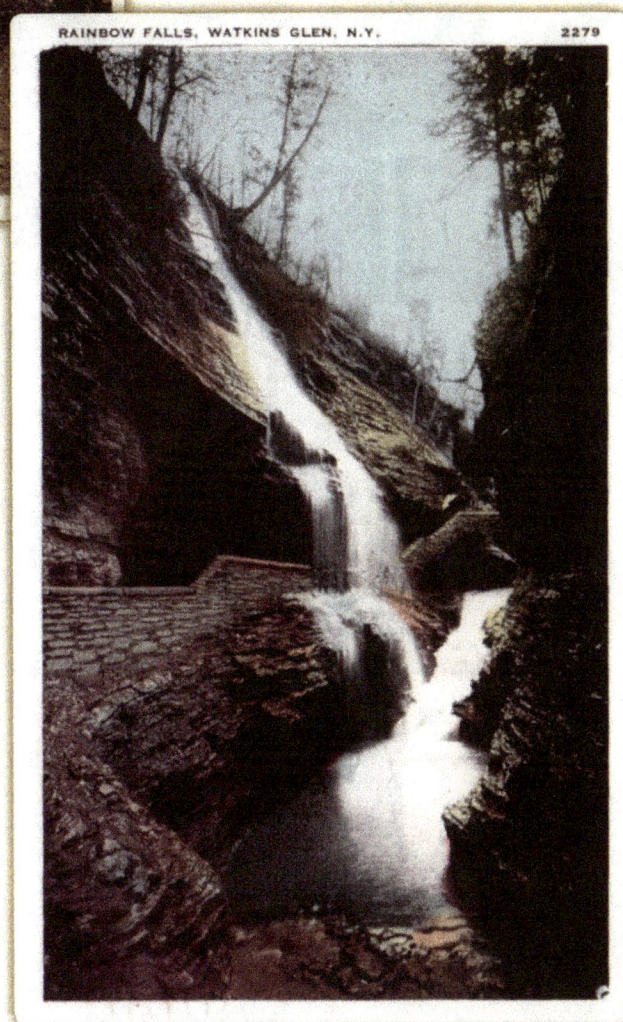

RAINBOW FALLS, WATKINS GLEN, N.Y.   2279

Left, above, and right: Most images of Schuyler County depict the scenic lakes, gorges, and waterfalls near Watkins Glen. We conjecture that, because the scenery is so dramatic, postcard producers have favored those views, often to the exclusion of other Schuyler County sites. These cards may suggest why.

COUNTY BUILDINGS, OVID, N.Y. 53.

The Seneca County Courthouse in Ovid dates from 1845. Although court is no longer held there, it houses various county offices.

Seneca County

Seventh Judicial District

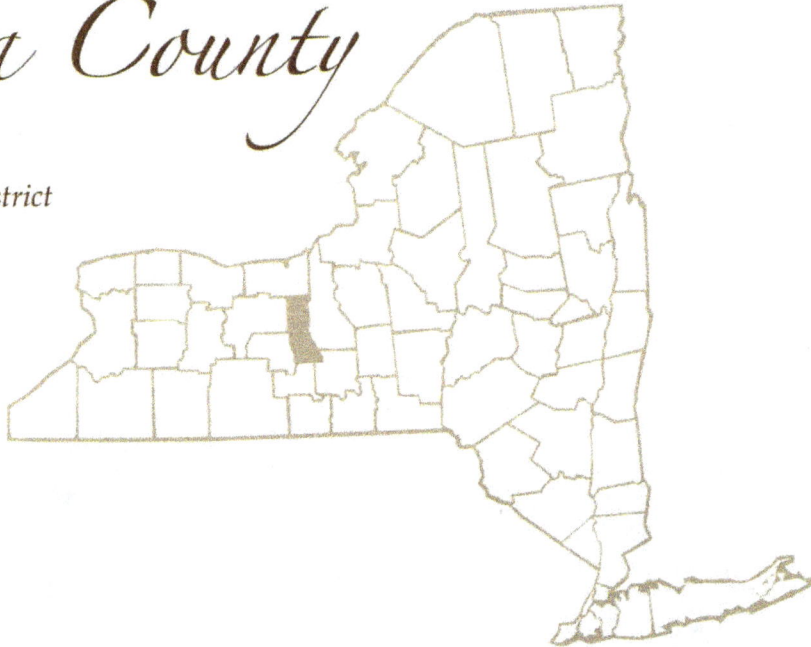

Many counties experience strife when selecting a county seat. Division of a county into two jury districts, or shires, typically effects an uneasy compromise between or among warring factions. The history of Seneca County, on the other hand, appears to reflect the accommodation of regional interests relatively peacefully.

Seneca County's first, and for more than a decade only, county seat was in Ovid. When the county was organized in 1804, court was held, most of the time, in the home of John and Eleanor Seeley of Ovid. Court was held there until 1808 when the courthouse was completed. On March 1, 1807, the Seeleys received $5.00, for the parcel of land on which the courthouse was built. Seeley was a pioneer settler in Ovid. He bought a 600 acres of land, in good faith. Some time later, someone else showed up with what looked like a good deed. Seeley paid him for it. Then a Revolutionary War veteran showed up with evidence that he had been granted this land by the government as compensation for his service in the war. Seeley bought his land yet a third time. Each time the price rose.

In the early 19th Century, Ovid was considered a long trek from the northern part of the county. Waterloo was near the geographical center. In 1817, major landowners Elisha Williams and Reuben Swift gave a parcel of land in the Village of New Hudson (now Waterloo) for a courthouse and jail. The residents of Ovid petitioned for half-shire status, and this was granted in 1822. From then on, Seneca County continued, reasonably contentedly, a half-shired county with two courthouses. Every three years, the county clerk transferred the county's records from one town to another, a distance of about 15 miles. Every six years, the Surrogate's records were transferred the same way.

Ovid's 1808 courthouse fell into disrepair, and in 1844 officials resolved to replace rather than to repair it. When the Greek Revival brick building was completed in 1845, the weathervane from the old courthouse was placed on it. During the days of the old building, the Courthouse Square was used for pig and cattle grazing. After the new building went up, the county regraded it, planted trees and grass, and fenced it in.

County Clerk's offices in both Waterloo and Ovid were begun in 1859, and both were completed in 1861. The County Clerk, County Judge, and Surrogate shared the buildings when each was in town. In 1900, the county ordered the Waterloo County Clerk's office sold and replaced it with a new one east of the courthouse.

The Waterloo courthouse dates from 1818. In 1914, severely damaged by fire, it was renovated and expanded. The county built a fireproof building for county records, demolished the old jail, and built a new one east of the old County Clerk's office, which became the Sheriff's residence. William J. Beardsley of Poughkeepsie served as architect, C.K. Benjamin of Geneva the contractor. The project cost $85,000.

A mini-scandal broke out in 1921 when 25 barrels of cider were discovered in the county buildings at Waterloo. This was the Prohibition era. Federal authorities were summoned, and after analysis, the contraband was consigned to the sewer. No one knew who stored the cider, and no one was going to own up to it. The Deputy Sheriff in charge of the county buildings lost his job over the incident.

The contraband cider did not deter the decision, in 1921, that Seneca should become a single-courthouse county at Waterloo, The residents, however, liked the status quo and objected. The county reverted to the half-shire arrangement, which continued until the

Court House, Jail and County Clerk's Office, Waterloo, N. Y.

The Seneca County Courthouse at Waterloo was built in 1818. It is shown here as it looked circa 1910.

COURT HOUSE, WATERLOO, N. Y.

The Seneca County Courthouse in Waterloo was rebuilt and renovated after a 1914 fire. It was renovated again in 1994.

early 1980's when Waterloo became the sole courthouse town. The Ovid courthouse now houses county department offices.

A second fire occurred in the 1940s, resulting in structural damage that was not discovered until the courthouse was again renovated in 1993-94. Fortunately, nothing collapsed in the interim. The county kept the original hardwood floor during these renovations, and a small burn from one of the fires is still visible. The 1993-1994 renovations added new lighting and a new ceiling in the main courtroom, a new Family Court courtroom, an elevator, holding cells, and more office space on the north side of the courthouse. Plans for further renovations are afoot.

Seneca County is distinguished by two great American institutions. In 1848, a watershed event in the women's suffrage movement took place when Lucretia Mott (1793-1880), Elizabeth Cady Stanton (1815-1902), and others gathered at Seneca Falls for the first women's rights convention in American history.

The event produced one of the nation's most revered documents, the Seneca Falls Declaration. Using the Declaration of Independence as a model, the writing was a historic step in advancing women's rights and equality.

We also credit Seneca County with the inauguration of Memorial Day (formerly Decoration Day). In 1866, when Henry C. Welles (1821-1868) and others formed a committee to honor the war dead, the Town of Waterloo observed the day of remembrance. It was one of the birthplaces of the celebration that led to our national holiday.

Thanks to Judge Dennis F. Bender.

8200. Court House, Bath, N. Y.

The Steuben County Courthouse at Bath, built in 1860, was completely renovated in 1989-90 and now houses all court functions.

Steuben County

Seventh Judicial District

For the convenience of far-flung residents, several counties in New York became half-shire (dual-shire) counties, with two county seats and, therefore two courthouses. Steuben County has them all beat with three courthouses. It became New York's only tri-shire county: Bath, Corning, and Hornell.

Baron Frederick William Augustus Henry Ferdinand von Steuben (1730-1794) arrived in Portsmouth, New Hampshire in 1777 and offered his services to Congress as a volunteer. He rose to become a Major General, and contributed greatly to the military tactics in the Revolutionary War. He was revered as a military hero, and when in 1796 a portion of land was taken from Ontario County, the new county was named after the Baron.

At the same time, Bath was designated county seat. Within a year or two, a one-story frame courthouse, built by Charles Williamson, was ready for occupancy. The supervisors sought to enlarge the courthouse with the addition of a second story and a steeple. The work proceeded over a couple of decades, and in 1824,

the addition of full two story pillars completed the project. The second story was leased to one Selah Bernard, in return for wood sufficient to heat the whole structure.

No sooner was the second story finished, than the Board of Supervisors wanted to the replace the wooden courthouse with a brick building. To make room for the new building, the frame building was sold in sections, which were removed and formed additions to other buildings in town. Bath's second courthouse was begun in 1827 and completed in 1828.

During these early days, people traveled far to attend court. The farmland near Bath did not yield great abundance. In his history of Steuben County, Guy Humphrey McMaster reported that one early settler compared the situation to the California Gold Rush, "Bath was just like San Francisco...Money was plenty, but they almost starved out. They once adjourned court because there was nothing to eat." Jurors, and others with business before the court, were wise to bring their own provisions.

One might think that the improvement in transportation and communication brought by the railroads would have pleased the residents by making travel easier. Instead, it increased dissatisfaction with the time and inconvenience to go to Bath for court and other county business. Bath would have a fight of it to remain as county seat.

In 1853, the State Legislature divided Steuben into two jury districts, with Corning winning the contest as the second shire town. Corning's first courthouse, built on a hillside in 1854 at a cost of $14,000, was a substantial brick building. Having this courthouse meant that Steuben was not without court facilities when disaster struck Bath.

Bath's second courthouse burned to the ground in 1859. Its third courthouse, which survives as a courthouse to this day, was built in 1860. The Board of Supervisors authorized $12,000 for the project, specifying that the building should be sufficient for the county's needs for future decades. They further advised that every dollar spent go to the function of the courthouse rather than for ornamentation. D. Rumsey and Reuben Nobel supervised the project. Using some bricks salvaged from the burned courthouse, they came in under budget, having $166.99 left before construction of a privy and a coal shed.

Bath did not achieve this courthouse, however, before facing a serious challenge to its primacy as county seat. In 1859, the State Legislature passed a bill dividing Steuben into three counties. The first, Cohocton, would have its courthouse in Cohocton. The second, Canisteo, would be seated in Hornellsville. The surviving Steuben County would have courthouses in Corning and Hammondsport. Bath's status survived only when Governor Edward D. Morgan vetoed the bill because none of the three counties would have the requisite population to qualify.

Corning was pleased to have a courthouse in 1854, but many complained of its hillside location. They found the walk uphill too arduous. In 1902, the Board of Supervisors allocated $25,000 for a new building. In 1903, they awarded the contract for building it to Drake and Company. The following year, they voted another $7,500 to complete it. The old courthouse was demolished in 1910.

Meanwhile, the residents of Hornellsville kept agitating for a courthouse of their own, noting that in 1876 the round trip from Bath to Corning took a day, but round-trip train travel from Bath to Hornellsville took two days because the railroad did not go directly between the two communities. Hornell made its plea before the Legislature at practically every session. The persistence gave Hornell's petition the status of a standing joke.

Surrogate Guy H. McMaster took the personal initiative in the 1880's to make the Surrogate's Court a rotating court. Although regular sessions were held in Bath, he would travel among the villages of Hornellsville, Addison, and Corning at least once a month, demonstrating that a tri-shire system with a rotating court could be a workable solution.

In the early 1900's the City of Hornell got its wish. The State Legislature provided for the third jury district. The Board of Supervisors balked at the cost of erecting yet another courthouse. Eventually, it agreed to appropriate $30,000 for the purpose, if Hornell would donate the land and pay for any cost overruns. Begun in 1907, the courthouse was completed in 1909. The first case heard in the building was "The State Commissioner of Excise v. Twelve Bottles of Lager Beer and Divers Other Liquors."

The 1860 Bath courthouse won praise as an example of courthouse architecture. In 1963, Steuben County Clerk Chilton Latham expressed surprise at that when he wrote in the local newspaper, "We've always classified the local hall of justice as a sort of antiquated monstrosity."

In particular, Latham noted that vaulted, high ceiling of the second-floor courtroom may have had its grandeur, but was drafty and uncomfortable. He reported that Justice John C. Wheeler of Corning complained, "that whenever he presided over the January term here, he usually was the victim of a losing bout with the cold bug."

Eventually, all court functions were consolidated in Bath and in 1989-90 the courthouse underwent a total renovation. The Family Court occupies the first floor. The drafty second-floor courtroom was divided into two stories. The top halves of the windows illuminate a new courtroom as well as the judge's chambers. The lower half serve the county clerk's offices and other rooms on the second floor. According to County and Family Court Judge Joseph W. Latham, nephew of the former County Clerk, there is a fourth floor, "mainly a storage area and access to the roof and belfry occupied (as in decades and centuries past) by Steuben County pigeons in great numbers."

Both the Corning and Hornell courthouses have been refurbished, Corning in 2001-2003 and Hornell in 1995-1996. Both accommodate the Department of Motor Vehicles on the first floor, and house other offices such as Probation, and the Department of Social Services. The courtrooms, jury rooms, and judges' chambers remain vacant.

The Bath courthouse has evoked imagery, but none more endearing than a young lad named Dominic (Mike) Gabrielli shining shoes for his customers on the front steps of the building. The lad went to high school in Bath, then on to college, and finally to Albany Law School, from which he graduated in 1936.

During the war Lt. Gabrielli served in Naval Intelligence, and after returning to Bath to practice law, he served as District Attorney of Steuben County. Gabrielli went on to be County Judge in 1957, Supreme Court Justice in 1966, and Appellate Division Justice in 1967. He capped his judicial career when he was elected to the New York Court of Appeals in 1972, where he enjoyed a lasting reputation. Others from Steuben County who sat on the Court of Appeals are Thomas A. Johnson (1804-1872) who served ex officio in 1847-1848, 1856, and 1864, and Henry Welles (1794-1868) who sat ex officio in 1852 and 1860.

Thanks to Judge Peter C. Bradstreet and Judge Joseph W. Latham.

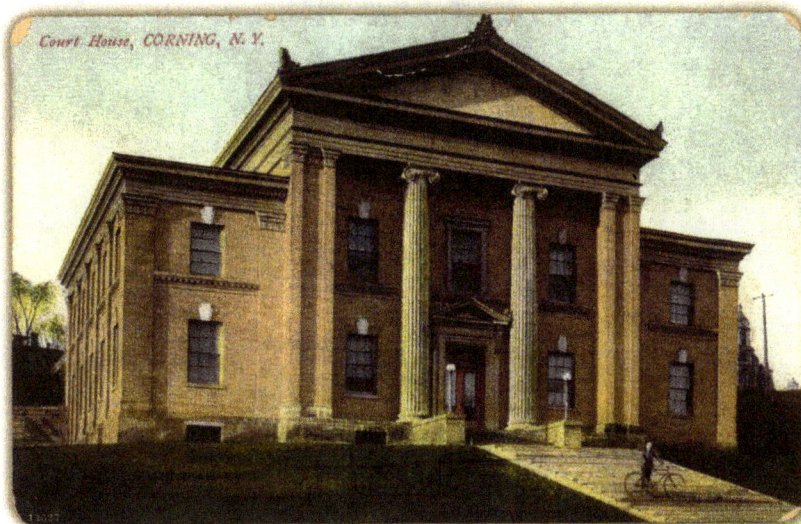

Above: The courthouse in Corning, built in 1903, was refurbished in 2001-2003 and houses several county offices.

Right: The courthouse in Hornell, completed in 1909, was refurbished in 1995-1996 to accommodate several county offices.

County Buildings and Jail, Riverhead, L.I.

This 1907 postcard shows Suffolk County's 1855 courthouse. The 1874 county clerk's office is to the right. The jail behind the courthouse was demolished in the 1990's to make way for a courthouse addition. The wrought iron fence was replaced by a stone fence, which survives.

Suffolk County

Tenth Judicial District

In 1729, having been a county since 1683, Suffolk County built a courthouse in Riverhead, and the county seat has remained there ever since. The small frame 1729 building sufficed as both courthouse and jail for a long time. After about 100 years, the county repaired the structure and built a separate jail.

By 1855, the county was ready for something more substantial. It constructed a two-story courthouse of Georgian style with a cupola on top and four pilasters supporting a portico and pediment in front.

That year, one of Suffolk's most eminent legal figures, Selah B. Strong (1792-1872) was serving on the State Supreme Court and very likely presided at the courthouse. He had been Suffolk County District Attorney for 10 years (1821-1841). He served on the New York Court of Appeals in 1849 and 1859 and later became a member of the 1867 Constitutional Convention. Strong's family is associated with a number of locations in Setauket, Suffolk County – Strong House, Strong Lane, and Strong's Neck.

As space needs increased, the county added buildings on either side of the courthouse. The first was a county clerk's office in 1874, designed by Tappan Reeve of Brooklyn. The county treasury building followed in 1916. It had grandeur, featuring four columns, extending a full two-stories which supported a portico and pediment, leading to a double door. On the second floor, a double door opened onto a wrought-iron balcony.

By the mid-1920's, the county needed still more space, and planned to build a new building across the street from the courthouse. In April 1927, however, the 1855 courthouse burned down.

Eight architects submitted plans. The winning architect, M. Vollney Liddell proposed a courthouse larger and grander than the one that had burned. In Classical style, it was designed to be a "Temple of Justice." The new courthouse was given three stories and a full basement. Columns supporting the portico and pediment extended the whole three stories. Eighteen granite steps, extending the whole length of the portico lead to a heavy double bronze door.

When it became apparent that the new building would take the place of the destroyed one rather than be located across the street, Liddell altered the plans so that it would harmonize with the two buildings on either side of it. The Manhattan firm of Wills-Egelhoff constructed the courthouse.

After World War II, the population of Suffolk County grew exponentially. To keep up with the needs of the government and the courts, the county has built several facilities at different sites, while keeping the Supreme Court in the 1929 courthouse. A jail, which had been built behind the courthouse, was demolished to make way for an addition to the courthouse. A Criminal Courts building was constructed in Riverhead in the mid-1980's. Between 1960 and 1990, several temporary court structures were built in Hauppage. The John P. Cohalan Court Complex at Central Islip went up in the early 1990's.

Thanks to J. Lance Mallamo Suffolk County Historian.

Mailed in 1919, this card shows a larger jail behind the courthouse and the stone fence that replaced the wrought iron one.

The County Treasury and Court House, Riverhead, L. I., N. Y.

Above: The 1929 Suffolk County Courthouse is connected to the 1916 county treasury building by a second-floor walkway.

Right: Depicting the Suffolk County Courthouse, this card was mailed on October 19, 1942, the day the *New York Times* reported that "the great battle for Europe is just beginning."

SUFFOLK COUNTY COURT HOUSE RIVERHEAD, LONG ISLAND, N.Y.

Court House Building, Monticello, N. Y.

This Federal style Sullivan County courthouse was built in 1846.

Sullivan County

Third Judicial District

Perhaps it is the Catskill Mountain air, but whatever the reason, Sullivan County has produced three Chief Judges of New York's highest court. William B. Wright (1806-1868), Lawrence H. Cooke (1914-2000), and Judith S. Kaye (1938-), all hail from Monticello. Judges Kaye and Cooke were born there; Judge Wright spent his adulthood there, having served as Sullivan County Surrogate (1840-1844) and delegate to the Constitutional Convention of 1846. He was Chief Judge in 1868. Judge Cooke joined the Court in 1976 and was Chief Judge from 1979 to 1984. Judge Kaye came to the Court in 1983, and for more than a year, the Court had two judges from Monticello. She will have been Chief Judge for the longest by far in the Court's history.

Separated from Pennsylvania by the Delaware River, the county was formed in 1809 from Ulster County and named after John Sullivan (1740-1795) a Revolutionary War General. At the outset, there was competition between Liberty, Thompsonville, and Monticello for county seat. Monticello prevailed, perhaps because it is on the thoroughfare between the Hudson and Delaware Rivers.

Shortly after Monticello was chosen, several buildings were erected there, including a tavern owned by Curtis Lindley. It doubled as a courthouse until 1814 when officials built a small wooden structure, Monticello's first actual courthouse. It lasted 30 years until it was destroyed by fire in 1846. Samuel Bull of Orange County erected its replacement, built in Federal style, at a cost of $6,790.00.

Sullivan County's courts were quiet in the 1830's and 1840's. As late as 1835, there were only six lawyers in Sullivan County, William B. Wright (later, Chief Judge) one of them. In 1845, two terms of Circuit Court were held and no cases tried; only two cases were tried in the County Courts, with aggregate amounts of verdicts being $85.00. In January 1847, there was not a convict from Sullivan County in the state prison.

This slow and peaceable pace was not to last, and eventually Sullivan County needed to expand its facilities. In 1909, the county replaced the 1846 building with the current courthouse, designed by Poughkeepsie architect William J. Beardsley. The building is made of Ohio sandstone and went up at a cost of $142,800, with Campbell and Dempsey of Kingston as contractors.

In 1997, the Sullivan County Legislature passed a resolution renaming the present courthouse after Chief Judge Lawrence H. Cooke. In addition to Judges Wright, Cooke, and Kaye, a fourth jurist from Sullivan County, Sydney F. Foster (1893-1973) of Liberty, New York, served on the New York Court of Appeals from 1960 to 1963.

Thanks to Sullivan County Historian John Conway, Judge Frank J. LaBuda, and Judge Burton Ledina.

William J. Beardsley designed the present Sullivan County Courthouse, built in 1909. In 1997, it was named for Chief Judge Lawrence H. Cooke.

SULLIVAN COUNTY COURT HOUSE AND PARK.   MONTICELLO, N. Y.

Park Showing Court House, Monticello, N. Y.

The 1909 building, still in use as a courthouse, was spanking new when horses and buggies traveled around it.

COUNTY COURT HOUSE, OWEGO, N.Y.

The cornerstone laying for the Tioga County Courthouse in 1871 brought thousands of people to Owego
to celebrate. Completed in 1873 at a cost of $65,000,
the courthouse is still in use today.

Tioga County

Sixth Judicial District

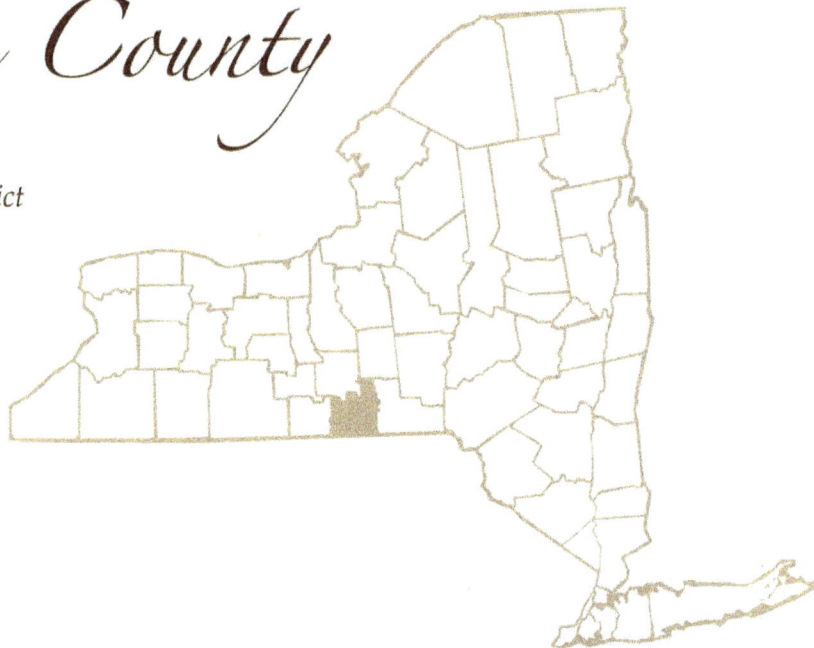

During Tioga County's first decades, there was a considerable amount of shifting of county seats. Formerly a part of Montgomery County, Tioga was formed in 1791. The shifting happened, in part, because of rivalries among various communities for the designation. Also, as land was taken from Tioga to form additional counties, a county seat sometimes went with it. In 1822, the legislature authorized courthouses to be built in both Elmira and Owego. When Chemung County was formed from a portion of Tioga in 1836, Elmira became part of Chemung, and Owego became Tioga's sole county seat.

Owego's first courthouse was completed in 1823. It included a sheriff's residence and a jail. The courtroom took up the second story. In 1852, the courthouse was remodeled after the county built a new sheriff's residence and jail next to the courthouse.

This first building soon became inadequate, and in 1868, a Tioga County Grand Jury issued a report calling the building "unsuitable and inconvenient for the transaction of legal business." Two years later, the Board of Supervisors authorized a new courthouse, appropriating $5,000 for the purpose.

The cornerstone laying in August 1871 was festive. The event, attended by thousands, was one of the single greatest celebrations in the county. Crowds poured into Owego on special trains that began arriving at 9:30 a.m. A mile-long parade lasted until 1:30 p.m. and the speeches until 5:30.

After the ceremonies, the crowd repaired to seven hotels and three restaurants for a special banquet. Each served the same menu, and a record of the bill of fare survives to this day: boiled corned beef and tongue; roast beef, lamb, veal and pig; baked veal pie, corn, turnips, potatoes, green peas, beets, string beans, onions, squash, relishes of cucumbers, tomatoes, and coleslaw. This was topped off by desserts of lemon, apple, and blackberry pies, tapioca pudding, melons, peaches, and vanilla ice cream. After the banquet, there came two toasts and dancing until 4:00 a.m.

The $5,000 that the Supervisors allocated was hardly adequate. By the time construction ended in 1873, the total cost including furnishings, came to $65,000. The investment however, resulted in a courthouse still in use today.

Seven years after Owego built its first courthouse, Benjamin F. Tracy (1830-1915) was born in that town. Tracy is known as the Father of the Modern American Fighting Navy, having served as United States Secretary of the Navy from 1889-1893. He was also a general in the Union Army during the Civil War and received the Medal of Honor in 1895 for action at Wilderness, Virginia in 1864. Tracy served on the New York Court of Appeals in 1881 to 1882.

Charles E. Parker (1836-1909) was born in Owego. A member of the 1867 Constitutional Convention, he became Presiding Justice of the Third Department in 1896 and served until he retired in January 1, 1907. His father, John M. Parker was a member of Congress and Justice of the State Supreme Court.

Thanks to Hon. Vincent Sgueglia, Tioga County Court Judge, Surrogate, and Family Court Judge.

Main Street, looking west from Court House Green, Owego. N. Y.

A view from the Tioga County Courthouse in this pre-1907 card shows a quiet Main Street in Owego.

The streets near the Tioga County Courthouse have become busy over the years, as these traffic signs show.

Park Showing Presbyterian Church and Court House.   Ithaca, N. Y.

One may well wonder why the Old Tompkins County Courthouse is so camera shy. It is regarded as a rather beautiful building. Here it hides behind a grove of trees in DeWitt Park.

Tompkins County

Sixth Judicial District

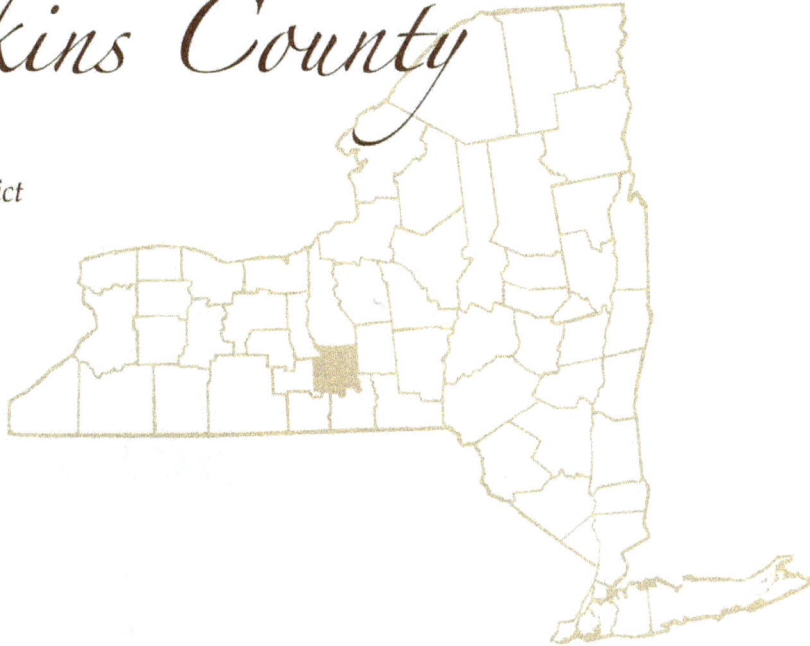

Tompkins County and its county seat Ithaca are known for Cornell University, founded in 1868 by Ezra Cornell, who had made his money by laying telegraph wire for Samuel F. B. Morse. Cornell University is the county's largest employer. In 1890, Ithaca College was founded, and it is safe to say that education is the county's chief industry.

Tompkins County was created in 1817 and named for Daniel Tompkins (1744-1825), who had just completed 10 years as New York's Governor, having brought the state through the difficult years of the War of 1812. In 1817, Tompkins took office as the nation's sixth Vice President, serving in the administration of James Monroe.

Many of the county's early settlers were Revolutionary War veterans who came to the Military Tract, by which the government bestowed parcels of land as compensation for veterans' service during the war. Some of them had remembered the very land itself, having participated in the campaign led by Major John Sullivan, who at the command of George Washington in 1779, led troops to suppress the Iroquois who had sided with the British. A contingent led by Colonel William Butler entered Cayuga territory into what became Ithaca. When the Cayuga ceded their land to New York State in 1789, thereby making it available for settlement, it became part of the Military Tract.

Simeon DeWitt, New York's Surveyor General, surveyed the acreage and set up his field office in Ithaca. He laid out the streets, sold lots to settlers, and encouraged development. When Tompkins County was established, DeWitt donated land for a courthouse. Ithaca raised $7,000 and built it hastily in order to win the race with other locations for the county seat. Becoming county seat gave Ithaca an advantage that prompted further growth.

Although constructed in haste, the wooden Greek Revival structure lasted until 1854 when it was replaced. Its replacement, a brick Gothic Revival courthouse built by John F. Maurice, cost $12,154. It is now known as the Old Courthouse, the oldest Gothic

Revival courthouse in New York. It is one of several buildings that surround a park, known as DeWitt Park because it is on land acquired by the Presbyterian Church from Simeon DeWitt. The church owns the land, but the city maintains the park.

The county built a new Neo-Georgian style courthouse in 1932 but continued to use the Old Courthouse for county offices and various public agencies. The DeWitt Historical Society maintained a museum in the building until 1974 when it moved the museum to other quarters. The Old Courthouse was completely renovated in 1975-1976 as a Bicentennial project and continues to house county offices. It was listed on the National Register of Historic Places in 1971.

Francis M. Finch (1827-1907) was one of Tompkins County's most eminent sons. An Ithacan throughout his life, he was Dean of Cornell Law School, and served on the New York Court of Appeals from 1880 to 1895. He is also remembered as a poet, having penned "The Blue and the Gray", a lament on the Civil War.

Alonzo B. Cornell (1832-1904), the son of Ezra Cornell, was New York Governor 1880-1883 after having been Assembly Speaker in 1873. Irving Vann (1842-1921) served on the New York Court of Appeals from 1896 to 1912. He was appointed the same day (December 31, 1895) Judge Francis Finch retired from the court.

Austin Blair (1818-1894), also known as "The War Governor," was born in Caroline, Tompkins County and served as Governor of Michigan from 1861 to1864. He was instrumental in the abolition of capital punishment in Michigan, the first state to do so.

Thanks to Judge John C. Rowley and to Donna Eschenbrenner of the History Center, Tompkins County.

Although the Conservatory of Music is the focus of this postcard view, the Old Tompkins County Courthouse can be seen, hiding behind the trees, the second building from the left.

DE WITT PARK, SHOWING CON

...ATORY OF MUSIC, ITHACA, N. Y.

COURT HOUSE, KINGSTON, N.Y.

10831.

The Ulster County Courthouse has always occupied the same site. The present structure was built in 1818.

Ulster County

Third Judicial District

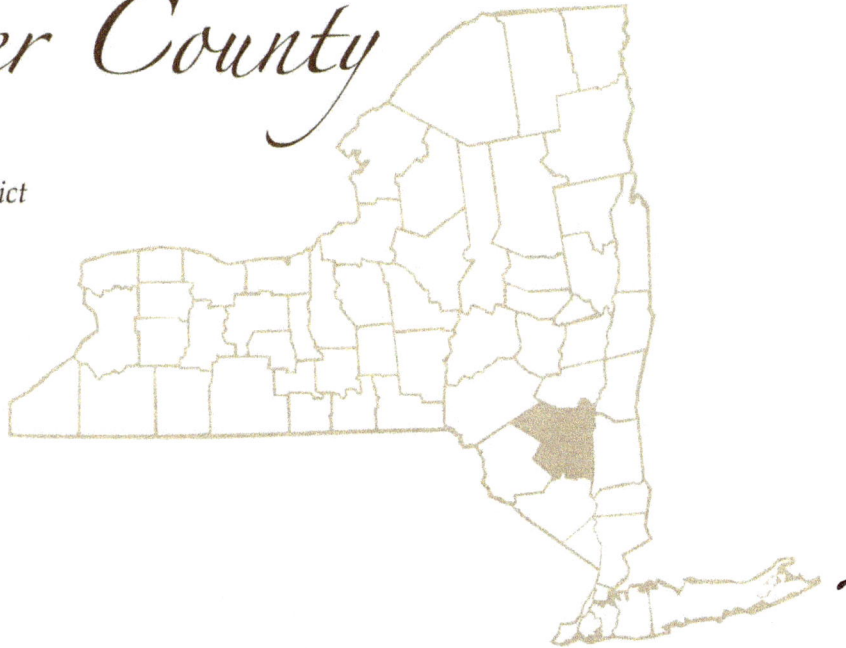

The Ulster County Courthouse has a prominent place in the history of New York State. After the British took New York City during the Revolutionary War, patriots headed north, first to White Plains and Fishkill, and then to Kingston, where at the courthouse, they adopted New York State's first Constitution on April 20, 1777. It was enacted ten years before the United States Constitution and in many ways served as its model.

Holding court in Ulster County dates from the days of the Dutch, with the first meeting of the court taking place on July 12, 1661 in Wiltwyck. After the English took over, Ulster became one of the original counties. The county took its first steps toward building a courthouse in 1688 on the site where the present courthouse stands. This humble, much repaired building became inadequate by 1732 when the county built a new courthouse and jail. The jail portion was damaged by fire in 1750 and was fixed. Before it met its end, the building, seemingly always in need of repair, was to serve the patriot cause during the Revolution.

The jail in the basement held Tories and British Military prisoners, so many that the patriots had to confine some on ships in the Rondout Creek. Kingston became the first Capital of New York when the Committee of Safety met in the courthouse on February 19, 1777. The stench from the jail in the basement, however, was so offensive that within a month, the Convention had moved to the tavern of Evert Bogardus. In May 1777, it elected John Jay the first Chief Justice of the Supreme Court of the State. Later, at the courthouse, George Clinton was sworn in as the first Governor of New York State. Several weeks later, the British burned the courthouse. The county, impoverished by the war, raised the money to rebuild with a lottery.

By the early 1800's, the county had recovered financially, and the rebuilt courthouse deteriorated into abject inadequacy. In June 1817, the demolition of the old courthouse began. The new courthouse, jail, and county clerk's office were ready to hold court in 1818.

By the 1890's, when the county needed more space, the courthouse was already valued for its historic character. In 1897-1898, the county built an addition, designed by Andrew F. Mason that kept the front and sides intact. A separate jail, built of limestone, was put up behind the courthouse in 1902.

Two monuments grace the lawn in front of the courthouse. One is to George Clinton (1739-1812). He was one of Ulster County's – and New York's – most memorable public figures. In addition to being New York's first Governor from 1777 to 1795, he was President of the convention that, in Poughkeepsie, ratified the United States Constitution in 1788. He also served as Vice President of the United States under Presidents Jefferson and Madison.

The second monument on the courthouse lawn is to Sojourner Truth, born Isabella Baumfree in Ulster County (c.1797-1883). She became an important figure in the anti-slavery movement. At the Ulster County Courthouse, she fought successfully to regain her son from slave traders.

John T. Loughran (1889-1953) served on the New York Court of Appeals from 1934 to 1953 and as Chief Judge from 1945 to 1953. Leonard Crouch (1866-1953) served on the Court of Appeals from 1934 to 1936. Both he and Judge Loughran were born in Kingston.

Thanks to Ulster County Historian Karlyn Knaust Elia and J. Michael Bruhn, County Court Judge.

Writing around the turn of the 20th Century, the sender asks Emma, in Brooklyn, whether Louise received the flowers.

Court House and Jail, Kingston, New York

K105

17275

This colorfully crafted card shows the Kingston Court House in the 1940's.

Court House and County Clerk's Office, Lake George, N.Y.

Although eventually cramped for space, the courts in Warren County enjoyed a beautiful lakeshore location for many years.

Warren County

Fourth Judicial District

The historic Warren County Courthouse occupies an extraordinarily beautiful setting on the shore of Lake George. This may be one reason why the users of the building endured overcrowding and the dispersal of various offices throughout the county before the consolidation of all the county services in the Warren County Municipal Center in Queensbury in 1963.

Named for Dr. Joseph Warren (1741-1775), who was killed at the battle of Bunker Hill in the Revolutionary War, Warren County was formed in 1813 out of part of Washington County. That year, the first Court of Common Pleas was held at an establishment known as the Lake George Coffee House. The officials who chose the site of the courthouse bypassed the populous Glens Falls and decided on the more scenic location north of the Coffee House in the Township of Caldwell.

The courthouse, built on this lovely lakeshore site in 1817, served the county's needs until it burned in 1843. The county built a replacement in 1844. The structure still stands, having been re-modeled and improved over the years. An 1878 remodeling gave it the appearance it has today.

A need for more space prompted the remodeling, but it did not happen until officials revisited the question of location. Glens Falls and Queensbury saw their opportunity to capture the county seat. They promised $50,000 toward the site and new buildings. The Board of Supervisors thought moving to be a good idea, but the State Legislature took no action on the matter.

The 1878 remodeling relieved the space problems for a time. As the courthouse again started bulging at the seams, the occupants turned to creative use of space. In the early 20th Century, the sheriff would open up his living quarters in the courthouse for the judge and lawyers when court was in session. He was even known to have served dinner during the noon recess. The notion of moving the county seat to Glens Falls kept cropping up, but each time it failed.

In the mid-1950's two prisoners escaped from the county jail in the manner of a Hollywood movie, using a teaspoon to dig mortar from between the bricks. This prompted the Board of Supervisors unanimously to recommend moving to Queensbury. The voters defeated it. By this time, the Supreme Court Chambers, Supreme Court library, County Treasurer, County Judge and Surrogate, County Attorney Civil Service commission, District Attorney, and Probation department all had offices in a rented building in Glens Falls. The need for new quarters was critical. Pressure from the State Department of Corrections and the recommendations of a Citizen's Advisory committee brought a narrow victory for the proposal in 1959.

Charles T. Whitney and William Bouton Bird of the firm Milton Lee Crandell designed a government center to house all county offices except the highway department. Groundbreaking for this complex, built in mid-20th Century modern style, took place in 1961. All court facilities moved there in 1963.

But the old Lake George courthouse has endured. Winifred Stranahan LaRose led a citizens' group that campaigned successfully to preserve it. Today, the Town of Lake George owns it, and it has new life as the Lake George Institute of History, Art and Science.

In Glens Falls, on Warren Street, tourists may visit the Enoch Rosekrans House. Rosekrans (1808-1877) served on the New York Court of Appeals in 1863. Glens Falls was also the birthplace of Charles Evans Hughes (1862-1848), Chief Justice of the United States Supreme Court, from 1930 to 1941. Glens Falls is the home of Richard J. Bartlett, New York State's first Chief Administrative Judge, former State Assembly member, and former Dean of Albany Law School. As a State Assemblyman, he led the State Temporary Commission of Revision of the Penal Law and Criminal Code, known as The Bartlett Commission.

Thanks to Retired County Judge and Surrogate John Austin.

This real photo card, printed on Kodak postcard paper, gives a remarkably unflattering image of this fine courthouse.

In 1963, the county consolidated all its offices at the Warren County Municipal Center, and court has been held here ever since.

Washington Co. Court House, Salem, N.Y.

Architect Marcus Cummings designed twin courthouses, similar but not identical, for Washington County. The first was built in Salem in 1869.

Washington County

Fourth Judicial District

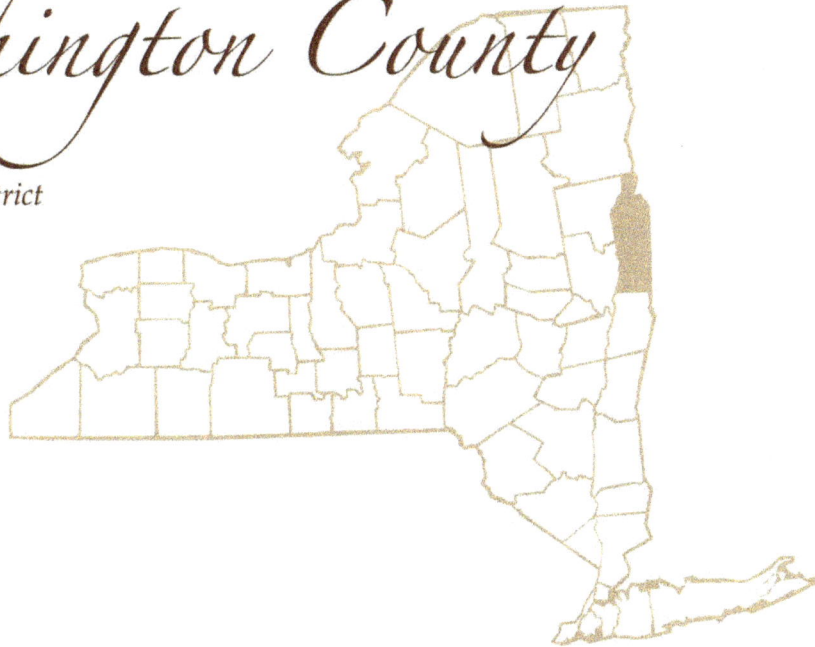

Washington County has two historic courthouses, of similar style, built four years apart. For most of the county's history, the two county seats acted much as siblings, although with few tales of rivalry. Salem, like the older child, would get the first courthouse, soon followed by Sandy Hill.

As one of the 12 colonial counties, Washington County had a different name. Created March 12, 1772 as Charlotte County, it extended northward to the Canadian border and eastward into what is now Vermont. The citizens of the county had no particular quarrel with Queen Charlotte after the Revolution, but they preferred not to have their county named for the wife of George III. They renamed it, in 1784, for George Washington. The settlement of the boundary of Vermont and the formation of Clinton and Warren Counties reduced Washington County to its present size, a strip about 15 miles wide and 61 miles long.

The selection of Salem brought little controversy nor did the notion that Washington would have two county seats. In 1792, the Board of Supervisors chose Salem as county seat, and arranged to build a courthouse there. They also directed that court alternate between Salem and Fort Edward, at the tavern of Adiel Sherwood.

Fort Edward lost the designation as county seat in an event recounted so often it has the status of legend. One evening, when court was held at his establishment, Col. Sherwood abruptly ordered the judges to leave so that he could set the table for dinner. A Revolutionary War veteran, Sherwood was an important figure in the community. Perhaps he felt he could get by with ejecting the court proceedings. In this context, however, the judges were even more important. They held Sherwood in contempt, fined him, and had him jailed for 15 days. They then moved the court to the hotel of Mary Dean in Sandy Hill. It took two centuries before court returned to Fort Edward.

Fort Edward, however, did not lose all vestiges of hosting county government. In 1806 a law provided that the county clerk's office be located in Fort Edward Village in the Township of Argyle.

The Salem courthouse and separate jail, begun in 1792, took four years to complete. Sandy Hill got its courthouse in 1806. As the 19th Century progressed, both wooden buildings fell into disrepair. In November 1867, a grand jury condemned the Salem building and ordered the county to replace it. The county engaged architect Marcus Cummings of Troy to design the new brick building to cost no more than $30,000. He created a building of Italianate style with Romanesque details and decorative brickwork. It featured circular and semi-circular stained glass windows, and a belfry. In 1906, Poughkeepsie architect William J. Beardsley designed a brick jail as an addition to the courthouse, to replace the old frame one, matching the style of the courthouse as closely as possible. Sometime in the 1930's the courthouse belfry was removed.

Sandy Hill, renamed Hudson Falls in 1910, got its new courthouse in 1892-3. Marcus Cummings designed a building similar but not identical to the one in Salem. Italianate in style, it was built of brick and cut stone and trimmed with cast iron and wood. Like its Salem sibling, it had a belfry surmounted by a cupola. The woodwork inside was of chestnut and black walnut. The basement was used as a temporary jail. Complete with gas pipes, plumbing, heat, and ventilation, the cost for the building came to $27,000.

The legacy of Adiel Sherwood no longer haunts Fort Edward. The two courthouses and jail could not be adapted readily to meet the standards set forth by the state in 1989. The courts have now moved to a new facility in Fort Edward.

Both the Salem and Hudson Falls courthouses are listed on the National Register of Historic Places. The Hudson Falls building was sold to a private developer who has used it as a movie theater, restaurant, and office space. The sheriff used the Salem Courthouse, and the attached jail housed prisoners until May 2003. It has been turned over to the Town of Salem. A local citizens group, the Historic Salem Courthouse Preservation Association, has plans to restore it. Architect John Waite of Albany, who designed the restoration of the Tweed Courthouse in New York City, has been engaged to do the feasibility and preservation studies.

Despite its small size, Washington County has contributed well to the state's juridical history. Its notable legal figures include Judge John Savage (1799-1863), Chief Justice of the (old) Supreme Court of New York in 1823; Judge Samuel Nelson (1792-1873), Chief Justice of the (old) Supreme Court of New York, 1837-1845; New York Court of Appeals Judge James Gibson (1902-1992); Court of Appeals ex officio Judges Hiram Gray (1801-1890) and Cornelius L. Allen (1800-1878); Esek Cowen (1787-1844) who served as state reporter, 1823-1828, and John L. Wendell (1785-1861) who succeeded Cowen in that office (1828-1841).

Thanks to Judge Philip A. Berke; Salem Town/Village Historian William A. Cormier, Washington Historian Edith M. Sparling, Washington County Historical Society Librarian Kathryn Taylor, and County Attorney Roger A. Wickes.

Washington County Court House, Salem, N.Y.

Washington County's Salem courthouse is viewed from afar.

Washington County Court House, Sandy Hill, N. Y.

Glad you are having such a lovely time. Hard work and more of it for me. Remember me to all of Mr. Swift's folks. CR.

In 1910 the name Sandy Hill was changed to Hudson Falls. The historic courthouse is now in private hands and has been at various times a movie theater, office building, and restaurant. Like its Salem sibling, it is listed on the National Register of Historic Places.

Above: Designed by Marcus Cummings of Troy, the Sandy Hill courthouse was built in 1892-3. It strongly resembled the one in Salem.

Right: The Salem courthouse lost its belfry sometime in the 1930's. Until May 2003, the sheriff used the building, and prisoners were housed in the jail attached to it. The Town of Salem now owns it. A citizens group, the Historic Salem Courthouse Preservation Association, plans to restore it.

Washington County Court House, Salem, New York

COURT HOUSE AND RESIDENCE OF DR. M. E. CARMER, LYONS, NEW YORK.

Designed by Rochester architect Henry Searle, the Wayne County Courthouse was
built in 1854. Dr. Myron E. Carmer bought the house next door in 1896.

Wayne County

Seventh Judicial District

Wayne County was named for Revolutionary War hero "Mad" Anthony Wayne (1745-1796), who was not mad, but as some thought, insanely courageous in his willingness to undertake missions. Much of the eastern portion of the county was in the Military Tract, land offered to Revolutionary War veterans as compensation for their service. The western part came from a land purchase negotiated by Oliver Phelps and Nathaniel Gorham and sold to Robert Morris, a financier of the Revolutionary War, who sold 1.1 million acres to British investor Sir William Pulteney. Pulteney never visited his lands but left the management from 1792 to 1802 to Charles Williamson, a Scottish immigrant.

Williamson had the land surveyed into lots, planned roads, and built gristmills, saw mills, taverns, stores, and houses. He spent so much on improvements and sold the land to settlers on such favorable terms that he lost $850,000 of Pulteney's money during his tenure. Pulteney's investment, however, undoubtedly yielded a long-term gain. The Pulteney Estate continued its land operation for 125 years, and sold its last parcel in 1915.

Wayne County was created April 11, 1823 from land coming from Ontario County and part of Seneca County. Lyons became the county seat. The county built a brick, almost square, two-story courthouse with a jail in the basement, offices on the first floor, and the courtroom on the second. Before the county built its courthouse, court was held in the Presbyterian Church and prisoners were sent to Ontario County.

Lyons was originally called "The Forks," but Williamson renamed it Lyons because it reminded him of the confluence of the Rhone and Saone Rivers in Lyons, France. The Erie Canal went through the southern portion of Wayne County in 1821, bringing industry and more settlers to the region.

In 1854, the county built its present courthouse, designed by Rochester architect Henry Searle. In 1860, in the second floor courtroom, William Fee was convicted of murder and sentenced to be hanged, the only execution to take place in Wayne County.

Taken after 1980, this view shows the Wayne County Courthouse after Dr. Carmer's house next door was removed.

The county built a new sheriff's residence and jail with 24 cells in 1855. After Wayne County built a new jail in 1961, this building got new life as a County Museum and office of the county historian. By that time the need for a new jail had become urgent. It was so overcrowded that prisoners slept wherever they could find a space, whether on the floor, a table, or any other spot with no segregation of prisoners by age, sex, or criminal charge.

One postcard shows the residence of Dr. Myron E. Carmer, who came to Lyons from Pennsylvania, wanting a small town practice. He bought the house next to the courthouse in 1896. The county bought it in 1971 to use for offices until 1980 when it was removed to make way for further development. The county built a new Hall of Justice behind the Old Courthouse in 1996. It was ready for occupancy in 1997. The Old Courthouse now houses the County Board of Supervisors and other county offices.

Ambrose Spencer (1765-1848), who was Chief Justice of the (old) New York Supreme Court from 1819 to 1823 died in Lyons, New York on March 13, 1848. Theron R. Strong (1802-1873) served on the New York Court of Appeals, ex officio, in 1858. Before that he had been Wayne County District Attorney from 1835 to 1839, and a Representative in Congress from 1839 to 1841.

Thanks to Wayne County Historian Peter Evans.

Wayne County Court House

The Wayne County Courthouse illuminated at night. Dr. Carmer's house can be glimpsed to the left.

A 6627   The Old Court House, Bedford, N. Y.

This place is about one and one-half miles from my present abode. A. G. B.

The 1787 Westchester County Courthouse in Bedford, NY survives today as the home of the Bedford Historical Society.

Westchester County

Ninth Judicial District

New York State was born in Westchester County on July 10, 1776. The Fourth Provincial Congress met on July 9, 1776 at the courthouse in White Plains. On the following day, the delegation, in recognition of its new-found status, changed its name from the Provincial Congress of the Colony of New York to the Convention of the Representatives of the State of New York.

In his Constitutional History of New York, Charles Z. Lincoln referred to it as "one of the most important bodies that ever assembled in this state. It had received a high commission from the people, namely to institute an independent government in such form and with such competent parts as might be best suited to the genius, the spirit, and the traditions of the colony."

The list of delegates included John Jay (1745-1829), who became the first Chief Justice of New York and of the United States Supreme Court. His homestead is in Katonah, Westchester County. It also included Robert R. Livingston (1746-1813), New York State's first

Chancellor, and Gouverneur Morris (1752-1816). These three men were the principal authors of New York State's first Constitution, which grew out of the White Plains Convention and was completed in Kingston in April 1777.

The history of Westchester County extends back to early colonial days. Two county courthouse buildings survive. The first dates from the late 18th Century when Bedford and White Plains were both half shire towns of Westchester. The second is the present courthouse, built in 1975.

Westchester was one of the original counties established in 1683. Its first county seat was the Village of Westchester, now part of The Bronx. Court met in various places until a courthouse was built in 1700. When this building burned down in 1758, the county seat was moved to White Plains, where a courthouse was built in 1759 on land donated by Dr. Robert Graham.

In November 1776, the courthouse was burned, not by the British, but by a contingent Continental troops from New England,

under the command of Major John Austin, who apparently acted on his own. The courts then moved to Bedford.

In 1786, the Legislature designated both Bedford and White Plains as shire towns and ordered the building of a courthouse in each location, with court sessions alternating between the two.

The 1787 Bedford courthouse, a frame building with gambrel roof and belfry, had a courtroom on the first floor and a couple of jail cells on the second. It functioned as a courthouse for close to a century. The county supervisors met in the building until 1829, and county court was held there until 1870. In the 1840's the railroad came to White Plains but not to Bedford. As travel to White Plains became easier for everyone, there was no need to maintain two county seats, and White Plains became the sole shire town.

The Bedford courthouse survives today, nonetheless, one of three 18th Century court buildings left in New York State. It was repaired and restored in 1965 and is the home of the Bedford Historical Society. The courtroom on the first floor remains much as it was, and the second floor houses the Bedford Museum.

The 1787 White Plains courthouse was built on the site of the one that burned. By the 1850's, it had become inadequate and was replaced in 1857 by a new courthouse and jail closer to the railroad.

Designed by R.G. Hatfield of New York City and built of brown granite in Italianate Revival style, the $120,000 courthouse had a tower crowned by a square cupola. A Hall of Records was added in 1894 and extended in 1904. In 1907, the county built a Supreme Court building designed by Lord and Hewitt of New York City in the Neo-Classic Revival style, as an addition to the 1857 building.

Eight years later, the county needed still more space. In 1915, the front portion of the 1857 courthouse was torn down, and a six-story Neo-Classical Revival building, designed by Benjamin Wistar Morris, was built in its place. It held four large courtrooms and several smaller ones. The county added an extension to the Hall of Records in the 1950's.

This entire complex of buildings achieved listing on the National Register of Historic Places, but despite this, all the buildings are gone. In this instance, Urban Renewal trumped the National Register. The county had built a new courthouse high rise "tower" on Grand Street in White Plains in 1975, and the old buildings were no longer needed. Two years later, the historic courthouse complex was razed to make way for the Galleria shopping center.

Thanks to Westchester County Historical Society Librarian Elizabeth Fuller, Town of Bedford Historian John Stockbridge, Edward W. Kelly, and attorney James M. Rose.

The 1907 State Supreme Court building in White Plains was designed by Lord and Hewitt of New York City. It was located adjacent to the 1857 courthouse.

This six-story Neo-Classical Revival Beaux Arts building was designed by Benjamin Wistar Morris and built in 1915. Despite being on the National Register of Historic Places, along with all the other government buildings on the block, all were demolished in 1977 to make way for the Galleria shopping mall.

CourtHouse 1842

Josiah Hovey and P. Pixley built Wyoming County's first courthouse in 1842. The county clerk's office, to the left of the courthouse, was separated by enough space that if one building burned, the other might survive. The belfry housed the county's first bell outside of a church. The bell is now in the village park.

Wyoming County

Eighth Judicial District

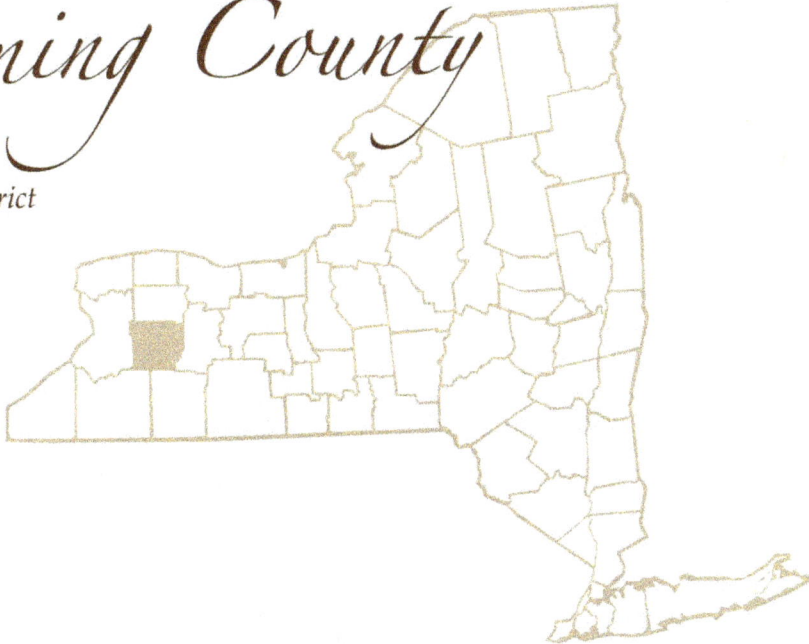

The Wyoming County Courthouse is a one-building architectural timeline, as each renovation added architectural style without supplanting the old. In his 1966 book, *Wyoming County, New York, An Architectural Tour*, James R. Yarrington described it as follows: "Seeming Georgian Revival, the County Court actually represents a radical remodeling of the Richardson Romanesque building erected by A.J. Warner in 1882, complete with belfries. The Court Street elevation reveals the joint of old and new buildings, and the truncated brick strapping which originally continued upward to large dormers. The 1936 face by Wallace P. Beardsley, architect of Auburn, sensitively aligns with the tower of the Frank/Smallwood-Cook mansion across Main Street."

The Smallwood-Cook mansion described by Yarrington is another window into the history of Wyoming County and New York State. It is the home and law office of Charlotte Smallwood, the first woman district attorney in New York State, one of the youngest persons ever elected to that post. Smallwood, now Charlotte Smallwood-Cook, was four years out of Columbia Law School when, in November 1949, as the mother of a five-year-old boy, she defeated her opponent by a decisive margin – 2,300 to 1,400. She is still practicing law in Warsaw, Wyoming County.

Wyoming County had been part of Genesee County until 1841. When, in 1840, the State Legislature approved a new courthouse and jail for Genesee, the residents of the southern part of that county wanted a county seat more convenient to them. The Legislature, however, voted to keep the county seat in Batavia, and the chagrined southern part asked permission to separate from Genesee. They succeeded, setting up a new county seat in the town of Warsaw.

Wyoming County built the jail first, in 1841. In 1842, a courthouse went up, built by Josiah Hovey, under the supervision of his son-in-law P. Pixley. The brick building housed the County Judge and Surrogate, and had a bell-tower believed to be the first in Wyoming County not in a church. A fire-proof county clerk's office was built to the south of the courthouse. The three buildings were separated with enough space between them so that if one burned, the other two might be spared. The sum expended for all three came to $10,000.

By 1877, these buildings had begun to get a little shabby. The Board of Supervisors passed a resolution that would have moved the county seat, and with it the courthouse and county buildings, to Gainsville. This was defeated in referendum, and a few years later the courthouse was replaced, with the bell the only surviving remnant.

It is no accident that architect Andrew Jackson Warner of Rochester designed the 1882 courthouse in the Richardson Romanesque style. He had worked with H. H. Richardson as supervising architect for Richardson's large Buffalo State Hospital project. Warner is responsible for many important western New York buildings. He practiced until 1894 and was succeeded by his son John Foster Warner.

During the 1936 renovation, the entire front of the courthouse was demolished, including the bell tower. Officials moved the bell to the village park where it hangs between two pillars south of the picnic pavilion.

Thanks to Doris Bannister, Wyoming County Historian.

County Court House and Jail, Warsaw, N. Y.

Above: The junction of Georgian Revival and Richardson Romanesque can be seen in this recent view of the Wyoming County Courthouse.

Left: Andrew Jackson Warner of Rochester designed this 1882 Richardson Romanesque courthouse for Wyoming County. The entire front of the building was demolished for the 1936 renovation.

COUNTY BLDGS., PENN YAN, N.Y.

The Penn Yan courthouse, built in 1835, has been remodeled and repaired several times. It now houses the County Legislature. The county built the building on the right in 1889 for the county clerk and surrogate. It was modified in 2002 as a new county office building.

Yates County

New York Governor Joseph C. Yates (1768-1837) was especially delighted to sign the bill creating Yates County, considering it was named for him. Yates, known as the Godfather of Yates County, had been a Justice of the (old) State Supreme Court (1808-1822) and served as Governor in 1823-1824. Yates County, created in 1823, was the direct offspring of Ontario County. The argument for its formation was the same as for most of New York's counties, the convenience of its residents.

Three towns bid to be county seat. Dresden touted its position on the shore of Seneca Lake with its convenience of access by water. Jerusalem claimed historical significance and centrality of location. Penn Yan, however, had the advantage. It was the most developed and centrally located, and it had influential men, including Abraham Wagener, who donated two acres for the county building. With such an irresistible offer, the choice was clear, and Penn Yan remains the county seat.

The name Penn Yan is said to be both geographical and cultural. Most of the settlers of the region had come from New England, and the town's name reflects its proximity to Pennsylvania and the Yankee heritage of its residents. At first, Yates County had no courthouse. Until one was constructed, court was held at the house of local resident Asa Cole, and prisoners were sent to the Ontario County jail. The first courthouse was a plain, brick building that included a jail. When that burned in 1834, the county put up a similar but larger courthouse, a stone county clerk's office, and a separate stone and frame jail. The 1835 courthouse, built initially for $12,500, has been remodeled and repaired several times, and serves today as the home of the County Legislature.

The Yates County jail did not fare so well. In 1857, a prisoner named Albert Hathaway, a known arsonist, set fire to it, and it was destroyed. At trial, Hathaway claimed insanity, and a jury acquitted him. The 1857 jail, built by Charles V. Bush of Penn Yan, was designed with fire resistance in mind and cost $10,200. In 1904, the county replaced this building with a new one to the north of the old building.

In 1889, the county budgeted $11,000 and engaged Hershel Pierce of Dundee to build a separate building near the courthouse, for the county clerk and surrogate, replacing a smaller building at the same site. The county demolished part of this building in 2002, leaving the façade, and built an addition to create a new county office building.

Judge Henry Welles (1794-1868) was one of Penn Yan's most eminent residents. Serving ex officio on the New York Court of Appeals in 1852 and 1860, he concurred in the Court's anti-slavery decision, *Lemmon v. People*, 20 N.Y. (6 Smith) 562 (1860). Frederick Collin (1850-1939), born in Benton, Yates County, served on the New York Court of Appeals from 1910 to 1920.

Thanks to Surrogate's Court Chief Clerk Michele Covert and Court Assistant Robert S. Peelle.

Above: A rear view of the buildings shown on p.250.

Right: Mailed in 1906, this card shows the courthouse and county clerk's building.

Bibliography

INTRODUCTION

Ogden, William D. "All for a Cent: New York Times, 8 June 1947, p. SM15.

Staff, Frank, The Picture Postcard and Its Origins, New York: F.A. Prager, 1966.

FIRST JUDICIAL DISTRICT (New York County)

Ackerman, Kenneth D. Boss Tweed: The Rise and Fall of the Corrupt Pol Who Conceived the Soul of Modern New York. New York: Caroll & Graf, 2005.

"Architect of the New Court House Defends His Circular Plan." New York Times 20 April 1913, p. sm2.

"Court House Plans Save 14,000,000…Circular Model Dropped." New York Times 14 Dec. 1919, p. S5.

"Court House Stone is Laid by Mayor." New York Times 29 June 1940, p. 24.

Folts, James D. Duely and Constantly Kept, A History of the New York Supreme Court, (1691-1847). Albany, NY: New York State Archives and Records Administration, 1991.

"Grand Jury Asks New Court House." New York Times 6 Nov. 1936, p. 11.

"Guy Lowell Dies; Noted Architect." New York Times 5 Feb. 1927, p. 15.

"The New Appellate Court: Justices Have a Housewarming With Greetings From the Bar. Women Among the Audience." New York Times 3 Jan. 1900, p. 5.

"The New Court House: A Plan by Architect J. W. Wilson Unanimously Chosen." New York Times, 27 July 1889, p. 8.

"New Court House Like the Coliseum." New York Times 14 April 1913, p. 2.

"New Court House Opened: Private View of the Home of the Appellate Division." New York Times 21 Dec. 1899, p. 8.

"New Court House Plans. Handsome Structure for Justices of the Appellate Division." New York Times 1 July, 1896 p. 9.

"New Criminal Courts Buildings." New York Times 9 Nov. 1889, p. 3.

"Old Court Block to be Razed Soon." New York Times 6 Oct. 1945, p. 28.

"Old Tombs Will Become a Fire College; Prison Bars to be Torn Out as War Scrap." New York Times 5 Feb. 1942, p. 23.

"Woes of 500,000 Recalled as Workmen Begin to Demolish the Old Bridge of Sighs." New York Times 24 July 1942, p. 21.

Rosenblatt, Albert M. "The Foundations of the New York Supreme Court (1691-1991): A Study in Sources." New York State Bar Journal 63. No. 4, (1991, May/June): 10.

"Tombs Prison Site Figured in Early New York History." New York Times 17 June 1934, p. xx20.

SECOND JUDICIAL DISTRICT (Kings County; Richmond County)

"Appellate Court Sits in New Brooklyn Home." New York Times 29 Sept. 1938, p. 4.

Bayles, Richard M. History of Richmond County, New York. New York: E. Preston, 1887.

"Brooklyn News – The New Court-House." New York Times 1 March 1865, p. 8

Chester, Alden. Legal and Judicial History of New York. New York: National Americana Society, 1911. [Kings County]

"City Waives Bids in Equipping Court – New Appellate Chambers in Brooklyn to be Fitted Just as Justices Want Them." New York Times 24 Nov. 1937, p. 25.

"Court House Bids Opened. Work Starts Soon on Brooklyn Appellate Division Quarters." New York Times 6 May 1937, p.51.

"Design for St. George Courthouse Must Still Be Finalized." The Staten Island Advance 23 Nov. 2005, p. A3.

Dickenson, Richard. Holden's Staten Island. New York: Center for Migration Studies, 2002.

Morris, Ira K. Memorial History of Staten Island. New York: Memorial Publishing Co., 1898.

"The New York and Brooklyn Court-Houses." New York Times 6 Aug. 1871, p. 4.

"The New York of To-Day; A Greater City Comes Into Being Without Any Visible Change in Conditions." New York Times 1 Jan. 1989, p.4. [Richmond County]

"Noble Line of Civic Buildings for Staten Island." New York Times 31 March 1912, p. SM9.

"Robert H. Bryson, Architect, 63, Dies." New York Times 11 Sept. 1938, p. 63. [Kings County]

"Staten Island Presents Object Lesson of Wise and Practical City Planning." New York Times 13 Oct. 1912, p. 21.

THIRD JUDICIAL DISTRICT (*Albany County, Columbia County, Greene County, Rensselaer County, Schoharie County, Sullivan County, Ulster County*)

"Abducted Last Thursday. Victim's Uncles are the Bosses of the Albany Democratic Machine." New York Times 11 July 1993, p. 1.

Chase, Emory A. Greene County: Courts and Officers. A General Historic View. Paper read at Second Annual Greene County Bar Association Meeting, Privately printed, 15 Feb. 1904.

Chester, Alden. The Legal and Judicial History of New York. Vol. 3. New York: National Americana Society, 1911. [Albany County]

Dedication Restored Schoharie County Courthouse. Commemorative Pamphlet. Schoharie, NY: Schoharie County Courthouse, 2002.

"Diamond Acquitted on Assault Charge." New York Times 15 July 1931, p. 1. [Rensselaer County]

"Diamond Acquitted by Jury at Troy." New York Times 18 Dec. 1931, p. 1.

"Diamond Gets Limit, 4 Years, $11, 000 Fine; Troy Trial Sep. 15." New York Times 13 Aug. 1931, p. 1.

"Diamond's Widow Murdered in Home." New York Times 1 July 1933, p. 1. [Rensselaer County]

"Diamond Witness Taken for Perjury." New York Times 22 July 22 1931, p. 3. [Rensselaer County]

"50-Year Sentence is Given to Strewl." New York Times 28 March 1934, p. 46. [Albany County]

Greene County Court House. The Greene County Court House. Its Diamond Jubilee 1910-1985. Catskill, NY: Greene County Court House, 1985.

Hoes, Roswell R. Old Courthouses of Ulster County. Kingston, NY: Board of Supervisors, 1918.

"Legs" Diamond Slain in Sleep at Albany by Two Assassins." New York Times 19 Dec. 1931, p.1.

McAdam, David. A History of the Bench and Bar of New York. New York: Historical Co., 1897.

New York Court of Appeals. Court of Appeals Hall: Construction, Restoration and Renovation 1842-2004. New York: New York Court of Appeals, 2005.

New York Court of Appeals. The Rededication of Court of Appeals Hall. October 5, 1959. New York: New York Court of Appeals, 1959.

"O'Connell Names Three as in Gang." New York Times 4 March 1933, p. 1. [Albany County]

Schoonmaker, Marius. History of Kingston, New York: Burr Printing House, 1888.

"War on Gangs Aim in Diamond Trial." New York Times 12 July 1931, p. N. [Rensselaer County]

Williams, Joseph C. Temple of Justice. Albany: Hall of Records, 1990.

FOURTH JUDICIAL DISTRICT (*Clinton County, Essex County, Franklin County, Fulton County, Hamilton County, Montgomery County, St. Lawrence County, Saratoga County, Schenectady County, Warren County, Washington County*)

Aber, Ted and Stella King. The History of Hamilton County. Lake Pleasant, NY: Great Wilderness Books, 1965.

Brown, William H. ed. History of Warren County. Glens Falls, NY: Board of Supervisors of Warren County, 1963.

Chester, Alden. The Legal and Judicial History of New York. Vol. 3. New York: National Americana Society, 1911. [Clinton County]

"Dutch is Freed." New York Times 4 Aug. 1935, p. E2. [Franklin County]

Fulton County Courthouse. Johnstown, NY: Board of Supervisors of Fulton County, n.d.

Gresham Publishing Company ed. History and Biography of Washington County. Richmond Ind.: Gresham Publishing Company, 1894.

Historical Fulton County Jail. Johnstown, NY: N.p., n.d.

"History Lives in Village." Post Star [Glens Falls, NY]: 1975, n.p.

Hough, Franklin B. History of Jefferson County in the State of New York. Watertown, NY: Sterling & Riddell, 1854.

Hough, Franklin B. A History of St. Lawrence and Franklin Counties. New York, Albany: Little & Co., 1853.

Loveday, William G. Jr. "Birth of a County." The Sunday Leader-Herald, 13 Jan. 2002, p. 8A. [Fulton County]

Maher, Joe. "County Celebrates Courthouse." Sunday Gazette. 19 May 2002, n.p. [Fulton County]

"Murderer Fled From Prison." New York Times 16 Dec. 1892, p. 6. [Saratoga County]

"New Trial is Set for July 23; Federal Judge Bryant Also Orders Case Moved from Syracuse to Malone." New York Times 14 May 1935 p. 41. [Franklin County]

"Oil Portraits Presented to Essex County at Supervisors' Meeting in Elizabethtown." Record Post 15 Aug. 1946, n.p.

Patton, Joan. "Courthouse Architecture Noted." Post Star [Glens Falls, NY]: 1989, n.p.

Seaver, Frederick J. Historical Sketches of Franklin County and Its Several Towns. Albany, NY: J.B. Lyon, 1918.

"The State Campaign." New York Times 6 Oct. 1875. p. 1. [Essex County]

Stone, William L. Washington County, New York, Its History to the Close of the Nineteenth Century. New York: New York History Company, 1901.

Sullivan, James. History of New York State, 1523-1927. Vol. 2. New York: Lewis Historical Publishing Co., 1927.

Sullivan, Robert G. "Schenectady County Digital Archive." 7 Oct. 2005. http://www.schenectadyhistory.org.

Thompson, Robert B. "Washington County Courthouses". Salem Press 12 Oct. 1972, p. 10.

FIFTH JUDICIAL DISTRICT (Herkimer County, Jefferson County, Lewis County, Oneida County, Onondaga County, Oswego County)

Bowen, Byron G. History of Lewis County 1880-1965. New York: Board of Legislators of Lewis County, 1970.

Case, Dick. "Tracing History of Black Lawyer." Post-Standard [Syracuse, NY] 2 Oct. 1999, n.p.

Chester, Alden. The Legal and Judicial History of New York. Vol. 3. New York: National Americana Society, 1911. [Jefferson County]

"A Complete Politician, Fred Anthony Young." New York Times 7 Aug. 1964, p. 12. [Lewis County]

"Courthouse Plans: Judge Tormey Made Wise Decision." Watertown Daily Times 6 May 2006, p. A8.

"Ex-Judge Merrell Dies Upstate, 77." New York Times 7 Dec. 1942, p. 27. [Lewis County]

"Fred Young Dies, Ex-State Judge." New York Times 17 Oct. 1973, p. 44. [Lewis County]

"Gillette Dies; Guilt Admitted." New York Times 31 March 1908, p. 6. [Herkimer County]

"Grace Brown's Letters Stir Audience to Tears." New York Times 21 Nov. 1906, p. 5. [Herkimer County]

Hardin, Evamaria. "Courthouse." Syracuse Scholar. 1988: 35-49.

Hough, Franklin B. History of Jefferson County in the State of New York. Watertown, NY: Sterling & Riddell, 1854.

Hough, Franklin B. History of Lewis County in the State of New York. Watertown, NY: Sterling & Riddell, 1883.

"Lewis Courthouse Project Moving Closer to its Start." Watertown Daily Times 9 Oct. 2005, p.B1.

Mariani, John. "County Seeks Aid to Repair Courthouse." Post-Standard [Syracuse, NY] 1 May, 2006, n.p.

"Mrs. Gillette Sees Hughes." New York Times 18 March 1908, p. 6. [Herkimer County]

Thomas, Arad. Pioneer History of Orleans County. Albion, NY: H.A. Brunner, 1817. [Oswego County]

Virkler, Steve. "Courthouse Figures: New Site Very Costly." Watertown Daily Times 28 April 2006, p. 4.

SIXTH JUDICIAL DISTRICT (Broome County, Chemung County, Chenango County, Cortland County, Delaware County, Madison County, Otsego County, Schuyler County, Tioga County, Tompkins County)

Bass, Gigi. (1980). Historical Analysis in Chenango County Courthouse. Norwich, NY: Chenango County Development and Planning Board, 1980.

Chester, Alden. The Legal and Judicial History of New York. Vol. 3. New York: National Americana Society, 1911. [Broome County]

Dieckmann, Jane M. A Short History of Tompkins County. Ithaca, NY: DeWitt Historical Society of Tompkins County, 1986.

Dieckmann Jane M. Tompkins County: The Towns of Tompkins County. Ithaca, NY: DeWitt Historical Society of Tompkins County, 1998.

Hugill, Peter J. Upstate Arcadia. Lanham, MD: Rowman & Littlefield, 1995. [Madison County]

Kieffer, Arthur J. "Chemung County's First Court House." Chemung Historical Journal (1971): 2011-2015.

Kieffer, Arthur J. "Lake St.'s First County Court House." Chemung Historical Journal (1971): 2083-2088.

Lawyer, William S., ed. Binghamton: Its Settlement, Growth, and Development, and the Factors in its History, 1800-1900. Binghamton, N.Y.: Century Memorial Publishing Co., 1900.

Liguori, Frank. Historic Preservation in Tompkins County. Ithaca, NY: Tompkins County Department of Planning, 1997.

Monroe John D. The Anti-Rent War in Delaware County. New York: Privately printed, 1940.

Oechsle, Russ. The Odyssey of the Courtroom Clock. The Ceremony to Rededicate the Main Courtroom. Binghamton, NY: Broome County Courthouse, 2003.

Sachae, Gretchen. "Ithaca: An Overview." Ithaca's Neighborhoods. Vol.1. Ed. Carol U. Sisler, Margaret Hobbie, and Jane M. Dieckmann, Ithaca, NY: DeWitt Historical Society of Tomkins County, 1980.

Smith, James H. History of Chenango and Madison County. Syracuse, NY: D. Mason & Co., 1880.

Sullivan, James. History of New York State, 1523-1927. Vol. 2. New York: Lewis Historical Publishing Co., 1927. [Broome County]

Varney, Elizabeth. "Introduction" and "Restoring the Courtroom". The Ceremony to Rededicate the Main Courtroom. Binghamton, NY: Broome County Courthouse, 2003.

Waid, Roy D. "Col. Hathaway, Whose Bust Adorns Courtroom Wall, Once Eminent Here." Elmira Telegram, 3 March 1940, n.p. [Chemung County]

SEVENTH JUDICIAL DISTRICT (Cayuga County, Livingston County, Monroe County, Ontario County, Seneca County, Steuben County, Wayne County, Yates County)

Aldrich, Lewis C. History of Yates County, N.Y. Syracuse, N.Y.: D. Mason & Co., 1892.

Becker, John. E. A History of the Village of Waterloo, New York and Thesaurus of Related Facts. Waterloo, NY: Waterloo Library and Historical Society, 1949.

Chester, Alden. The Legal and Judicial History of New York. Vol. 3. New York: National Americana Society, 1911. [Cayuga County]

Doty, Lockwood. A History of Livingston County. Geneseo, NY: Edward E. Doty, 1876

Storke, Elliot G. History of Cayuga County New York. Syracuse, NY: D. Mason & Co., 1879.

Latham, Chilton. "On Ancient Court Houses." Steuben Courier Advocate 10 Jan. 1963, n.p.

"Livingston Gives its Courthouse New Life." The Rochester Democrat and Chronicle 29 March 1995, n.p.

McKelvey, Blake. Rochester on the Genesee. Syracuse, NY: Syracuse University Press, 1993.

McKelvey, Blake. Rochester: An Emerging Metropolis, 1925-1960. Rochester, NY: Christopher Press, 1961.

McKelvey, Blake. Rochester the Flower City, 1855-1890. Cambridge, MA: Harvard University Press, 1949.

Mulford, Uri. Pioneer Days and Later Times in Corning and Vicinity 1789-1920. Corning, NY: Uri Mulford, 1920. [Steuben County]

Near, Irwin W. History of Steuben County. Vol. 1. Chicago: Lewis Publishing Co., 1911.

Peck, William F. An Historical Sketch of Monroe County and the City of Rochester in Landmarks of Monroe County. Boston, MA: The Boston History Company, 1895.

Penn Yan, New York. Penn Yan, NY: Peerless Printing, Co., n.d.

Perez, Marjory and Mary A.Bleik. Wayne County Looking Back. Lyons, NY: Wayne County Department of History and Archives, 1980

Pierce, Preston. E. "Liberian Dreams, West African Nightmare: The Life of Henry W. Johnson." Rochester History. 66 (Fall 2004) and 67 (Winter 2005). [Ontario County]

Pierce, Preston. E. Seat of Justice: Witness to History. Canandaigua, NY: Office of the County Historian, 2003.

"Siegel in a Cell, Serving His Term." New York Times 22 June 1915, p. 24. [Livingston County]

"Siegel in Geneseo Ready for Trial." New York Times 9 Nov. 1914, p. 1. [Livingston County]

EIGHTH JUDICIAL DISTRICT (Allegany County, Cattaraugus County, Chautauqua County, Erie County, Genesee County, Niagara County, Orleans County, Wyoming County)

Bishop, Lewis. "'Ringing Through the Valley' Tower Clocks and Bells of Warsaw." Historic Wyoming. 27. 2 (October 1980): 43.

Cattaraugus County 1808-1985. Little Valley, NY: Cattaraugus County, 1985.

Chautauqua Historical Company. The Centennial History of Chautauqua County. Vol. 1 Jamestown, NY: The Chautauqua History Company, 1904.

Chazanof, William. Joseph Ellicott and the Holland Land Company. Syracuse, NY: Syracuse University Press, 1970 [Genesee County]

Chester, Alden. The Legal and Judicial History of New York. Vol. 3. New York: National Americana Society, 1911 [Chautauqua County]

"County Courthouse Combines Old and New Lockport." Union-Sun and Journal Aug. 28, 1971, n.p.

"80,000 HUD Grant Given for Ellicottville 'Courthouse' Project." Salamanca Republican Press 23 June, 1971, n.p. [Cattaraugus County]

"Election of Woman District Attorney Is Believed to Be the First in This State." New York Times 10 Nov. 1949, p. 5. [Wyoming County]

Ellis, Franklin. History of Cattaraugus County, New York. Philadelphia: L.H. Everts, 1879.

Henry, Michelle. "New York's Last Hanging." (Summer 2005). The New York Archives. 5.1., n.p. [Chautauqua County]

History of Wyoming County, NY. New York: F.W. Beers & Co., 1880.

Laidlaw, William K. The Old Cattaraugus County Court House and Ellicottville Town Hall. Privately printed, n.d.

Lewis, Clarence O. "Goddess of Justice Graced Courthouse in Former Years." Union-Sun and Journal 9 Feb. 1953, n.p. [Niagara County]

Lewis, Clarence O. "Court House 'Attic' Reveals Many Historical Treasures." Union-Sun and Journal 23 June, 1955, n.p. [Niagara County]

Lewis, Clarence O. "Historian Receives Pleas to Save County Building." Union-Sun and Journal 27 March, 1958, n.p. [Niagara County]

Lyman, Curtis L. Historical Sketch of the Orleans County Court House. Albion, NY: New York State Bar Association, 1959.

McAllister, Arden. County Organizations and Government 1900-1976 in Orleans County History, Past to Present, Bicentennial Year, 1976. Albion, NY: Orleans County Supervisors, 1976.

"Once a Pioneer, Now One of the Crowd." New York Times 16 Dec. 2001, p. A41. [Wyoming County]

Richardson, Chuck. "Courthouse Project Finds Link to Past." Union-Sun and Journal 11 July 1987, n.p. [Orleans County]

Rosenblatt, Albert. An Illustrated History of The New York State District Attorney's Association. New York State District Attorney's Association, 1998. [Wyoming County].

Seymour, Whitney N. Jr. Line Drawing on cover page, Historical Sketch of the Orleans County Court House. Albion, NY: New York State Bar Association, 1959.

Thomas, Arad. Pioneer History of Orleans County. Albion, NY: H.A. Brunner, 1817.

Yarrington, James. R. Wyoming County, New York, An Architectural Tour. Canandaigua, NY: The Humphrey Press, 1966.

Young, Andrew W. History of Chautauqua County, New York. Buffalo, NY: Matthews & Warren, 1875.

Young, Andrew W. History of the Town of Warsaw, New York. Buffalo: Sage, Sons, & Co, 1869

NINTH JUDICIAL DISTRICT (Dutchess County, Orange County, Putnam County, Rockland County, Westchester County)

Board of Supervisors. County of Dutchess Proceedings of the Board of Supervisors. Poughkeepsie, NY: Dutchess County Board of Supervisors, pp. 45, 213-216 (1902); pp. 224-229 (1903).

Budke, George H. The County Seat at New City, New York. Nyack NY: Rockland Record, Rockland County Historical Society, 1930. [Rockland County]

Chester, Alden. The Legal and Judicial History of New York. Vol. 3. New York: National Americana Society, 1911. [Orange County]

Haviland, John. C. "A Very Special Courthouse in Dutchess County." Poughkeepsie Journal (1988): n.p.

Kaye, Judith S. "Commentaries on Chancellor Kent," 74 Kent-Chi L. Rev. 11 (1998-2000). [Putnam County]

Lamb, Martha J. History of the City of New York: Its Origin, Rise, and Progress. Vol. 2. New York: A. S. Barnes, & Co, 1880. [Dutchess County]

Langbein, John H. "Chancellor Kent and the History of Legal Literature," 93 Colum. L. Rev. 547 (1993). [Putnam County]

Lincoln, Charles Z. The Constitutional History of New York. Vol. 1. Rochester, NY: Lawyers Cooperative Publishing Company, 1906.

The 100th Anniversary of the Dutchess County Courthouse. Commemorative Pamphlet Poughkeepsie, NY: Dutchess County Bar Association, 2003.

Pomares, Henry. 1841 Courthouse. Orange County, NY: n.p., n.d.

"Preserving Our History. Restoring 1928 Courthouse Boost for County Heritage." Journal News 26 Dec. 2002, n.p. [Rockland County]

"Restore Grandeur to Courthouse." Poughkeepsie Journal (1987): 22a.

Rheingold, Paul D. and Joyce B. Rheingold. "The Courthouses of Westchester County, Part One." Westchester Historian 61. 4 (Fall 1985): 92-99.

Rheingold, Paul D. and Joyce B. Rheingold. "The Courthouses of Westchester County, Part Two." Westchester Historian 62. 1 (Winter 1986): 20-23.

Pryslopski, Christopher. "A Thoroughly Modern Conundrum: Paul Rudolph's Orange County Government Center." The Hudson River Valley Review 21. 1 (Autumn 2004): 72-83.

Sullivan, James. History of New York State, 1523-1927. Vol. 2. New York: Lewis Historical Publishing Co., 1927. [Rockland County]

White, Justin. The New Rockland County Courthouse at New City. Nyack, NY: Rockland Record, Rockland County Historical Society, 1930.

TENTH JUDICIAL DISTRICT (Nassau County, Suffolk County)

Chester, Alden. The Legal and Judicial History of New York. Vol. 3. New York: National Americana Society, 1911. [Suffolk County]

"Legality of Nassau County." New York Times 8 Oct. 1898, p. 2.

"Mineola Chosen Nassau County's Seat." New York Times 10 Nov. 1898, p. 4.

"Nassau County Buildings' Site." New York Times 25 May 1898, p. 4

"Sites for Nassau County Buildings." New York Times 29 Sept. 1989, p. 5

ELEVENTH JUDICIAL DISTRICT (Queens County)

Chester, Alden. The Legal and Judicial History of New York. Vol. 3. New York: National Americana Society, 1911.

Kerson, Paul E. "The Very Troubled History of the Queens County Courthouses." Queens Bar Bulletin April 2001: n.p.

"Mayor to Dedicate [Jamaica] Court." New York Times 1 March 1939, p. 12.

"New Court House Started in Queens." New York Times 15 Oct. 1936, p. 15.

"The New Queens County Court-House." New York Times 9 Feb. 1874, p. 3.

"Queens County Court House." New York Times 14 Feb. 1870, p. 3.

"Rushing Work on New Court House for Queens." New York Times 11 April 1909, p. 13.

"Wins [Queens] Court House Contract." New York Times 19 May 1937, p. 42.

TWELFTH JUDICIAL DISTRICT (Bronx County)

"Above the Harlem River." New York Times 29 April 1883, p. 14.

"Big Granite Structure at 161st Street and Third Avenue, Started During the Louis F. Haffen Administration, Will Probably Cost Taxpayers $2,000,000 Before Finishing Touches Are Put to it – Original Plans Called for $800,000." New York Times 11 Jan. 1914, p. xx2.

"Bronx County Created." New York Times 7 Nov. 1912, p. 12.

"Bronx Grand Juries Distracted by Noise." New York Times 26 July 1914, p. 9.

"Bronx Out Again for Countyhood." New York Times 14 Dec. 1911, p.2.

"Bronx County Law is Constitutional." New York Times 15 March, 1913, p. 4.

"Bronx Would Save By Being a County." New York Times 17 Dec. 1911, p.7.

"Bronx County – Vote 'No.'." New York Times 5 Nov. 1912, p. 12.

"Enlarged New York." New York Times 2 May 1873, p.4.

"Francis Martin, Jurist, Dies at 68." New York Times 2 June 1947, p. 25.

"Give Godspeed to Bronx County." New York Times 2 Jan. 1914, p. 16.

Gonzalez, Evelyn. The Bronx. New York: Columbia University Press, 2004.

Hansen, Harry. North of Manhattan. New York: Hastings House, 1950.

Jenkins, Stephen. The Story of The Bronx. New York: G.P. Putnam's Sons, 1912.

"New Bronx Court House." New York Times 27 July 1902, p. 22.

"Plan to Dedicate New Bronx Court." New York Times 10 June 1934, p. RE1.

Williams, Timothy. "Old Halls of Justice Yield to Halls Full of Children." New York Times 6 June 2006, p. B4.

Postcard Publishers

Duchess Co. Leather
Hy-Sil Manufacturing Boston.

Syracuse Tin
Owens Bors-Hillson Co., Boston, Mass.

Treaty Rock, Ontario Co.
"Tichnor Quality Views" Reg. U.S. Pat. Off. Made Only by Technor Bros. Inc., Boston, Mass.

Ontario Co.
No Publishing Information Available

Wayne Co.
Published by Moore & Moore, Lyons, N.Y. Printed in Germany.

Albany
647-Published by Albany News Co., Albany, N.Y. Made in U.S.A.

Albany
No Publisher Information Available.

Albany
Published by Chas. W. Hughes, Mechanicville, N.Y.

Albany
Made in Germany. A.C. Bosselman & Co., N.Y.

Albany
Published by New York State Court of Appeals

Allegany
No. 5 Published by B.B. & H.W. Slade, Belmont, N.Y., Made in Germany.

Allegany
No Publisher Information Available

Allegany
Published by Scott Studio, Rochester, N.Y.

Bronx New Court House
Published by The Williamsburg Post Card Co., New York City.

Bronx
143: -Bronx County Court House, Bronx, New York, N.Y.

Court House Binghamton, N.Y.
Published by Walther R. Miller Co., Binghamton, N.Y. Made in the U.S.A.

Binghamton, N.Y. Court House Square
Fowler, Dick and Walker, Binghamton, N.Y. Germany

Broome County Courthouse
Published by the Manhattan Card Publishing Company.

Broome County Courthouse
Published by C.S. Woolworth & Co., Made in Germany.

Cattaraugus Co.
McLouth's Drug Store Hand Colored

The Courthouse
Published by E.L. Campbell, Little Valley, N.Y.

Cattaraugus Bell from Old Home
No Publisher Information Available.

Cayuga County
G 4285, Copyright 1905 by the Rotograph Co., N.Y., City. (Germany).

Cayuga County Court House
Published by O.M. News Company Geneva, N.Y. 127570.

Genesse Street Scene
Published by Wm. Juss Co., Inc., Syracuse, N.Y.

Mayfield Old Holland Land Co. Vault
The Hugh C. Leighton Co., Manufacturers, Portland, ME, 4833; Made in Germany.

Old Court House Mayville
No Publisher Information Available.

1908 Chautauqua Court House
No Publisher Information Available.

Modern Chautauqua
McClenathan Printery Inc., Dunkirk, N.Y.

Chemung County Courthouse
Buffalo News Company, Buffalo, N.Y., Leipnig-Berlin.

Chemung Courthouse West Lake Street
Souvenir –Post Card Co., New York Printed in Germany

Chenango Courthouse
FLB by Carmen Co., Binghamton, N.Y.

Chenango 1903
Valentine Souvenir Co., New York, N.Y. Printed in U.S.A.

Chenango Aerial view
Published by WM Jubb Co., Syracuse, N.Y.

Chenango 1996
New Image Photography and Video Services, Wayne A. Osterhout, Norwich, N.Y.

Clinton Courthouse
O.T. American Art Colored.

Clinton Park and Courthouse
Valentine Souvenir, New York. Printed in U.S.A.

Columbia
The Hugh C. Leighton Co., Manufactured Portland, ME U.S.A, Printed in Frankfort Main Germany N11368.

Columbia
The Valentine & Sons Publishing Co. Ltd, New York, Printed in Great Britain.

Cortland
The Leighton & Valentine Co., N.Y. City, Printed in United States

Cortland County Courthouse
Published by Wm Jubb Co., Inc. Syracuse, N.Y.

Cortland
Published by WM. Jubb Co., Inc., Syracuse, N.Y.

Delaware County
Published by Chas. W. Hughes, Mechanicville, N.Y. Made in U.S.A.

Delaware County
Published by Bob Wyer Photo Cards, Delhi, N.Y.

Dutchess County
54524 Published by Jake B. Flagler Poughkeepsie, N.Y., Germany.

Dutchess County
The Reuben Publishing Co., Newburgh, N.Y.

Erie
No Publisher Information Available.

Erie County and City Building
5242 Published by the Buffalo News Company Buffalo, N.Y., Leipzig, Dresden

Essex
JGH C. Leighton Co., Manufacturers, Portland, ME, U.S.A. 27481; Made in Germany.

Essex
No Publisher Information Available.

Franklin
The Hugh Leighton Co., Manufacturers, Portland, ME U.S.A., Made in Germany 2678.

Franklin
134861, Tichnor Quality Views.

Franklin
$5 Photo Co., Photo Park, Canton, New York.

Fulton
Published by Utica Paper Co., For R.G. Dewitt & Co., Johnstown, N.Y.

Fulton
Published by C.W. Hughes and Co., Mechanicville, N.Y.

Fulton
No Publisher Information Available.

Genessee
500Y2, Washington & Wood Batavia, N.Y. (Germany).

Genessee
Published by The Acmegraph Co. Chicago

Genessee
N.E. Curteich-Chicago "C.Y. American Art" Post Card (Reg. U.S. Pat. Off)

Greene
The Rotograph Co. N.Y. City, Printed in Germany, E 3115a.

Greene
J. Ruben Publisher, Newburgh, N.Y.

Greene
Published by H.H. Smith, 5& 10c. Store, Catskill, N.Y.

Hamilton
Published by Marks & Fuller, Inc. Rochester, N.Y.

Hamilton
Eastern Illustrating & Publishing Co., Belfast, ME.

Herkimer
Photochrome (letters 'N', 'Y' and 'C' in leaves of a clover), N.Y, Leipzig, Dresden, Berlin; Printed in Germany.

Herkimer
No. 2140 Published by The Rochester News Comp., Rochester, N.Y., U.S.A., Leipzig, Berlin.

Jefferson
The Leighton & Valentine Co., N.Y., City, Printed in the United States.

Jefferson
The Leighton & Valentine Co., N.Y. City, Printed in the United States.

Kings
Illustrated Post Card Co., N.Y.

Kings
No. 3036 The Rotography Co., N.Y. City. (Germany).

Kings Supreme Court
No Publisher Information Available.

Lewis
No. D 7587 by Miss H.G. Reed, Lowville, N.Y.

Lewis
Genuine Natural Color Made By Dexter Press Inc.

Lewis
Published by Miss H.G. Reed, Lowville, N.Y.

Livingston
Post Cards of Quality – The Albertype Co., Brooklyn.

Livingston
John Balding & Son, Printed in Germany.

Livingston
Published by Ulmer's Drug Store, Geneseo, N.Y.

Madison
Published by W. Jubb, Syracuse, N.Y.

Madison County Clerk's Office
No Publisher Information Available.

Madison
E 13456, Published by A. M. Wiggins, Oneida, N.Y. Made in Germany.

Madison
Published by A.M. Wiggins, Oneida, N.Y. Made in U.S.A. L-2421.

Monroe
Tuck's Post Card, Raphael Tuck & Sons Series No. 2029 Rochester, N.Y. Art Publishers to their Majesties the King and Queen; Photochromed in Saxony.

Monroe
Published by The Rochester News Company, Rochester, N.Y., Made in Germany.

Monroe 3rd Courthouse
Published by the Rochester News Company, Rochester, N.Y.

Monroe County Hall of Justice
Published by Manson News Distributors Inc., Rochester, N.Y.

Montgomery
C 3816 Published by The American News Company, New York, Leipzig, Berlin and Dresden

Montgomery
Published by John W. Davis, Fonda, N.Y. , Printed in United States.

Nassau
1801, Illustrated Post Card Co., N.Y.

Nassau
Published and imported by H. Agnew, Stationer, Hempstead, N.Y., Made in Germany.

New York Tombs
No Publisher Information Available.

New York Bridge of Sighs
No Publisher Information Available.

New York Tweed Courthouse No. 150
No Publisher Information Available.

New York Palace of Justice
The American Art Publishing Co., New York City.

New York
C.T. Art Colortone Made only by Curt Teich & Co., Inc. Chicago U.S.A., The Union News Co. Copyright by Irving Underhill, Inc., N.Y.C.

New York Supreme Court Appellate Division
Printed in Germany

New York Jefferson Market Courthouse
Acacia Card Company, 258 Broadway, New York 7, N.Y.

Niagara
The Rotograph Co., N.Y. City

Niagara
Published by Robert Stephanski, Lockport, N.Y.

Niagara
Plaster News Company, Lockport, New York. Technor Quality Views Reg. U.S. Pat. Off. Made only by Technor Bros. Inc. Boston

Oneida
Published by Wm. Jubb Co., Inc., Syracuse, N.Y. C.T. American Art

Oneida
Famous Quality Throughout the World, The Leighton & Valentine Co., N.Y. City. Printed in United States

Oneida
Published by Margo Studio; Rome N.Y. 13440

Onondaga
Made in Syracuse, N.Y. by American Publishing Company.

Onondaga
Published by Wm. Jubb Co., Inc., Syracuse, N.Y.

Onondaga
Published by William E. Shoudy, Syracuse, N.Y. Made in Germany

Ontario
Published by Robinson and MacFarlane (Germany).

Ontario
The Rotography Co., N.Y. City, Printed in Germany, E 4221.

Ontario
The Hugh Leighton Co., Manufacturers, Portland, ME U.S.A. Made in Germany 2902.

Ontario
Published by Wm. Jubb Co., Syracuse, N.Y.

Orange
By Greenberg's Cigar & Stationery Shop, Gosen, N.Y. Eagle Post Card View Co., New York 1, N.Y.

Orange
159-14 Illustrated Postal Card Co., New York-Germany.

Orange
Published by Greenberg's Cigar & Stationery Shop, Goshen, N.Y.

Orleans
C.T. Doubletone

Orleans
Published by Wm. Jubb Co., Syracuse, N.Y.

Orleans
No Publisher Information Available.

Oswego
Published by Wm. Jubb Co., Syracuse, N.Y.

Oswego
Published by Wm. Jubb Co., Syracuse, N.Y. 9-2337.

Oswego
WM. Jubb Co., Inc., Syracuse, N.Y.

Oswego
Published by The American News Company, New York.

Otsego
No. C 13466 Published by Lippitt & Augur, Coopertown, N.Y.

Ostego
Published by Peter L. Hollis, Cooperstown, N.Y.

Ostego
Published by Oneonta Dept Store, Oneonta, N.Y., Made in Germany.

Putnam
Published by Pendor Natural Color Box 33, Pearl River, N.Y.

Putnam
Published by Haddon Hall, 14 Palmer Ave., Nanuet, N.Y.

Putnam
Published by S.G. Cornish & Son, Carmel, N.Y.

Queens
Published by Bergman & Pinkus, Astoria, N.Y. Printed in the United States

Queens 1939
Interborough News Co., 525 West 52nd Street., New York, N.Y. Genuine Curteich-Chicago "C.T. Art Colortone" Postcard (Reg. U.S. Pat. Off.)

Queens
The Valentine-Souvenir Co., New York, Printed in the U.S.A.

Queens
No Publisher Information Available.

Rensselaer
Souvenir Post Card Co., New York and Berlin

Rensselaer
P.J. Shea, Troy, N.Y., Made in Germany.

Rensselaer 1914
Superior Quality Throughout the World, The Valentine-Souvenir Co., New York. Printed in U.S.A. He National News Company, New York, Leipzig, Dresden; Poly Chrome.

Richmond
Published by Weitzman's Photo Shop, Inc. Stapleton, S.I., N.Y. 15031. Colourpicture Cambridge, Mass. U.S.A. Sales Office –Fifth Ave., N.Y.C.

Richmond
American Souvenir-Card Co., New York.

Richmond
No Publisher Information Available.

Rockland
Made in Germany, A.C. Besselman & Co. New York

Rockland
The Ruben Publishing Co., Newburgh, N.Y., Ruben Quality Views

St. Lawrence
Made In Germany A.G. Besselman & Co., N.Y.

St. Lawrence after 1925 Fire
128309, Tichnor Quality Views

Saratoga
The PCK Series, Published by J.S. Wooley, Baliston Spa, N.Y. Printed in Germany.

Saratoga
Feeney Bros. & Co., Pub. (Germany)

Schenectady 1909
Souvenir Post Card Co., New York and Berlin.

Schenectady 1913
Published by C.W. Hughes & Co. Inc., Mechanicville, N.Y., C.T. American Art Colored.

Schenectady
No Publisher Information Available.

Schoharie
Published by J.L. Harrington, Schoharie, N.Y., Hand Colored; Made In France.

Schoharie
No Publisher Information Available.

Schuyler No. C10892
Published by the Buffalo News Company, Buffalo, N.Y., Dresden-Leipzig-Berlin Made in Germany; Litho Chrome.

Schuyler
"C.T. Photo Colorit", Made only by Curt Teich & Co., Inc., Chicago, U.S.A.

Schuyler
No Publisher Information Available.

Schuyler
Santway Photo-Craft Company, Watertown, N.Y.

Seneca
C. Stern Illustrating & Publishing Co., Belfast.
  All Reproduction Rights Reserved.

Seneca
Published by James E. Batsford & Son, Waterloo,
  N.Y.. Dresden-Leipzig-Berlin Trade Mark
  Germany; Litho Chrome.

Seneca 128003
Tichnor Quality Views

Steuben
Published by The Acmegraph Co., Chicago

Steuben
Souvenir Post Card Co., New York Printed in
  Germany

Steuben 1909
No Publisher Information Available.

Suffolk
Published by. Mc Cabes Central Store.

Suffolk
No Publisher Information Available.

Suffolk
Published by Manhattan Post Card Co., New
  York City, Made in USA.

Suffolk
Published by The Tomlin Art Company,
  Northport, Long Island, N.Y.

Sullivan
226a Publishers, Tichenor & Rucolph,
  Middletown, N.Y. Made in Germany.

Sullivan
Post Cards of Quality The Albertype Co.,
  Brooklyn, N.Y.

Tioga
The Rotograph Co., N.Y. City, Printed in Great
  Britain.

Tioga
Published by The American News Company,
  New York.

Tioga
No Publisher Information Available.

Tompkins
Published by the Rochester News Company,
  Rochester N.Y. U.S.A. Leipzig-Berlin

Tompkins
No Publisher Information Available.

Ulster # 127
No Publisher Information Available.

Ulster
No Publisher Information Available.

Ulster
A "Colourpicture" Publication, Boston 15,
  Mass., U.S.A.

Warren
Published For Lake George Souvenir Co., Lake
  George, N.Y.

Warren
No Publisher Information Available.

Warren
Published by Dean Color, Glens Falls, N.Y.
  12801

Washington
No Publisher Information Available.

Washington
R.A. Cruickshank, Publisher, Salem, N.Y.,
  Printed in Great Britain.

Washington
United Art Publishing Co., New York City,
  Printed in Germany.

Washington
The Valentine Souvenir Co., New York, Printed
  in U.S.A. Superior Quality Famous
  Throughout the World.

Washington
Portland Lithograph Co., 252 Spring St.,
  Portland, ME., 1301-F.

Wayne
Published by W.E. Bourne & Co., N.Y.

Wayne 69733
Don Hunt, Wolcott, N.Y.

Wayne
No Publisher Information Available.

Westchester
The Rotograph Co., N.Y. City, (Germany)

Westchester
No Publisher Information Available.

Westchester
No Publisher Information Available.

Westchester
No. 409 Printed in Germany.

Westchester
The Ruben Publishing Co., Newburgh, N.Y.

Wyoming
No Publisher Information Available.

Wyoming
61213, J. C. Hofstetter & Co. Printed in
  Germany.

Wyoming
Published by Wm. Jubb Co., Inc., Syracuse, N.Y.
  13224.

Yates
The Rotograph Co. N.Y. City, Printed in
  Germany, 54970.

Yates
Published by The Buffalo News Company,
  Buffalo, N.Y., Made in Germany

Yates
The Rotograph Co., N.Y., City. (Germany)

Index